CHARLES RENOUVIER
PHILOSOPHER OF LIBERTY

CHARLES RENOUVIER
PHILOSOPHER OF LIBERTY

William Logue

LOUISIANA STATE UNIVERSITY PRESS
Baton Rouge and London

Copyright ©1993 by Louisiana State University Press
All rights reserved
Manufactured in the United States of America
First printing
02 01 00 99 98 97 96 95 94 93   5 4 3 2 1

Designer: *Glynnis Phoebe*
Typeface: *Sabon*
Typesetter: *Graphic Composition, Inc.*
Printer and binder: *Thomson-Shore, Inc.*

Library of Congress Cataloging-in-Publication Data
Logue, William, 1934–
    Charles Renouvier, philosopher of liberty / William Logue.
      p. cm.
    Includes bibliographical references and index.
    ISBN 0-8071-1788-9
    1. Renouvier, Charles, 1815–1903. I. Title.
  B2357.L58   1992
  194—dc20   92-15585
                                                  CIP

To the memory of
S. William Halperin and Louis R. Gottschalk,
gentlemen, scholars, teachers

Always remember that men are not governed by facts
but by what they believe.
—Desmond Bagley, *The Snow Tiger*

CONTENTS

PREFACE

The book I have chosen to write on Charles Renouvier has taken the form of a historical essay, or rather a closely related set of essays. As a result, it has a more obviously personal quality than is the norm in twentieth-century historical scholarship. For this reason it seems desirable to say something at the beginning about how I became interested in Renouvier and how I came to write this book.

My interest in French social and political thought formed a significant part of my decision to pursue an academic career. My preference for thinkers who were considered promoters of freedom in the modern world was perhaps less an individual choice than an unconscious acceptance of the spirit of the time. That preference has not changed, though my evaluation of who belongs in that distinguished group has certainly altered, as have the views of most of my contemporaries. In my case, this involved primarily a change in my view of the past, for I was always skeptical of the utopian promises congealed in the political ideology of the Left. My preference was always for liberal solutions, stressing individual initiative and responsibility. My deepest interest was in the history of ideas. Understanding that history has always been a hard enough challenge, even without the delusion of believing it could be understood well enough to grasp the necessary course of history.

But it was my academic ambitions that first brought me into contact with the thought of Charles Renouvier. My dissatisfaction with the only substantial history of French political thought in the nineteenth century, that of Roger Soltau (1931), planted the seed of the idea that I might someday produce a volume that would supplant this venerable work. It would be a long time before I could seriously contemplate an undertaking of such dimensions. Before that ambition could take more concrete form, I was diverted by the university upheavals of the late 1960s and early 1970s into an examination of the political thought of French university professors in the nineteenth century, wondering if parallels with the present could be detected and any lessons drawn. Alas, this did not prove to be a fruitful line of inquiry, but the research it involved did point me in a useful direction.

I became aware for the first time of a substantial current of liberal thought that was largely neglected because Western scholarship had been fixated on exploring the origins of twentieth-century socialism and fascism. That I was not immune to that fascination can be seen in my *Léon Blum: The Formative Years, 1872–1914* (1973). Liberal thought had been devalued since World War I because of the failures of liberal political leadership in Europe and America. The world appeared to be heading in new directions—or in *a* new direction after the defeat of Nazi Germany—and historians were naturally inclined to scrutinize the past to understand better the apparent wave of the future. Fascination with the horror of nazism also provoked a substantial vein of scholarship in intellectual history, generating a new interest in thinkers and movements of the Far Right.

An awareness of the greatest challenge to the interpretation of nineteenth-century thought came only slowly: How could that century have produced what most assumed to be the absolutely contrasting poles of communism and fascism? Those writers who pointed out the similarities of the two movements were not well received in the academic community and perhaps did sometimes fall into exaggeration. Intellectual history, so absorbed by the study of Left and Right, forgot that the dominant mode of nineteenth-century political thought belonged, so to speak, to the Center. Any attempt to write a global history of nineteenth-century French political thought would, if it was to tell us more about the nineteenth than the twentieth century, have to make a substantial place for the history of liberalism.

It soon became evident to me that the greatest deficiency in the secondary literature on liberalism concerned the last half of the century.

With no ready-made interpretations to fall back on, I was going to have to construct my own before I could think of moving on with my larger project. The result of this observation would be my *From Philosophy to Sociology: The Evolution of French Liberal Thought, 1870–1914* (1983), which advanced the hypothesis that the early Third Republic saw the emergence of a New Liberalism, which turned its back on laissez-faire and sought ways the state and society could promote social justice without the loss of freedom inherent in the socialist program. In the process of this development I detected a parallel evolution in the intellectual underpinnings of liberalism that moved from a reliance on philosophy to a utilization of the concepts of a newly emerging sociology.

At the hinge point of this transformation I found Renouvier, who provided the last major effort to build a philosophical foundation for liberalism that could withstand the ravages of the social-science challenge. In the course of writing a chapter on Renouvier I became convinced that there was much more that needed to be said about him than would fit into the framework of that chapter. It proved easier to decide to write a book about Renouvier than to decide exactly what kind of book and what audience—if there was to be one other than myself.

My awareness of the attraction of Renouvier's thought for me had been awakened some years earlier by a seminar paper produced by an M.A. candidate at Northern Illinois University, Sally Zerbe. Contrary to the clichés of the profession, I have rarely found students the source of ideas significant for my research. I think there is little doubt that the constraints of the teaching profession are harmful to literary and artistic creativity. In philosophy the record is mixed, creativity having found a home in German universities in the nineteenth century but flourishing in France only outside them. This was largely true in Great Britain too. Whether scholarship is generally more benefited than harmed by its present academic setting is an open question, at least regarding quality, for it certainly does promote quantity. Nonetheless, I want to acknowledge the real influence of a student paper, if only as a starting point.

When I first began to read Renouvier for myself, I was staggered by the immense volume of his work. My chapter in the liberalism book was made possible only by a judicious (I hope) selection of the most obviously relevant writings, and even in the present work I cannot claim an intimate acquaintance with much more than half of the results of his sixty years of nearly continuous labor. Nor will I claim a profound grasp of everything that I have read. Renouvier was a philosopher, and I am not. What I will claim is that he can be read with interest and intellectual benefit by people who are not philosophers. I hope this work will persuade others to share that conviction. Some knowledge of Renouvier's thought seems essential to any understanding of the intellectual history of nineteenth-century France. This is true not merely because of his important position in the development of French liberalism but also because he offers a useful perspective from which to examine all the intellectual trends of his day—and many of ours.

Finally, I must confess to being attracted to Renouvier because of the ways his thought supports my positions on many of the political, social, and intellectual issues of our time. As I tried to emphasize in my previous book, there are many connections between the issues of the twentieth century and those of its predecessor, the most striking difference being the fertility of the nineteenth century in proposing answers. Our century has largely been living on the intellectual capital of the last century, despite the illusion of novelty created by our mass-consumption society.

Twentieth-century social and political thought on the whole has been so impoverished that it seems renewal can come only from a return to earlier sources of inspiration. Many, it is true, have condemned the nineteenth century for being the progenitor of the twentieth—a charge amply confirmed by Renouvier's analysis of his time—but it seems unnecessary to return with Leo Strauss to Aristotle and worse than futile to return with Hannah Arendt to Heidegger. For the nineteenth century contains antidotes for some of its poisons, and what Luc Ferry and Alain Renaut have found in Fichte can also be found in Renouvier, without the need to penetrate a smoke screen of Teutonic obscurity. Renouvier offers a philosophical defense of liberty and responsibility that is capable of supporting the renewed reflection we need so much today.

My thanks to Linda L. Clark and Benjamin F. Martin, who read this manuscript in various stages of its development and made numerous valuable suggestions. They are not responsible for the weaknesses of this work, but they helped make it better than it would otherwise have been.

CHARLES RENOUVIER
PHILOSOPHER OF LIBERTY

INTRODUCTION
Renouvier in His Day and Ours

Charles Renouvier was born in the year of Napoléon's dramatic return from Elba and the turmoil of the emperor's "Hundred Days" that culminated in his final defeat on the plains of Waterloo and the second restoration of the Bourbon monarchy. Renouvier would die with the Third Republic well launched into its career as the longest lived of modern French regimes and just two years short of the adoption of the law for the separation of church and state for which he had so long argued. In those eighty-odd years, French political life was studded with traumatic episodes great and small that form the landmarks of her nineteenth-century history: the "Three Glorious Days" of the July revolution in 1830; the February revolution of 1848, with its echoes of the great Revolution; the protracted agony of the Second Republic (1848 to 1852), which ended in the coup d'état that established the Second Empire of Napoléon III (nephew of the great emperor), "Napoléon the Little," as Victor Hugo called him; the fall of Napoléon III on September 4, 1870, in the wake of his defeat by the

1

Prussians at Sedan; the bloody tragedy of the Paris Commune of 1871. The Third Republic, established in the wake of defeat, would have to face and surmount a series of challenges after its compromise constitution was finally adopted in 1875, but neither the Boulanger crisis nor the Dreyfus affair could prevent the new regime from going its plodding way.

Through all these changes of regime, civil and political liberty advanced, but only by fits and starts and not without relapses. The restored Bourbon monarchy was much different from its Old Regime predecessor: The old dynasty ruled, in the persons of the brothers of the late lamented Louis XVI, but under the terms of a written constitution that granted a limited form of representative government much like what many reformers had been seeking in 1789. Fundamental civil liberties were established but were constantly under threat, especially when freedom of the press was used to attack the government. The July revolution left the constitution largely unchanged. Though doubled in numbers, the electorate continued to include only a tiny minority of the adult population. The main change was that the new king, Louis Philippe, head of a distant branch of the Bourbon dynasty, was much more in tune with "modern" ideas and was ready to accept a greater, if by no means predominant, role for the bourgeoisie in government. He and his ministers, especially the liberal historian François Guizot, stoutly resisted the growing pressure for a sharply expanded electorate and paid the price of exile in the 1848 revolution.

The Second Republic proved no more stable or enduring than the First. It brought universal manhood suffrage and a broader commitment to civil liberties but foundered in the quarrel between those who wanted a socially conservative republic (who controlled the provisional government) and those who sought some form of socialist regime (who took to the streets when they were thwarted at the polls). Renouvier would have his first experience of political life in those exciting days, and it would leave a permanent mark on his thought.

Louis-Napoléon Bonaparte established a regime that has defied all the usual categories: It called itself democratic and maintained manhood suffrage, but elections were manipulated by the system of official candidates, and the power of the elected representatives to act contrary to the wishes of the prince-president (later emperor) was extremely limited. Civil liberties were repressed as long as the regime feared for its security but began to be restored in the 1860s, and indeed before its abrupt end people were beginning to speak of the new "liberal empire." Whatever virtues such a regime might have come to possess were canceled for Renouvier and many others by its suicidal plunge into an ill-considered war with Prussia.

A genuinely liberal regime was established with the Third Republic: a democratic parliamentary government (though women were still denied the right to vote) based on a broad commitment to liberal values. It successfully fought off challenges from the monarchist and clerical Right, which rejected those values, only to face a new challenge from the Left, which argued that the liberal regime benefited only the bourgeoisie. Renouvier developed his fundamental philosophical positions during the Second Empire and applied them to political questions in the context of the Third Republic's struggles.

Of course, it was not political developments alone that provided the context. The intellectual climate of opinion was the most important influence on him. After the Revolution, French philosophy in the areas of ontology, epistemology, logic, and aesthetics was in the doldrums. The rationalist tradition that began with Descartes was unchallenged; the prestige of the Enlightenment, with its Newtonian ideal of a mechanistic science and its Lockean psychology of sense impressions, weighed heavily on the new century. The philosophy of the state school system, France's official philosophy, was controlled by Victor Cousin, whose successors would continue his benevolent dictatorship nearly to the end of the century. This official philosophy is generally known as Eclecticism because of its insistence on finding and incorporating the elements of truth it believed existed in all past systems of philosophy, but its practitioners generally preferred to call it *spiritualisme,* emphasizing its commitment to, its participation in, the long historical development of the human mind. It must not be confused with what came to be called spiritualism in English in the nineteenth century—the belief in telepathy, communication with the spirits of the departed, poltergeists, and so forth. While decidedly rationalist, the Eclectics were politely deferential toward religious orthodoxy and accepted the constitutional monarchy as the best of all possible regimes. They would make no significant contributions to the evolution of Western philosophy.

Outside of the schools, French social and political thought in the first half of the century was exhibiting a vitality and originality that has no parallel. The Revolution destroyed the old certainties and showed that it was possible not only to think about different social and political orders but to change the existing ones. Anything seemed possible. This understandable if erroneous assumption called forth the most diverse responses imaginable. These ranged from the "constitutional liberalism" of those who wanted to salvage the good from wreckage of the Revolution to the technocratic authoritarianism of the Saint-Simonians, to the structured libertarianism of Charles Fourier, to the various socialist sectarians—all more or less authoritarian—to the scientistic positivism of Auguste Comte (first phase) or his Religion of Humanity (second phase), to the sui generis conservative anarchism of Pierre-Joseph Proudhon. Renouvier would grow up in the midst of this heady confusion, and it is not surprising that it took him some time to find his own way. His earliest philosophy was shaped by the historical interests of the Eclectics, but by and large his sympathy would be with the independent innovators, no matter how severely he criticized their ideas.

In this atmosphere of intellectual upheaval—and limited political stability—the main vehicle of intellectual reaction in France was the Roman Catholic church. Defender of the rationalist philosophy of Thomas Aquinas and the medieval Scholastics, it was, understandably, hostile to the increasingly secular rationalism that had flourished during the Enlightenment. This hostility would not diminish in the course of the century, and some of the Church's strongest statements against the major trends of Western thought—the *Syllabus of Errors* and the encyclical *Rerum Novarum*—came late in the century. The efforts of the Church leadership to combat the development and dissemination of new ideas, to maintain control of elementary education and seek power over secondary and higher education, to claim a monopoly on moral truth and its teaching, would form a backdrop without which it is impossible to understand the intellectual and political struggles that shaped Renouvier and most secular thinkers of his century.

As we will see in the course of this study, Renouvier's mind was engaged with almost all the leading intellectual developments of his century and concerned with all its leading political developments. The breadth of his interests would be impressive, even in that age of far-reaching intellectual ambition.

Introduction

Renouvier's Place in the History of Philosophy

When Charles Renouvier died in 1903 at the age of eighty-eight, he was hailed in France as one of the three or four greatest thinkers of the nineteenth century, and it was confidently predicted that he "would remain between Comte and Bergson, and at the same level, one of the greatest glories of French philosophy in the 19th century." The obituary writers did not hesitate to place him with "Descartes, Spinoza, Leibniz, Berkeley, Hume, Kant, Schopenhauer, Spencer," and this recognition came as readily from critics as admirers. Across the Rhine it was recognized that Renouvier was "the most important systematic thinker in France since Malebranche" and that "a new era in the history of French philosophy in the 19th century begins with Renouvier's *Essais de critique générale.*" [1] The neocriticist movement that Renouvier established almost single handedly upheld the honor of French philosophy when teaching in the schools was dominated by a cut-rate Eclecticism and the larger public was under the spell of thinkers like Ernest Renan and Hippolyte Taine—brilliant minds and powerful writers but dilettantes in philosophy. Taine and Renan continue to be read for what they reflect of the major characteristics of nineteenth-century intellectual life: a dogmatic positivism in the former case and an aristocratic skepticism in the latter. On the other hand, Renouvier can be read both for what he tells us about his century and for the insight he offers into some of the perennial problems of the modern world. He has that power of "posthumous productivity" that Julian Benda, following Goethe, noted as one of the signs of a great mind.[2]

Any reader who has picked up this book without having heard of

1. Paul Archambault, *Renouvier* (Paris, 1911), 60; Jean Arnal, *L'Hypothèse suprême en théodicée d'après Charles Renouvier* (Mazamet, France, 1904), 4–5; Ludwig Baur, Obituary on Renouvier, *Philosophisches Jahrbuch*, XVIII (1905), 452; see also Überweg-Heinze, *Grundriss der Geschichte der Philosophie* (1903), Pt. IV, p. 375, cited by Roger Verneaux, *L'Idéalisme de Renouvier* (Paris, 1943), 328; Maurice Ascher, *Renouvier und der französische Neu-Kriticismus* (Bern, 1900), 6.

2. Léon Brunschwicg and Elie Halévy, "L'Année philosophique en 1893," *Revue de métaphysique et de morale*, II (1894), 474, cited by Henri Miéville, *La Philosophie de M. Renouvier et le problème de la connaissance religieuse* (Lau-

Charles Renouvier is likely to be surprised, even shocked, to find him named in the same breath with Spinoza, Hume, and Kant, acknowledged as great names even by those who know nothing of their thought. I do not claim that his rank in the history of philosophy is comparable to theirs, but I assert that the quality of his thought can stand comparison with theirs and insist even more strongly that he should be considered a major figure in the history of modern French thought, in the lineage that includes Descartes, Malebranche, Rousseau, Maine de Biran, Auguste Comte, and Henri Bergson.[3] Believers in the verdict of history (to put it less charitably, consumers of received opinions) will no doubt be skeptical. How could this be true if they have not heard of him, a condition common enough in France and nearly universal among American and English philosophers? This is a legitimate question. Outside my special fields of competence, I too am inclined to define a famous person as somebody I have heard of. It therefore seems necessary to say a little about why Renouvier was important and why he has been largely forgotten. (This is not, as some may imagine, a self-contradictory statement.)

To justify this claim, we must first examine some of the reasons why Renouvier is not accorded the place he merits. Most of these will prove extrinsic to the question of the stature of his thought. Given the nationalism prevalent in Western thought after the passing of Latin as the common language of philosophy, it will not be surprising to find different reasons affecting his fate in different countries. The central question is thus why Renouvier has not secured the place in the French pantheon of thinkers for which he seemed destined in his lifetime. But before going into that, we will briefly look at his reputation abroad.

---

sanne, 1902), ix; Julien Benda, "Les Idées d'un républicain en 1872," *Nouvelle Revue française*, XXXVII (1931), 24.

3. See also Louis Foucher, *La Jeunesse de Renouvier et sa première philosophie, 1815–1854, suivi d'une bibliographie chronologique de Charles Renouvier* (Paris, 1927), 3; Marcel Méry, *La Critique du christianisme chez Renouvier* (Paris, 1952), I, 61; Beurier, "Renouvier et le criticisme français," *Revue philosophique* (1877), 322.

Because of the explicit attachment of his thought to that of Kant and Leibniz, you would expect Renouvier to have generated some interest in Germany, but he came a century too late for that. The influence of the French Enlightenment in Germany was considerable, and Kant could openly acknowledge his debt to Rousseau. But in the nineteenth century the tables were turned: The dominant French philosophical school, Eclecticism, attracted little respect outside the country, and philosophy was flourishing in Germany. After national unification in 1871 raised German self-esteem to the heights, there were few who saw any reason to look across the Rhine, and indeed the French were coming to Germany to study. This did not prevent the few Germans who took an interest in French thought from recognizing Renouvier as a major figure on the French scene, especially since he appeared to be a disciple of Kant.[4] The only German philosopher of note to write on Renouvier was Ernst Cassirer. The Danish historian of philosophy Harald Höffding confessed in his survey of modern thought to being ill informed about the contemporary situation in France and showed an awareness of only a fragment of Renouvier's work.[5] His position was typical.

Across the Channel, the situation was more problematic. Exchanges of ideas among the avant-garde of the two countries had been common in the eighteenth century, and there was a convergence of approaches between the Anglo-Saxon empiricism and the French *sensationnalisme*. But in the nineteenth century the French strain seemed to lose its vigor when the utilitarian school was dominant in Britain. Though a persistent

4. For example, a thesis at Leipzig, Friedrich K. Feigel, *Charles Renouvier's Philosophie der praktischen Vernunft: kritisch beleuchtet* (published at Wittenberg in 1908); another, at Bern, by Maurice Ascher, *Renouvier und der französische Neu-Kriticismus* (Bern, 1900), stresses the contribution of neocriticism to the revival of philosophy in France.

5. Ernst Cassirer, Review of Charles Renouvier's *Essais de critique générale. Premier essai. Traité de logique générale et de logique formelle*, in *Die Geisteswissenschaften*. XXIII (1913), 634–35. Cassirer also wrote an essay, "Das Problem des Unendlichen und Renouviers Gesetz der Zahl," *Philosophisches Abhandlungen, Hermann Cohen zum 70. Geburtstag gewidmet* (Berlin, 1910), which I have not seen. Harald Höffding, *Philosophes contemporaines,* trans. A. Trémesaygues (Paris, 1908), 79–81.

critic of utilitarianism, Renouvier also acknowledged a considerable debt to the empiricism of David Hume, and he continued to have a lively interest in English thought (English being the one modern foreign language he read reasonably well).[6] The English showed an interest in French positivism, but neither England nor Scotland was a fertile ground for the neo-Kantian approach. Timing was also a factor. The one English philosopher with whom Renouvier could have had a fruitful interaction was John Stuart Mill, who was unfortunately near the end of his career before Renouvier's works began to be known. A brief discussion in one of Mill's letters to a French friend is all we have from his side—a tantalizing might-have-been.[7] The only extensive discussion of Renouvier's thought in Britain was the work of one Shadworth Hodgson, William James's mentor in London but hardly a household name, though his article was published in the prestigious journal *Mind*.[8]

The most fruitful influence Renouvier had outside France was on the American philosopher and psychologist (the two were not clearly distinguished until the twentieth century) William James. While studying in Germany as a young man, James was converted to belief in free will by reading Renouvier.[9] A correspondence eventually developed from which both men drew substance. Their strong mutual admiration was based on

6. Renouvier's testimony, in *Critique philosophique* (1888-II), 406; Renouvier to Charles Secrétan, April 13, 1869, in *Correspondance de Renouvier et Secrétan* (Paris, 1911), 23; *Revue philosophique et religieuse*, VII [1856?], 405, cited by Méry, *Critique du christianisme*, I, 222n7. Renouvier said he drew great help from Max Müller's English translation of Kant, *Critique de la doctrine de Kant*, ed. Louis Prat (Paris, 1906), 28, cited by Maximilien Vallois, *La Formation de l'influence kantienne en France* (Paris, 1924), 225n72.

7. John Stuart Mill to Emile Honoré Cazelles, October 23, 1869, in *The Later Letters of John Stuart Mill, 1849–1873*, ed. Francis E. Mineka and Dwight N. Lindley (Toronto, 1972), IV, No. 1489.

8. Shadworth Hodgson, "M. Renouvier's Philosophy," *Mind* (1881), 31–61, 173–211. Renouvier published a translation of Hodgson's articles as "Examen critique des *Essais de critique générale*," *Critique philosophique* (1881-I), 161–69, 177–86, 193–98, 209–16, 241–45.

9. See Henry Blumenthal, *American and French Culture, 1800–1900: Interchanges in Art, Science, Literature, and Society* (Baton Rouge, 1975), 168–69.

a number of common views: their rejection of an impersonal reason, their understanding of the role of belief in philosophy, their desire to make philosophy useful. They were also united by a concern for the future of religion and an interest in the "varieties of religious experience." [10] Unfortunately, James remained isolated in his admiration for Renouvier, and none of Renouvier's work was ever translated into English, although Renouvier would publish some translations of James in the pages of his *Critique philosophique*.[11] The eclipse of pragmatism would close off this possible line of influence for Renouvier.

In the twentieth century, the direction taken by Anglo-American philosophy caused a loss of interest in all modern French schools of thought. English-language histories of philosophy tend to act as if nineteenth-century France did not exist, and indeed it had no influence on the main Anglo-American trends. George Boas, one of the few Americans well informed about modern French thought, lamented that when he tried to bring French thinkers to the attention of his students, he was severely rebuked by his colleagues for "wasting their time." [12] Renouvier would be known in the twentieth-century United States only to a few historians, not to practicing philosophers.

10. Renouvier quotes James in *Esquisse d'une classification systématique des doctrines philosophiques* (Paris, 1885–86), II, 177, hereinafter cited as *Esquisse*. Both Dominique Parodi (*Du positivisme à l'idéalisme: philosophies d'hier, études critiques* [Paris, 1930], 76, hereinafter cited as Parodi, *Philosophies d'hier*) and Léon Brunschwicg (*Le Progrès de la conscience dans la philosophie occidentale* [Paris, 1927], 627) see Renouvier as having had a considerable influence on James. See the Renouvier–James published correspondence in Ralph Barton Perry, "Correspondance de Charles Renouvier et de William James," *Revue de métaphysique et de morale*, XXXVI (1929), 1–35, 193–222. Isaac Benrubi (*Les Sources et les courants de la philosophie contemporaine en France* [Paris, 1933], I, 293–96) suggests another possible connection when he sees Kant as a precursor of James.

11. William James, *The Varieties of Religious Experience* (New York, 1902).

12. George Boas, "The History of Philosophy," in *Philosophic Thought in France and the United States,* ed. Marvin Farber (2nd ed.; Albany, 1968), 397. Boas cites Maine de Biran, Cournot, Renouvier, and Cousin as almost totally ignored in the United States.

The potentially self-destructive tendency of Anglo-American philosophy to reduce philosophy to a language game on the one hand or symbolic logic on the other was only an aggravated example of the general crisis of Western thought, which in philosophy has taken the form of loss of meaning in favor of a preoccupation with signs. The mathematical approach of Russell and Whitehead's *Principia Mathematica* threatened to exclude from meaningful knowledge everything that could not be fit into the procrustean bed of their symbolic logic, fruitful though this was in understanding the nature of mathematics. The philosophy of language threatens to drive us into an even deeper dead end, one in which we are forced to recognize that all communication is impossible. Man having been banished from philosophy, Renouvier's concerns would not seem part of the relevant history of thought.

The loss of confidence by twentieth-century philosophy has erected a psychological barrier between most practicing philosophers and those of the nineteenth century, whose ambitions have come to seem grotesque and naïve. It is true that those ambitions were often excessive, a fault that Renouvier did not entirely escape, but we have certainly suffered from the loss of a conviction that philosophy considers something relevant to our lives, our society, and our destiny. At a time when television stars and automobile-company executives are consulted for their opinions on all the issues of the day, the absence of thinkers from the public domain is all the more acutely felt.[13] The Western country that seems to have best resisted the diminution of philosophy in the twentieth century has been Italy, perhaps because of the example of Benedetto Croce, who so brilliantly carried the banner of philosopher-in-the-world into our time. It is thus no accident that the most significant non-French works on Renouvier since World War II have come from Italy and have tended to focus on his social and political thought.[14]

13. For more sophisticated discussion of the relevance of philosophy, see the last section of Jacques Bouveresse, *Rationalité et cynisme* (Paris, 1984), and W. V. Quine, "Has Philosophy Lost Contact with People?" in his *Theories and Things* (Cambridge, Mass., 1981); see also Bernard-Henri Lévy, *Eloge des intellectuels* (Paris, 1987).

14. See especially Giovanna Cavallari, *Charles Renouvier, filosofo della liberal-democrazia* (Naples, 1979), and Vittore Collina, *Plurale filosofico et rad-*

The single factor that has the greatest influence on the reputation of a thinker outside his homeland is his reputation inside. Thus Renouvier was best known outside France during the height of his influence within France during the early years of the Third Republic. Recognition as a major philosopher came very slowly to Renouvier. His writings did not have the stylistic qualities needed to attract attention among the educated strata of society in nineteenth-century France, where rhetorical effect was still highly appreciated. Access to the more select audience capable of forming a serious opinion of his work was blocked by the hostility or indifference of the academic establishment, to which he did not belong and indeed often ridiculed. His first work had received only one review, and that in a Swiss Protestant review, the *Semeur,* by Charles Secrétan, later one of his best friends.[15]

Renouvier would come to the general attention of French intellectuals only with the publication of Felix Ravaisson's report on the status

---

icalismo: saggio sul pensiero politico di Charles Renouvier (Bologna, 1980). For earlier Italian work on Renouvier, see Nicola Abbagnano, *Storia della filosofia* (Turin, 1950), Vol. II, and Gallo Galli, *Studi storico-critico sulla philosofia di Ch. Renouvier* (Gubbio, 1933; Rome, 1935). There has also been some interest in Spanish Latin America; see Antonio Pasquali, *Fundamentos gnoseològicos para una ciencia de la moral: Ensayo sobre la formacion de una theoria del conocimiento moral en la filosofias de Kant, Lequier, Renouvier y Bergson* (Caracas, 1963). Renouvier's *Les Dilemmes de la métaphysique pure* and *Esquisse* were published in Spanish translation in Buenos Aires in 1944 and 1948, respectively. I would like to thank my colleague Samuel Amaral for pointing out that Renouvier's *Uchronie* is well known to Argentine historians because of its influence on the leading figure of modern Argentine historiography, Bartolomé Mitre; see, for example, Natalio R. Botana, *La Libertad politica y su historia* (Buenos Aires, 1991), 119–21.

15. Charles Secrétan, in his Review of Renouvier's *Manual de philosophie moderne* (*Semeur: journal religieux, politique, philosophique et littéraire,* XI [1842], 378–79) recognized in this early work some of the virtues and defects that would mark most of Renouvier's later work: his lack of precision, clarity, and organization on one hand; his understanding of doctrines and his "*coup d'oeil philosophique*" on the other.

of French philosophy in 1867.[16] Political developments would also play no small part in the growth of his reputation after 1870 as the Third Republic sought to establish its moral legitimacy and its intellectual bona fides.[17] With good reason, Renouvier suddenly seemed very relevant. To be sure, this is a precarious benefit for a philosopher, for political circumstances change, and what they give they can take away. More seriously, they have the disadvantage of leaving behind the suggestion that a thinker's success was due merely to a conjunction of circumstances.

Renouvier would certainly suffer from being *démodé* in this fashion, with the further unfortunate effect, for France, that the elements of continuing relevance in his thought would be neglected when they would have been useful. In general, his reputation, like that of Alexis de Tocqueville, would suffer from the post–World War I eclipse of liberalism in France. It remains to be seen whether the current circumstances that have made possible a revival of interest in Tocqueville will also prove favorable to Renouvier.

There were also more specifically philosophical factors in the rise and fall of Renouvier's status in France, some intrinsic to his work, oth-

16. Félix Ravaisson, *La Philosophie en France au XIXe siècle* (Paris, 1868). There is a general consensus that French philosophy as a whole underwent a revival after 1867. Paul Mouy (*L'Idée de progrès dans la philosophie de Renouvier* [Paris, 1927], 191–93) credits Renouvier with having single-handedly kept French philosophy alive. Renouvier (*Philosophie analytique de l'histoire: les idées; les religions; les systèmes* [4 vols.; Paris, 1896–98], IV, 550–51, hereinafter cited as *Histoire*) thought that the lack of serious philosophical construction by the most popular thinkers of the day—Michelet, Quinet, Renan, and Taine— contributed to the general disinterest in philosophy. On the impact of Ravaisson's report, see Louis Prat, *Charles Renouvier, philosophe: sa doctrine, sa vie* (Pamiers, France, 1937), 254; Jules Thomas, Introduction to Renouvier, *Manuel républicain de l'homme et du citoyen* (new ed.; Paris, 1904), 6. Emile Boutroux ("La Philosophie en France depuis 1867," *Revue de métaphysique et de morale,* XVI [1908], 683–84) claimed that the dominance of the Eclectics was such that original thinkers like Renouvier and Comte were still little known in 1867.

17. Marcel Prélot (*Histoire des idées politiques* [8th ed.; Paris, n.d.], 444) credits Renouvier's neocriticism with introducing Kant's political thought into dominance in France.

ers coming from the outside. While Victor Cousin's influence prevented anything but Eclecticism from taking root in the "University," a feeling gradually penetrated among young French philosophers that they were missing out on a major trend of modern thought, the "return to Kant." Kant had been recognized in France and absorbed willy-nilly into Eclecticism even though Cousin's articles on Kant show that he did not understand the first thing. But as developments in Germany had shown, Kant's work was too powerful to be absorbed this casually. The serious teaching of Kant for his own sake in France would begin at the Ecole normale supérieure in the courses of Jules Lachelier, and the Ecole normale would remain the hotbed of Kant studies in France.[18]

At this point, the French were ready to discover that they already had a Kantian of their own in Renouvier.[19] Because of their limited knowledge of Kant, it would not be obvious to them at first just how heterodox a Kantian he was. Renouvier demonstrated to a younger generation that it was possible not just to study Kant historically but to be a Kantian; there was even a certain grandeur in his having been a Kantian when they did not officially exist. Furthermore, he offered the model of a French Kantian, which made it unnecessary to identify oneself with excessively Germanic models such as Schelling, Fichte, or Schopenhauer.

At the same time, Renouvier's reputation as a Kantian was bound to become tarnished as the progress of academic Kant studies produced a

18. On the introduction of Kant into France from the beginning through the Eclectics, see Vallois, *Formation de l'influence kantienne;* Lionel Dauriac, "Un épisode de l'histoire de la philosophie française en la fin du XIXe siècle: souvenirs personnels," *Critique philosophique* (1887-II), 280–86.

19. Benrubi, *Sources et courants,* I, 298: "The works of Charles Renouvier form, in some fashion, the link which unites Kantianism with the present day." The first substantial exposition of the whole of neocriticism was the series of articles by Beurier in the *Revue philosophique* of April, May, and June, 1877. The first university recognition apparently was the inaugural lecture of one Nolen at the Faculté des lettres de Montpellier according to Beurier ("Renouvier et le criticisme français," 322). The first recognition of neocriticism by the Eclectics was in an article by Paul Janet, "Le Mouvement philosophique," *Temps,* March 8, 1876.

more accurate knowledge of Kant's work and a body of clearer, more polished exegesis.[20] After the work of Lachelier, Emile Boutroux, and Victor Delbos, no one would read Renouvier to find out what Kant thought.[21] Just as interest in Kant was the path by which Renouvier had entered the university, so would it be the path by which he left. In one sense this was perfectly reasonable. Renouvier had never set himself up as a exegete of Kant; what mattered to him was the role Kant played in the formation of his thought and his conviction that it was not possible to be a philosopher in the nineteenth century without taking Kant's critiques into account.[22]

Renouvier's example as a living philosopher was as important in its own way as Lachelier's superior exposition and interpretation were in theirs.[23] Lachelier would lament that many of his best students became disciples of Renouvier, but *disciples* is too strong a word. Still, there were around the turn of the century a gratifying number of young men who identified themselves with neocriticism.[24] That they would mostly be het-

---

20. Elizabeth Waelti, *La Morale kantienne de Charles Renouvier et son influence sur la constitution de la morale laïque dans la deuxième moitié du XIXe siècle en France* (Geneva, 1947), 121–22, 131–32. If Renouvier's lack of German was one source of his weakness as an interpreter of Kant, it was a weakness shared with most French philosophers of his age (Vallois, *Formation de l'influence kantienne*, 47–48).

21. Waelti, *Morale kantienne*, 121–22, 131–32; Brunschwicg, *Progrès de la conscience*, 629. Even Renouvier's faithful colleague François Pillon would call Victor Delbos' *Philosophie pratique de Kant* the best French work on Kant's ethics (Review in *Année philosophique* [1905], 267).

22. Waelti, *Morale kantienne*, 120. Numerous philosophers have examined the ways Renouvier differed from Kant or "misunderstood" him, how he was ahead of earlier French interpreters but not entirely free of their errors. The most thorough discussion is Roger Verneaux, *Renouvier, disciple et critique de Kant* (Paris, 1945).

23. Secrétan, incidentally, thought he saw an influence of Renouvier on Lachelier (Secrétan to Renouvier, March 17, 1869, in *Correspondance de Renouvier et Secrétan*, 19).

24. Verneaux, *Idéalisme de Renouvier*, 5–6; for example, Dauriac, Liard, Brochard, and Evellin were like disciples. Renouvier (*Histoire*, IV, 677n1) rec-

erodox neocriticists did not bother Renouvier, for whom the essence of philosophy was to learn to think for oneself. As he fought for the acceptance of his ideas, he expected other philosophers to fight for theirs. Among the young neocriticist philosophers three names stand out as most highly esteemed by their contemporaries: Octave Hamelin, whose lectures on Renouvier are the most sophisticated and whose personal contribution to neocriticism was the most original; Henry Michel, whose early death was a serious blow to the neocriticist movement, especially to the development of Renouvier's reputation as a political philosopher; and Henri Marion, who introduced Renouvier's moral philosophy to the Sorbonne and the training of future teachers.[25] Only slightly less distinguished intellectually were Gaston Richard, holder of the first chair of social science in a French university, who demonstrated Renouvier's importance for social thought, and the highly influential education reformers Louis Liard and Félix Pecaut.[26] Nor should one forget the popularizer Gabriel Séailles, whose book on Renouvier's philosophy does more than

---

ognized Dauriac, Liard, Pillon. See also Waelti, *Morale kantienne,* 105–10. Secrétan (*Correspondance de Renouvier et Secrétan,* 19) noted as neocriticists in the university Lionel Dauriac and Jules Thomas.

25. I should also mention among those who showed some affinities with Renouvier, while basically standing on their own: Emile Boutroux and Victor Brochard (Prat, *Renouvier,* 263–64). Dauriac ("Un épisode de l'histoire," 293) insisted on the philosophical similarities of Renouvier and Boutroux. On Hamelin, see Foucher, *Jeunesse de Renouvier* [1]; Brunschwicg, *Progrès de la conscience,* 627; Dominique Parodi, *Du positivisme à l'idéalisme, Etudes critiques: philosophies d'hier et d'aujourd'hui* (Paris, 1930), 185–86, hereinafter cited as Parodi, *Du positivisme à l'idéalisme.* Renouvier saw Michel as a possible successor to carry on the message of his *personnalisme* (Charles Renouvier, *Les Derniers entretiens recueillis par Louis Prat* [Paris, 1930], 106). On Marion, see Waelti, *Morale kantienne,* 105–107.

26. See Pt. II, Chap. 4, of Gaston Richard, *La Question sociale et le mouvement philosophique au XIXe siècle* (Paris, 1914). Renouvier praised Liard (*Histoire,* IV, 678–79); Father Lucien Laberthonnière (*Critique du laïcisme* [Paris, 1948]) found Renouvier's influence in all the laic reformers: Pécaut, Steeg, Liard, Buisson, Séailles, Jaurès. On Pécaut, see François Pillon, "Un ouvrage récent sur la philosophie de Charles Renouvier," *Année philosophique* (1905), 127.

any other to make it accessible to the generally educated reader.[27] Only specialists will recognize most of these secondary names today, but their work was easily equal to that of the leading scholars of today.

It must be recognized that despite this impressive array of talented followers, Renouvier's work did not lead to the establishment of a durable neocriticist school of philosophy in France. There was even a certain recession in the wave of his influence by the time of his death in 1903. A number of factors were involved in this: the emergence of a bright new star more attractive to the general public, perhaps, but also producing new food for thought—Henri Bergson;[28] the premature death of some promising neocriticists; the difficulties of adapting Renouvier's thought to the mechanics of the French university.

The rise of Bergson seemed to many to close a parenthesis in the history of French thought, to return to a tradition whose last great representative had been Maine de Biran (1766 to 1824). The nineteenth century thus appeared as a kind of positivist deviation, and Renouvier's insistence that only phenomena are real, however modified by contact with Kant, was swept away in the discredit of the positivism against which he had so bitterly fought. Standing between idealism and empiricism, Renouvier's philosophy suffered a kind of parallel fate to that of liberalism, which also stands in a middle position opposed to both the extremes that enter into its composition.[29]

27. Pillon ("Un ouvrage récent," 97) praised Séailles' study. Foucher (*Jeunesse de Renouvier*) also mentions the phenomenology of Victor Egger, as does Prat (*Charles Renouvier*, 264). Also worthy of mention is Dauriac (Roger Verneaux, "Le Criticisme de Dauriac," *Revue philosophique de la France et de l'étranger*, CXXXIII [1942–43], 97–98). Isaac Benrubi (*Contemporary Thought of France*, trans. Ernest B. Dicker [New York, 1926], 113) points to parallels in the work of Gaston Milhaud, who also wrote a book on Renouvier's philosophy: *La Philosophie de Charles Renouvier* (Paris, 1927).

28. Waelti (*Morale kantienne*, 112–13) saw Bergson as further expanding the use of liberty as the basis of philosophy.

29. Waelti (*ibid.*, 132) argues that Bergson revived the French spiritualist movement, which was naturally hostile to Renouvier's phenomenism. Benrubi (*Contemporary Thought of France*, 115–16) argues for the appearance of a rad-

The final blow, which produced a definitive eclipse of Renouvier's philosophy despite a spate of scholarly studies in the 1920s, was undoubtedly World War I. The real end of the nineteenth century—the Great War, as the French persist in calling it—occasioned a radical break in so many aspects of European life and culture that it would take a book to enumerate them. The postwar culture would have many evident roots in the Belle Epoque, but the war caused a radical separation in people's minds between those things that seemed to look forward to the new world and those irremediably identified with a century that suddenly appeared very remote indeed. Renouvier was in too many of the more obvious ways a man of the nineteenth century to seem relevant in the postwar world. Yet if more people had paid attention to his message, the war would have come as less of a shock, and their cultural disorientation might have been less severe.

Thinkers forgotten by generations immediately following are sometimes revived, by way of reaction, in those that follow. This did not take place in Renouvier's case, despite the impact of another war that instead brought down the remaining shaky foundations of French thought. No post–World War II French philosopher seems to have thought of Renouvier as a precursor. The reasons for this are partly philosophical and partly political, with the latter dominant. A superficial knowledge of Renouvier—and there was some—would naturally have associated him with the liberalism of the early Third Republic, anticlerical and antilabor. Even if one was familiar, which was seldom the case, with his hostility to laissez-faire and his support for a variety of reforms to aid the working class, this would have been overbalanced by his hostility to Marxist collectivism and his rejection of social revolution.

Thus a thinker like Jean-Paul Sartre, who ought to have been at-

---

ically new stage of "inwardness" in French philosophy. Léon Brunschwicg and Elie Halévy ("L'Année philosophique en 1893," 495) had already heralded a similar development. Jean Lacroix (*Vocation personnelle et tradition nationale* [Paris, 1942], 161), on the other hand, thinks Renouvier lost out because he remained too individualist. The peculiar character of liberalism is explored in depth by Thomas A. Spragens, Jr., in *The Irony of Liberal Reason* (Chicago, 1981).

tracted by Renouvier's emphasis on man's freedom and by his phenomenology, was blinded after 1945 by his own political commitment to anti-anticommunism. Few have pushed intellectual incoherence as far as Sartre—"esprit faux, if there ever was one" [30]—but there is no doubt that postwar Marxism in all its many variants tended to sever French philosophy from its past. An exaggerated respect for certain German models, whether Hegel, Husserl, or Heidegger, was also a factor, as was a diffused sense of guilt.

Still, we should not altogether discount the role of philosophical factors among professional thinkers. [31] Postwar French phenomenology would be more narrowly phenomenological in its approach than Renouvier's effort to blend it with Kantian criticism had been. His concern for systematic construction would also be foreign to their approach to philosophizing. [32] There was an opening of new subjects to philosophic inquiry, just as new areas were being explored by historians. Both developments would have been all to the good were it not for a parallel tendency to consider the new subjects the only ones worthy of attention and to neglect the perennial areas of interest, areas to which Renouvier had been attached. He and other French philosophers of the late nineteenth and early twentieth centuries would be made even more unfashionable by the domination in the 1960s and 1970s of the "self-consuming" strain

30. This description has been attributed to Claude Lévi-Strauss.

31. Renouvier's work is, after all, not without its internal contradictions, most of which derive from his position astride two sharply conflicting traditions: idealist rationalism and empiricism. See Verneaux, *Idéalisme de Renouvier*, 325–29.

32. The question of Renouvier's place in the history of modern phenomenology has been raised by Verneaux (*Idéalisme de Renouvier*, 3) and Ascher (*Renouvier*, 2), but as far as I know, no one has seriously tried to answer it. Surely this is a subject worth exploring, given its potential for correcting the common history of philosophy, but it is outside my interests and my capacity. Verneaux (*Idéalisme de Renouvier*, 1) argues that it would be wrong to dismiss Renouvier's work as one of those vast nineteenth-century syntheses "more broad than deep," because he finds in it a deep center: Renouvier's theory of knowledge. One might contrast Renouvier with Sartre, whose efforts to develop a systematic exposition of his own thought were always abortive.

of philosophic activity, which virtually abandoned the pursuit of truth as an ideal.[33]

If practicing philosophers would not be interested in Renouvier for a variety of reasons, some legitimate, it is harder to understand why he is altogether absent from French philosophical education, which still has a substantial historical element. Undeniably lesser contemporaries still find a place in the education manuals and anthologies, thus perpetuating a distorted picture of their time and his. It is true that Renouvier's work is not easily adapted to the French instructional method: Though it would be only difficult and not impossible to discuss his thought in the highly compressed and artificially structured style of French manuals, it is extremely difficult to present his main ideas in the kind of little extracts used to introduce French students to the classics of philosophy.[34] On the other hand, his work offers many opportunities for the imaginative teaching of philosophy. In the course of a very long career, he touched on virtually every subject then recognized as belonging to the domain of philosophy and some that went beyond it. And he was particularly con-

33. How similar is Renouvier's fate to those of Emmanuel Mounier and Albert Camus, which Etienne Borne (*Les Nouveaux Inquisiteurs* [Paris, 1983], 21) attributes to their effort "to articulate [their ideas] in a coherent discourse"? Julien Benda ("Les Idées d'un républicain en 1872," *Nouvelle Revue française*, XXXVII [1931], 24) attributed neglect of Renouvier to his propensity to demand choices where most people prefer to avoid them, to bring certain fundamental conflicts out into the open.

While many observers have tried to make a virtue out of the antihumanism and irrationalism of much of contemporary French philosophy (Foucault, Derrida, Serres, Deleuze) by celebrating its pluralism and its originality, it has also come increasingly under attack (*e.g.,* Jean-Paul Aron, *Les Modernes* [Paris, 1984]; Jacques Bouveresse, *Le Philosophe chez les autophages* [Paris, 1984]; Luc Ferry and Alain Renaut, *La Pensée 68: essai sur l'anti-humanisme contemporain* [Paris, 1985]; David Lehman, *Signs of the Times: Deconstruction and the Fall of Paul de Man* [New York, 1991]). Louis Prat in Renouvier, *Derniers entretiens*, 79–80, was already complaining of a tendency to dilettantism in 1930.

34. That it can be done is illustrated by Paul Théveau and Pierre Charlot, *D'une république à l'autre: la période réaliste* (Paris, 1981), 235–45, in Vol. XII of Théveau and Charlot, *Histoire de la pensée française*.

cerned with interpreting the history of ideas. As a subject for research at the university level, Renouvier's work presents the grave inconvenience of its enormous volume, estimated at 25,000 pages by Marcel Méry, the last scholar to have read a large part of it.[35] Modern standards of scholarship make Renouvier's philosophy a subject not lightly undertaken. Méry's magisterial *thèse* shows that such an effort can be rewarding, but there is also ample room for less ambitious works dealing with selected aspects of that vast corpus.

It would be beyond my capacity and outside my intentions to argue that French philosophy should go "back to Renouvier," in the way that German philosophy has periodically made a "return to Kant." On the other hand, it would be hard to deny that French philosophy is in need of a new spirit.[36] The belated discredit into which Marxist ideology has fallen and the intellectual limitations of the structuralo-linguistic approach have created an opportunity for a philosophy that would renew its links with Western tradition or, to go even further, reassert the value of that tradition despite the failures of the twentieth century. Renouvier's example at least suggests one possible line of inquiry. The revival of interest in political philosophy has been the most promising development of the 1980s.[37] Once the exclusive domain of conservatives, French political philosophy has shown a new opening to liberalism, which by its very nature calls for a reexamination of the nineteenth century.

The combination of the declining intellectual vigor of Marxism (another nineteenth-century doctrine, it must be remembered) and the rise to power of a socialist-communist coalition in France in 1981 stimulated

35. Méry (*Critique du christianisme*, I, 11) notes that Ravaisson, Lachelier, and Boutroux are still covered on exams partly because they wrote little and are thus manageable.

36. At the very least, it should introduce real discussion between conflicting viewpoints, as so many philosophers have preferred to talk only to the converted (Walter Kaufmann, *Goethe, Kant, and Hegel* [New York, 1980], 264, Vol. I of Kaufman, *Discovering the Mind*).

37. Cavallari (*Charles Renouvier*, 186–87) sees views close to Renouvier's on political questions in Eric Weil, *Philosophie politique* (Paris, 1956), and Evelyne Pisier-Kouchner, "L'Obéissance et la loi: le droit," in *Histoire des idéologies*, ed. François Châtelet (Paris, 1978), III, 125.

a remarkably broad spectrum of thought about liberty, political and civil, and the conditions and nature of political democracy. Evidence of this new interest in liberty is to be found in the works of historians, political scientists, sociologists, and philosophers. Particularly notable have been the efforts of Luc Ferry and Alain Renaut to construct a political philosophy of freedom on the basis of a rereading of Fichte and that of Claude Lefort to revalue democracy in part from a rereading of Tocqueville.[38]

Interest in Tocqueville is particularly symptomatic of this new spirit. Long ignored in France except by Raymond Aron, who saw in him one of the precursors of sociology, and a few law professors, Tocqueville has also been rediscovered by historians, especially François Furet, who has made effective use of his analysis of the French Revolution.[39] The history of liberalism itself has received more attention than ever with André Jardin's big survey, Louis Girard's study of the early nineteenth century, and Pierre Guiral's biography of Adolphe Thiers. Pierre Manent has just edited a two-volume anthology of liberal thinkers and written a collection of essays on the origins of our ideas of liberty.[40]

These are all very hopeful signs and especially encouraging after the years when so many French intellectuals were distinguished by either their open support for Stalinism, as with Sartre and Simone de Beauvoir, or their efforts to prop up the shaky edifice of Marxist socialism by more or less ingenious and (dis?)ingenuous injections of Freud or structural-

---

38. Luc Ferry and Alain Renaut, *Philosophie politique* (Paris, 1984–85); Claude Lefort, *Essais sur le politique (XIXe–XXe siècles)* (Paris, 1986). See my paper on Lefort, Ferry, and Renaut, "French Political Thought in the 1980s: Return to the Rights of Man?" *Proceedings of the Annual Meeting of the Western Society for French History,* XVI (1989), 283–90.

39. François Furet, *Penser la révolution française* (Paris, 1978).

40. André Jardin, *Histoire du libéralisme politique, de la crise de l'absolutisme à la constitution de 1875* (Paris, 1985), and a biography of Tocqueville (1984). The late Jean-Claude Lamberti's *Tocqueville et les deux démocraties* (Paris, 1983) was the first French doctoral dissertation on Tocqueville. Louis Girard, *Les Libéraux français, 1814–1875* (Paris, 1985); Pierre Guiral, *Adolphe Thiers: ou la nécessité en politique* (Paris, 1986). Pierre Manent, *Les Libéraux* (Paris, 1986), and *Histoire intellectuelle du libéralisme: dix leçons* (Paris, 1987); see also *Tocqueville et la nature de la démocratie* (Paris, 1982).

ism, as with Louis Althusser. Even those who broke, however cautiously, with the Soviet model continued by their quasi-religious devotion to Marxism to favor the decline of liberty. Though these intellectual types are still common, they are no longer dominant, and the widespread, erroneous belief that to be a socialist meant to be on the side of progress, the future, and freedom has been broken. This is a development of more than local interest, for the intellectual prestige of France in the world is still great, however much it has been undermined since 1945. A foreign observer may therefore be excused for wanting to make a contribution to the rediscovery of liberalism in France.

The Development of Renouvier's Philosophy

As an intellectual historian, I have been especially surprised by the failure of the French to rediscover their most profound thinker about liberty (and a good many other things) since the Revolution—Charles Renouvier. Having written briefly about his place in the development of liberal thought in the last half of the nineteenth century, I am proposing to broaden and deepen my study in this work. Renouvier's example, like that of Tocqueville, reminds us that the nineteenth century showed more originality and depth in its efforts to cope with the political, social, and intellectual problems posed by the American and French revolutions than has our century. A renewed reflection on such nineteenth-century thinkers is proving an effective way out of the doldrums and self-distaste of current Western thought. Renouvier offers a particularly vital example because he shows us why the search for final solutions will always be vain and how we need to orient ourselves if we want to secure the maximum of freedom and justice in our highly imperfect world.

French public life since 1789 has regularly been a battleground of ideas, interests, and persons. As a result, men of ideas have figured more prominently in the political history of France than in other Western countries. The roles they played have been varied, the ideas they defended in the political arena more varied still. Men of ideas occasionally became men of action to the point of losing their quality as intellectuals, as with François Guizot, and the frustration of political ambitions was often valuable for the development of thought, as with Tocqueville. Renouvier's political activity was that of a thinker, mobilized to action as a liberal publicist by the crises facing his country. His family tradition was one of even more direct political involvement. His paternal grandfather was a member of the departmental assembly during the Convention, his maternal grandfather a member of the Council of Five Hundred and the Senate during the Consulat, his father and elder brother deputies under the constitutional monarchy.[41] The young Charles was active in groups of intellectuals promoting social reform on the eve of the 1848 revolution and had a brief contact with the realities of revolutionary government during the Second Republic. After the establishment of the Second Empire, he would find the role, more congenial to his philosophical temperament, of the solitary promoter of ideas.

This first period of his political activity also brought to a close the first phase in Renouvier's development as a philosopher. I am not going to examine what is generally called his "first philosophy" in any detail, but a few observations need to be made. Like most of the original minds of the nineteenth century, Renouvier was self-educated as a philosopher. After receiving formal training as an engineer and mathematician at the Ecole polytechnique (1834 to 1836), he declined the naval commission to which his (low) rank in the graduating class entitled him and spent the next four years trying to discover what he wanted to do with his life. Though the family fortune, patiently amassed by generations of lawyers on both sides of the family, made it unnecessary for Renouvier to pursue a profession, he understood the importance of giving a serious purpose to his existence.[42] As with Rousseau nearly a century earlier, the decisive turning came to him in the form of an essay competition: The Académie des sciences morales et politiques announced a prize for a paper on the

41. On Renouvier's family, see Foucher, *Jeunesse de Renouvier*. This work is essential for the comprehension of the first part of Renouvier's life and thought. Indispensable for the researcher is Foucher's *thèse complémentaire*, a complete bibliography of Renouvier's published works, included in *Jeunesse de Renouvier*.

42. Renouvier's family fortune permitted him to live as he pleased, modestly, and was also important in subsidizing the publication of his many books.

theme of Cartesianism. Having already dabbled a little in philosophy, Renouvier began serious work at the age of twenty-five and produced a *mémoire* (1840) that won him an honorable mention.

Thus encouraged, he began to read more widely and expanded that *mémoire* into his first book, the *Manuel de philosophie moderne*,[43] which appeared the same year as the last volume of Auguste Comte's *Cours de philosophie positive,* 1842. Now thoroughly committed to a philosophical vocation, Renouvier expanded his self-education by producing a *Manuel de philosophie ancienne,* which was published in the same year as the first volume of that monument of the Eclectic school, Adolphe Franck's *Dictionnaire des sciences philosophiques,* 1844. Both *Manuel*s demonstrate that Renouvier was not mistaken in his vocation: He showed a capacity to get at the heart of other people's philosophic systems but no disposition to be content with historical erudition as an end in itself.

The *Manuel*s also contain the expression of their author's emerging philosophy. It was not yet a very original philosophy, owing a great deal to the very Eclectics he despised, but it was already an eclecticism that sought to be consequent and coherent well beyond the aspirations of the dominant school.[44] A variety of influences are to be found, reflecting his wide reading: Descartes, Malebranche, Leibniz, Kant, Hegel, Berkeley, Hume, and even Lamennais. The overall tone was Saint-Simonian.

Like his first philosophy, Renouvier's first political activity was under the aegis of the Saint-Simonian groups to which he had been introduced by his elder brother, Jules, the future archaeologist. The Saint-Simonian movement had been fractured by the schism between the epigoni Enfantin and Bazard, and weakened by prosecution under the July Monarchy, but its influence was still felt in many reformist circles.[45] The political

---

43. It was more an essay than a manual, but "an essay full of merit" (Secrétan, Review of Renouvier's *Manuel de philosophie moderne,* 366).

44. This was Renouvier's later evaluation (*Esquisse,* II, 368–69).

45. The classic works on Saint-Simonism are still valuable. Frank E. Manuel, *The New World of Henri St. Simon* (Cambridge, Mass., 1956); Sebastien Charléty, *Histoire du Saint-Simonisme* (Paris, 1896); Maxime Leroy, *La Vie véritable de comte Henri de Saint-Simon* (Paris, 1925).

thrust of this movement remained, as before, the establishment of a rationalized system of "government" that would close the era of chaos opened in 1789. Political philosophy was to be replaced by science and political authority in the old sense by the authority of knowledge and the techniques of administration.[46] Clearly, the existing form of government stood in the way of such a development, and most Saint-Simonians thought that a republic would open the way to the diffusion and acceptance of their ideas. As a result, they enthusiastically welcomed the February revolution and saw in the formation of the provisional government ample opportunities to exert an influence on the course of events. Renouvier was swept along in their wake.

One thing the French Left had learned from the experience of the July revolution in 1830 was that unless there was a strong and enlightened public opinion behind the republican cause, the dominant political elites would be able to confiscate any upheaval for the preservation of their positions. As a result, there was in 1848 a sense of being involved in a desperate race against time. The fall of the July Monarchy gave the republicans a chance to "educate" the country but little time to do it, for the exercise of the new democratic institutions was likely to return a conservative government determined to abort the reformist movements. The socialists were caught in a trap where it seemed that the implementation of their political program would spell the death of their socioeconomic program. Hence their very embarrassing attempts to delay national elections, efforts that made it possible for their opponents to present them as insincere democrats and emboldened the conservatives to take the risk of universal manhood suffrage. Renouvier's friends had little confidence in the efficacy of street demonstrations and sought to work from inside the provisional government. The futility of the violence of the 1848 revolution would leave a permanent mark on Renouvier's political thought.

The Fabian tactics of the Saint-Simonians were aided by the presence, as minister of public instruction, of Hippolyte Carnot whose status as son of the "Organizer of Victory" had enabled him to survive the

46. See Spragens, *Irony of Liberal Reason*, 117, *passim*, on the technocrats.

purge of more radical elements from the government following the election of the Constituent Assembly in April, 1848. A former Saint-Simonian himself, Carnot established a committee on scientific and literary studies under the direction of Jean Reynaud, who named his thirty-three-year-old friend Renouvier as secretary. Other members of the committee included pamphleteer Beranger, the philosopher-economist A.-A. Cournot, Tocqueville's companion in America Elie de Beaumont, the historian Henri Martin, the Catholic sociologist Frederic LePlay, and the freethinking intellectuals Jules Michelet (who declined the honor) and Edgar Quinet. In response to Carnot's call for a manual of civic rights and duties for use in the education of the newly enfranchised masses, Renouvier dashed off his *Manuel républicain de l'homme et du citoyen,* of which fifteen thousand copies were rapidly distributed throughout the country at government expense.[47]

At this point Renouvier received a rude shock, and he would never forget how naïve his expectations had been. When the leaders of the conservative majority in the new Constituent Assembly had gotten wind of the contents of the *Manuel,* they were perhaps not as shocked as they publicly claimed, but they certainly saw an opportunity to remove Carnot from the government. A parliamentary maneuver was organized, the more scandalous bits of Renouvier's text read out—much was made of a reference to the rich as *mangeurs* (devourers) of the poor—and Carnot was faced with the alternative of agreeing wholly with the *Manuel* (which neither he nor 99 percent of the deputies had read) or appearing to lack adequate control over his ministry. After defending its basic approach while regretting some excesses of language, the minister saw the hopelessness of his position and resigned. Renouvier, now out of government for good, republished the *Manuel républicain* on his own.[48] It was the closest he would come to the corridors of power, perhaps a good

47. "The clergy being by reputation hostile to the progress of the Enlightenment, it is not surprising that the first attempts to instruct the people in the direction of Reason took the form of counter-catechisms" (Maurice Agulhon, Introduction to Renouvier, *Manuel républicain* [Paris, 1981], 15)

48. There have been two "modern" editions, one edited by his philosophical follower Jules Thomas (1904) and one by Maurice Agulhon (1981). For a detailed account of the affair, see Thomas' introduction; Agulhon's is more brief but quite adequate. See also Foucher, *Jeunesse de Renouvier,* 140–54.

thing for the development of his philosophy. He also learned a lesson about the limited power of sound ideas and sincere goodwill, a lesson he would absorb in his mature philosophy.

Renouvier's shock at finding himself, however incidentally, the object of political vilification did not drive him immediately out of politics. Until the founding of the Second Empire put a definitive end to his hopes, Renouvier continued to try to exert political action through the printed word. His most significant output was a little book coauthored with Charles Fauvety, *Gouvernement direct et organisation communale et centrale de la république* (1851).[49] Because of the notoriety surrounding the affaire of the *Manuel républicain* and perhaps because of the enormous volume of his later work, this early treatise has been neglected until recently, when its value as a reflection on the conditions of democratic government has been recognized. Still convinced of the necessity of building democracy from the base, Renouvier turned his attention to the question of how to structure a democratic regime at the level of the commune and the department as well as the state.

While motivated by the desire to present practical programs that could be implemented from the starting point of society as it then existed, the *Gouvernement direct* was nonetheless a utopian document that went against the main lines of French history, indeed against the main trends of Western democracy. It marked, however, a break with the more socialist aspirations of the *Manuel républicain* and did not propose to create a new society, only to establish freer political institutions. Its main thrust was the decentralization of political power to the level of the "commune" (conceived as equivalent in size to the administrative canton of that period), the largest unit in which people could really know those they chose to lead them. A national government would still be needed, but a radically different one from any that had existed. The National Assembly would do little in the way of legislation (and Renouvier remained a man of the eighteenth century in this respect; for him as for

49. Ostensibly the collective effort of several authors, all critics have accepted that it was largely written by Renouvier. There were a number of works on direct democracy published at that time. See Jacques Julliard, *La Faute à Rousseau: essai sur les conséquences historiques de l'idée de souveraineté populaire* (Paris, 1985), 127.

Rousseau the multiplication of laws was an evil), and the bulk of their time would be devoted to administration. Committees of the Assembly would replace all the ministries, which were identified with the authoritarian traditions of government. The whole proposal was coherent, and essential matters like taxation and finances were not neglected. But like most such proposals of the nineteenth century it was conceived in terms of a largely static society. It was not that the authors were unaware of growing change, but like many they doubted man's capacity to master it rationally.

The marginality of Renouvier's political activity saved him from having to take the route of exile from 1851 to 1852, but the coup d'état would leave its permanent marks on him. His integration into Parisian intellectual life came to an end; in giving it up for the smaller social world of provincial life, he would also escape from its fads and fashions and enter into a deeper contact with the wider world of philosophy. His sense of being a *méridional* would be reinforced by the violent repression of southern republicanism by the new empire. When it again became possible to think of living in Paris during the "liberal empire," Renouvier returned but found that it no longer attracted him as in his youth.

In 1866 he definitively established himself in the south of France, though long maintaining a pied-à-terre for use when publishing affairs made it necessary to visit the capital.[50] Unlike some enemies of the Napoleonic regime, Renouvier did not waste time in vain regrets or nostalgia for life in Paris. Indeed, he soon came to recognize the benefits of his separation from the pre-1848 intellectual life of Paris. Though he was originally a minor figure on the fringes of Parisian Saint-Simonianism, his isolation from his earlier associates gave him the opportunity to develop the originality of his thought. He would seize the opportunity to become a philosopher in his own way and would escape the fate of becoming another one of the "prophets of Paris."[51]

50. On Renouvier's later changes of residence, see Méry, *Critique du christianisme.*

51. See the brilliant psychological interpretation of the French social reformers of the eighteenth and early nineteenth centuries by Frank Manuel, *The Prophets of Paris* (Cambridge, Mass., 1962).

In the next two decades Renouvier would lay the solid foundation of his neocritical philosophy in a series of thick volumes under the general heading *Essais de critique générale*.[52] This period would reach its culmination in the publication of his *Science de la morale* in 1869. Freed from the distractions of everyday public affairs and having to earn a living, he was able to work out his position on the most fundamental questions and yet maintain the importance of philosophy for the everyday questions of this world. Out of that effort would emerge the prototype for Julien Benda's ideal of a modern *clerc,* and Benda would recognize him as the model of a *"clerc qui n'a pas trahi."* [53]

Renouvier demonstrated that a single-minded pursuit of truth free from considerations of party, sect, or person need not lead to a sterile detachment from the affairs of contemporary society. He showed, on the contrary, the value that independent thinking can have for contemporary society. It is true that the degree of Renouvier's solitude in these years is sometimes exaggerated, for while his human contacts were relatively limited in number, they compensated in intensity. But he was not involved with any organized groups whose interests he had to take into account. It was particularly important that he had no connection with the university and would feel nothing in common with the *"philosophes salariés"* who dominated official thinking.[54]

---

52. Charles Renouvier, *Essais de critique générale. Premier essai. Analyse générale de la connaissance. Bornes de la connaissance. Plus un appendice sur les principes généraux de la logique et des mathématiques* (Paris, 1854); Renouvier, *Essais de critique générale. Deuxième essai. L'homme: la raison, la passion, la liberté, la certitude, la probabilité morale* (Paris, 1859); Renouvier, *Essais de critique générale. Troisième essai. Les principes de la nature* (Paris, 1864); Renouvier, *Essais de critique générale. Quatrième essai. Introduction à la philosophie analytique de l'histoire* (Paris, 1864). Hereinafter cited as *Premier essai, Deuxième essai, Troisième essai,* and *Quatrième essai,* respectively. (See the Bibliography regarding a second edition of the four *essais.* All references herein are to the first editions noted above.)

53. "An intellectual who has not betrayed his calling." See Julien Benda, *La Trahison des clercs* (Paris, 1927).

54. For Renouvier's observation on his relations with the Eclectics, see Renouvier to Secrétan, August 14, 1869, in *Correspondance de Renouvier et Secré-*

Renouvier's philosophical position had begun to evolve even before 1848, as could be seen clearly in the article "Philosophie" he wrote for Jean Reynaud's *Encyclopédie nouvelle* in 1847. But with the first of the *Essais,* Renouvier emerged as defending a philosophy distinctly his own, a philosophy that came to be known as neocriticism, or as Renouvier preferred to say, "French criticism." The term *criticism* indicates the filiation of his philosophy with that of Emmanuel Kant, especially with Kant's famous critiques—the *Critique of Pure Reason,* the *Critique of Practical Reason,* the *Critique of Judgment.* Renouvier gave himself the same mission as Kant—to provide a method for establishing the limits of rational knowledge and faith. He aspired to carry on what Kant had started, not to be content with what Kant had achieved. Despite his differences with Kant, which were explicit and major from the beginning, Renouvier maintained his fidelity to the spirit of Kant's criticism and bitterly opposed the German Kantians, whom he accused of a return to metaphysics.[55]

Kant's critique of knowledge freed Renouvier from the simplicities of empiricism and positivism, but Renouvier also took from the English empiricists, especially David Hume, the tools to prevent himself from backsliding into "realist" metaphysics, as he thought Kant had tended to do. Rejecting the noumena—the hidden realities behind the phenomena that were alone present to our senses—Renouvier proposed to build all our understanding on phenomena, which may not be the ultimate reality, whatever that means, but are the only reality humans can know, thus paving the way for a phenomenology that would not be just another name for empiricism or materialism.[56] Even if one agrees that Renouvier's genius was not up to the task of reconciling idealism and em-

---

tan, 28, and *Premier essai,* vi–vii. He continued to attack them at the end of his career (*Esquisse,* II, 143–55; *Dilemmes de la métaphysique,* 261). Méry (*Critique du christianisme,* I, 49) notes that Renouvier was even more severe on the thinkers of his youth in 1897 than he had been in 1868.

55. *Premier essai,* viii–ix; *Deuxième essai,* 413. (All citations with no author's name are to Renouvier.)

56. See Verneaux, *Renouvier, disciple,* 26–35, 95, 118; Benrubi, *Sources et courants,* I, 305.

piricism,[57] it can be recognized that his heroic efforts opened up worthwhile lines of inquiry. The two traditions may be ultimately irreconcilable, but Renouvier's choice of a middle path was no more unreasonable than choosing exclusively to adhere to one or the other.

In constructing a phenomenological, some would even say positivist, version of Kantianism,[58] Renouvier had finally found his own way:

> Our existence flows through time; our thoughts and our beliefs change as time passes. . . . But a moment comes for us to finally know ourselves and to give our intelligence a steady direction. Then we collect our forces, we fix our sentiments, and it is only then that—marching straight along the path of life we have chosen—we become our true selves. To thus transform plurality into unity is to make a contract with ourselves in order to place the government of our innermost spirit in the hands of a single idea.[59]

Renouvier's understanding of freedom and rejection of an impersonal Reason will be considered in more detail later. They grew out of his personal experience as well as his reading and reflection. Renouvier liked to stress the role of reflection on certain mathematical problems concerning infinities in giving this definitive direction to his philosophy,[60] and he gave full, perhaps even excessive, credit to his friend Jules Lequier for his conversion to free will.

Most important, he came to realize that a philosophical position is a choice, a choice in which one cannot, without self-delusion, achieve

57. Miéville, *Philosophie de Renouvier*, 68–70.

58. Benrubi, *Contemporary Thought of France*, 85–87; Jean-Louis Dumas, "Renouvier," *Dictionnaire des philosophes* (Paris, 1984), 2216; Léon Ollé-Laprune, *De la certitude morale* (Paris, 1880), 320–21; Verneaux, *L'Idéalisme de Renouvier*, 148; Waelti, *Morale kantienne*, 17–18. Victor Delbos (*La Philosophie française* [Paris, 1919], 364) goes so far as to call Renouvier a "sort of Hume corrected by the idea of the necessity of a priori categories."

59. *Deuxième essai*, 547.

60. *Esquisse*, II, 363, 372, 374–75.

apodictic certainty.[61] Philosophers have reacted to this problem in various wáys. Few have been able to resist the temptation to *prove* their positions and have wound up, like Kant, in an often impenetrable obscurity as a result. Others have been content with skepticism, or the proclamation of antitheses. Renouvier was prepared to choose, in the knowledge that no one can hope to put an end to the fundamental disagreements that have marked—that in a sense *are*—the history of Western philosophy. He would spend much of his career defending the rationality and the probable truth of his choices. Free will formed the central core of Renouvier's mature philosophy, and we will examine it in some detail in Chapter II.

In the first of his *Essais,* Renouvier described the presentation of his philosophy as a history of his thought. Near the end of his career he would write a lengthy chapter on "how I came to these conclusions" in his *Esquisse d'une classification systématique des doctrines philosophiques* (1886). He admirably summed up the philosophical position of his maturity:

> Having finally succeeded in freeing my mind from the prestige of the three idols of philosophy, . . . the actually existing infinite, the idea of substance behind all phenomena, and the absolute causal connection between successive events, I found myself at the same time protected from [the error of] empiricism by that admirable theory of the understanding in which Kant has reconciled recognition of the existence of synthetic a priori judgments and the definition of the laws governing the mind with the facts of experience; I was protected from all skeptical doctrines by one of my oldest and most deeply rooted convictions about the moral nature of statements about every kind of reality and about the legitimacy—or even the duty of belief with respect to everything outside the immediate evidence of our senses, whose certainty is the only certainty which can be purely and exclusively intellectual.[62]

61. On "*croyance,*" see *Esquisse,* II, 360–61.
62. *Ibid.,* 390.

Introduction

The technical philosophic questions raised by every phrase in this paragraph, some of which I'll try to explain later, give some hint of the importance of Renouvier's neocriticism. He brought his critical perspective to bear on all the main issues in the history of Western philosophy, and even where his solutions are not convincing, his grappling with these problems is full of stimulating insights. We are not, however, writing the history of philosophy here, and what matters most is that Renouvier's philosophy was also a philosophy of combat. It was a struggle against the errors common to his day (and not so absent as some seem to think from our own) and a battle in defense of fundamental values: reason, freedom, the individual.

Renouvier's Philosophical Combat

The philosophic effort and the political struggle were never completely separable for Renouvier. He would show that there is no necessary contradiction between a deep immersion in the traditional (and often very technical) issues of Western philosophy and a commitment to apply one's intelligence to the issues of contemporary society. Knowing the limits of the power of sound thought to affect the conduct of man in society, Renouvier was not tempted to sacrifice his values in the name of social or political efficiency. Philosophical reflection would be applied where it could do the most good—the critique of contemporary ideas. The defense of individual freedom was the main objective of Renouvier's philosophical politics, and in the context of nineteenth-century intellectual-political affairs this especially involved him in a combat against historicism. The truth of J. M. Keynes's famous remark that statesmen are all ruled by some dead economist was understood in a more general and truer form by Renouvier, who was acutely conscious of how men's actions are shaped by the way they understand the world and that this understanding is never the direct product of personal experience but is shaped by the interpretation common in the intellectual milieu. For instance, one of the dominant intellectual attitudes of that time was historical determinism; even those who did not give it any thought were under its spell. The common form of this determinism was the idea of progress, and most people thought of progress as an evident fact of experience rather than what it really is, a philosophical interpretation of that experience based on certain presuppositions that have not been demonstrated to be true.[63]

After 1848, Renouvier was embarrassed to admit that he ever shared in the belief in progress as understood by most of his contemporaries. He would not deny that progress in some respects had taken place at some times in human experience or that it was to be desired and worked for in the present. What had to be repudiated was the idea of a necessary progress in this world, whether that necessity rested on Newton's laws of motion, God's providence, Hegel's world spirit, Darwin's natural selection, or Marx's historical materialism. This idea of necessary progress had to be combated both because it was false, false to history and false philosophically, and because of its political and social consequences. In his experience, belief in progress had perhaps raised unrealistic expectations and thus heightened the disappointments of 1848, but this was a minor aspect of the problem, and true believers are rarely discouraged when things do not turn out as they expected. More vital for Renouvier was the moral impact—or rather the immoral impact—that belief in progress has on our interpretation of the past and our actions in the present.

One of the unfortunate effects of the rise of historical studies in the nineteenth century, it seemed to Renouvier, was an increased tendency to apologize for all the crimes of the past on the grounds that they ultimately contributed to progress. He did not deny that good may some-

---

63. Renouvier did not see any cumulative advance in philosophy, only a prolongation of ancient quarrels. Rather than dying out and being replaced by superior ideas, all basic systems of thought have survived (with some changes in form to be sure) into the present (*Quatrième essai*, 754; *Esquisse*, II, 149). This empirical observation was one of the factors in shaping Renouvier's concept of the role of belief in philosophy. He did recognize some distinctiveness in the modern configuration: "That which gives modern methods or systems their new physiognomy, besides the changes of form and of language in the position of problems, is the state of advancement of the natural sciences, . . . the philosophy of history and . . . the enormous progress made by psychological analysis" (*Esquisse*, II, 39).

times come out of evil; if it did not, good would surely have disappeared from this world. But he knew the importance of rejecting the idea that whatever happens, however bad it seems at the moment, is necessarily for some future good. It is understandable, a sort of professional weakness, that historians see the past as a chain of causes and effects that could not have been other than what they were. That this easily becomes apology for tyrants perhaps has little effect on the quality of historical research, but it has a dangerous impact on the way our understanding of the past affects our actions in the present.

Out of Renouvier's critique of the historicist idea of progress came his conception of the political utility of philosophy and the content of his political positions. It gave him a more realistic or restrained conception of the good that can be accomplished at any particular moment without weakening his sense of obligation to promote that good. It did not lead to political quietism or the substitution of a pessimistic fatalism for the optimistic one. Such an attitude can, of course, lead to an excess of conservatism, to a preference for clinging to the good one has out of fear of losing that in the effort to reach something better. Renouvier's political practice during the Third Republic did not always escape from this temptation, but his political philosophy always contained an antidote in his devotion to liberty.

Very few people in the nineteenth century would share Renouvier's understanding that the penetration of Western thought by historicist assumptions was not favorable to the construction of earthly paradises but on the contrary would pave the way to new despotisms. This analysis has become almost a commonplace of today's French political thought now that the bankruptcy of the effort to keep Marxism alive with injections of Freud, Weber, phenomenology, or even self-transfusions of Young Marx has finally been recognized. Nobody, however, has yet given Renouvier credit for seeing through the illusions of his contemporaries and showing why those illusions were leading to disaster. It would be an exaggeration to claim that Renouvier had a fully developed idea of totalitarianism, but he understood that the age of personal despotism could give way to a new social despotism claiming to be scientific. The attack on liberty carried out by Auguste Comte under the banner of "Order and Progress" was explicit and overt, but the emotional power of "progress" was so strong that many continued to believe they could combine positivism and political liberty.[64] (This is another point I will deal with in a later chapter.) Few, even among *fin-de-siècle* pessimists, could detach themselves from historicist illusions.

As we shall see when we deal with Renouvier's moral philosophy, he understood that the basic problem of modern thought was to combine universal and permanent values with an awareness of historical relativity and change. He was not a syncretist—a type common in the nineteenth century—because he remained attached to the superior character of universal values while grasping the constraints that real-world conditions impose on their pursuit. He was not a political opportunist or a philosophical pragmatist, though he had affinities with both groups. For Renouvier, the political ideal is not something for which we are justified in sacrificing the interests and happiness of present generations, nor is it an anodyne with which to mute present distress. It is something we are obliged to pursue while remaining conscious of our inability to attain it. Politics, for all its moral shortcomings, remains essential, as does a limitation of its domain. The democratic republic as a form of sociopolitical organization seemed to Renouvier the only framework in which man's enduring ideals could be effectively pursued. The effort to establish such a regime on the ruins of the Second Empire called him out of the provinces for another period of involvement in national politics.

The sense of impending change that marked the end of the 1860s and the emergence of the "liberal empire" reached Renouvier and drew him back toward the public arena without causing him to leave his character as a philosopher. His collaboration with François Pillon in launching the *Année philosophique* in 1868 was an anticipation of the role he would play in the early years of the Third Republic. The slide of the empire into an ill-prepared war came as no surprise to Renouvier, who had not slackened in his contempt for the regime of Louis-Napoléon. The ease with which the empire was overthrown, on the other hand, probably came as a surprise, given his pessimism at that moment.

Like many republicans, Renouvier had a moment of excusable

64. *E.g.*, Emile Littré, "Education politique," *Philosophie positive*, XVII (1876), 421–27.

Schadenfreude at the hated emperor's downfall, but any pleasure was soon replaced by anxiety over what sort of regime was to follow. He had no desire to return to the July Monarchy or the upheavals of 1848, though he would later argue that the republicans of 1870 could have avoided the five years of travail it took to produce a new constitution by simply proclaiming the continued validity of the 1848 constitution. The tragedy of the Paris Commune filled him with the deepest sorrow. He had little sympathy for the aims of the communards, whose socialist elements appeared hostile to liberty, but he placed most of the blame for the outburst of violence on the Thiers government and more generally on the ruling classes, whose ineptitude and immorality he denounced in the strongest terms.[65] For Renouvier as for most liberal republicans, the defeat of 1871 called forth an effort for the moral renewal of France.

Unlike most of them, however, his upsurge of feeling for suffering France had its limits.[66] Despite his contribution to that renewal, some of the more ardent young nationalist republicans like Daniel Halévy would never forgive Renouvier for a few expressions of a less-than-unqualified admiration for France and the French.[67] While making clear his contempt for Prussianism, Renouvier insisted on drawing attention to the responsibility of France for the war. The France that had to be uplifted was not an innocent victim, and no good could come from pretending that it was.

Renouvier's position on the fate of Alsace-Lorraine did not please the unconditional nationalists either: If Germany had no right to decide the fate of those provinces, neither did France. The land and people that had become German in 1871 by "right" of the strongest had earlier become French on the same grounds. Only the Alsatians and Lorrainers, he insisted, could be said to possess any right to determine their national affiliation. France could claim no right based on great moral superiority. On the other hand, Renouvier was moved by the war to find more virtues

65. For one example, see Renouvier to Charles Secrétan, April 11, 1871, in *Correspondance de Renouvier et Secrétan*, 57.

66. Albert Thibaudet ("Réflexions," *Nouvelle Revue française*, XXXV [1930], 547) saw in Renouvier's "Europeanism" a valuable message for the post–World War I period.

67. See Daniel Halévy's response to Thibaudet, "Une lettre de Daniel Halévy," *Nouvelle Revue française*, XXXV (1930), 719–20.

than he usually did in the Latin nations as compared to the Germanic. Like many French intellectuals, he modified his image of Germany with the emergence of Bismarck's reich.

His belief in free will always led Renouvier to reject providential interpretations of history, but he was tempted to see in the defeat of 1871 and the Commune a merited punishment for the sins of the French. He was dubious that they would draw any salutary lessons from the experience, however, and the election of the National Assembly filled him with gloom. Republicanism was stronger in the country than it had been in 1848, but its enemies were still numerous and apparently more effectively led. The division of the monarchists soon revealed that there was hope in the situation, and he began to think of intensifying his effort to influence republican thinking. With Pillon he decided to turn the *Année philosophique* into a weekly aimed at an elite audience. Renouvier's independent financial resources enabled him to contemplate this commitment that would absorb much of his income and his time for several years. The new *Critique philosophique,* launched in 1872, was explicitly announced as an organ of combat.

The *Critique philosophique* would publish, especially in the 1870s, commentaries on current political and social issues and give its support to various reform proposals. However current the issue under discussion, Renouvier and his collaborators generally took a longer view, examining political decisions in the light of philosophical principles. They had no partisan connections, no inside information, but were determined to show the utility of a philosophically informed perspective. Renouvier was aware of his limitations and rarely strayed outside subjects where he could make a contribution to the national debate.

Above all, *Critique philosophique* was an organ of philosophical combat. It tirelessly attacked those ideas and systems of thought he believed both false and harmful. He proposed to

combat common tendencies which show themselves under so many names and in so many forms in our century: pantheism, Hegelianism, Saint-Simonianism, positivism, communism, altruism, evolutionism, monism, Buddhism, religious utilitarianism, sacerdotalism, transcendental immoralism, rehabilitation of the Middle Ages, justification of evil as a necessary cause of good, abandonment of the historical and moral principles of the Revolution, all tendencies that are harmful and threaten to sweep everything away.[68]

Political action for Renouvier was never divorced from the examination of ideas and their long-term consequences.

In the practical sphere of the application of ideas, Renouvier's *Critique philosophique* was mainly concerned with questions of national education, especially moral and civic instruction. The missed opportunity of 1848 had been paid for, and the republicans were not going to let it slip away again. Renouvier was now prepared, as he had not been in 1848, to make an original contribution to the debate. He would not miss the chance to show the relevance of the neo-Kantian moral philosophy he had developed in the 1860s. If he could not expect many people to work through the two substantial volumes of his *Science de la morale*, he could use the pages of the *Critique philosophique* to present his philosophy in handy doses and in the context of current issues. The substance of his moral philosophy and the social action Renouvier based upon it form the subject of the next chapter. What is important to note here is that the form of his actions enabled Renouvier to remain faithful to his role of laic "*clerc.*"

The successful implantation of the democratic republic in France in the later 1870s and early 1880s responded to Renouvier's aspirations while falling well short of his ideals. In the 1890s he would receive a belated public recognition for his work on behalf of the republic and his contribution to the revival of French philosophy in the second half of the nineteenth century. The Ministry of Public Instruction underwrote the publication costs of his mammoth four-volume *Philosophie analytique de l'histoire* (1896 to 1898), and the Institut de France awarded him the Prix Estrade Delcros (1899) "for the ensemble of his philosophic work, and especially for the *Philosophie analytique de l'histoire* and for the *Nouvelle monadologie.*" He was elected to the Académie des sciences morales et politiques in 1900, succeeding the Eclectic philosopher Paul Janet.[69] Renouvier declined an offer of the Légion d'honneur.

68. *Critique philosophique* (1876-I), 370–71.
69. Méry, *Critique du christianisme*, II, 15–16.

The real satisfaction he derived from this recognition was tempered by the conviction that he had had a very limited success in checking the spread of false and harmful ideas. What distressed him most and contributed to the growing pessimism of his last years was not so much the failure of the republic to grapple successfully (or even seriously) with the immense social problems facing the country (see Chapter IV) but the feeling that his fellow Europeans were living in a fools' paradise because their optimistic historicism blinded them to the growing dangers facing the West (see Chapter V).

It is hard to imagine today the enormous popularity enjoyed at the end of the last century by the evolutionary optimism of Herbert Spencer, one of Renouvier's bêtes noires, and the general belief that Spencer offered a scientific view of the world. Especially comforting was Spencer's assurance that Europe had passed from a military age into an industrial age. He shared the common nineteenth-century view that economics was destined to supplant politics—and that this was a good thing because it promoted an era of peace and prosperity. Renouvier saw little reason to believe that the conditions for lasting peace were ever likely to be established in this world. The prejudices of an optimistic philosophy prevented men from making realistic judgments about what was going on in the world around them.

Renouvier would not fall into the error of an excessive rationalism either; his philosophical outlook embraced the whole of human nature and was thus less open to unrealistic expectations.[70] Contemporary developments seemed to Renouvier the most ominous he had witnessed in a long lifetime. Europe was moving toward a general war that Spencer's vaunted industrial society would make more destructive than ever. It was also facing a social upheaval for which the Commune had been only a mild anticipation. The twentieth century, alas, would correspond only too well to his expectations.

The remaining chapters of this book are devoted to an examination of several important themes in the intellectual life of nineteenth- and twentieth-century Europe, taking Renouvier's reflections as our base. I

70. See, *e.g.*, Miéville, *Philosophie de Renouvier*, 209–10.

hope that in the process of this examination we will learn something about Renouvier, the nineteenth century, and ourselves and the problems we face today.

The central theme of this work, as it must be in any work on Renouvier, is liberty. At various stages of his career, Renouvier labeled his philosophy as neocriticism, French criticism, or *personnalisme,* but at all periods it can be most accurately called a philosophy of liberty.[71] I will examine what liberty meant to Renouvier at the levels of ontology and psychology as well as in the domains of social life and politics, freedom in the abstract and in the concrete. We will see how Renouvier defended his conception of freedom and applied it to the study of historical and philosophical questions, especially to the intellectual and sociopolitical questions of his day.

I will argue from his example that the menace to freedom in the twentieth century has been aggravated by the absence of an adequate philosophical reflection on liberty, which has led to the acceptance of certain assumptions that have turned out to be hostile to practical freedom. The twentieth century has discovered that the natural sciences and the social sciences are incapable of furnishing a solid foundation on which to defend liberty; indeed, both have easily been used for purposes hostile to liberty. If philosophy becomes part of the dead past of Western civilization, the cause of freedom would appear to be doomed. Belief in freedom at least permits the conclusion that such is not the necessary or the only possible outcome of present affairs.

Freedom for Renouvier was the necessary basis for moral philosophy, just as it appears to be in common sense, and moral philosophy is the core of any philosophical enterprise. The construction of his basic philosophical positions—his epistemology and his psychology—had the primary purpose of laying a foundation for his moral philosophy. Once this was established in his *Science de la morale,* the main part of his later work was devoted to examining its ramifications in areas ranging from politics to poetics, cosmology, and history. To seek to construct a laic moral philosophy was in the mainstream of nineteenth-century concerns,

71. Paul Glaize, "La philosophie de M. Renouvier," *Morale indépendante,* September 13, 1869, pp. 50–51.

though Renouvier's approach is distinctive and not simply a reflection of that mainstream.[72] Today's moral thought is diverse in the extreme, ranging from permissive hedonism to social-science relativism to efforts to revive a certain Protestant "puritanism." What is rarely found is a belief in the possibility of a rationally based moral philosophy having a universal human value, even if diversely applicable.[73] In the light of the experiences of the twentieth century, the application of a moral doctrine to political life and international relations has seemed both more needed than ever and a more vain utopian hope than in the past. One result has been an incoherence in efforts to think about public morals, with sentimentality of the most uncritical kind and the most cynical *Realpolitik*— practiced, it sometimes seems, by the same people. Attempts at a philosophically thought-out position have been rare, apparently requiring the heroism of a Sidney Hook to remain loyal to a rationalist faith.

Renouvier's moral reflection anticipated some of the difficulties that have assailed the twentieth century. While critical of Catholic moral teaching, which he considered hostile to freedom, and convinced that religion should be founded on morals rather than morals on religion, he was concerned that the evident decline of religious faith in the West would lead not to the triumph of rationalist secular morals but to moral anarchy or the domination of new ethical systems of heteronomy based on social-scientific doctrines. What we have had in our century has been both, and if to most people the alternative of a rational moral doctrine has seemed unworkable and old-fashioned, no viable alternatives have emerged. This also justifies a renewed reflection on Renouvier's effort.[74]

One problem with many social-science approaches to moral questions is their tendency to absorb the individual in the community and to undermine the sense of individual responsibility that is basic to the West-

72. I recently saw a new anthology of French laicism that included nothing of Renouvier in its section on the nineteenth century. But see Phyllis Stock-Morton, *Moral Education for a Secular Society: The Development of Morale Laique in Nineteenth Century France* (Albany, N.Y., 1988).

73. Some recent French writers have begun to react against this anomie, but it is a reaction that risks being associated with the Right in politics.

74. This would be helped if some French publisher can be persuaded to bring out a new edition of Renouvier's *Science de la morale*.

ern moral tradition. Thus, another main theme of this book is the problem of the relations of the individual and the community in the nineteenth century, with emphasis on Renouvier's effort to build community on the primacy of the individual without falling into anarchist or libertarian illusions. The originality of his analysis has not been fully appreciated, and his concept of "*solidarité dans le mal*" (solidarity of evil) can still bear useful fruit for social thought.

In nineteenth-century France it was generally recognized that individualism was the increasingly dominant characteristic of modern Western mentalities. It was accepted as a fact even by those who lamented it and hoped to make it a passing fancy, whether traditionalists longing for the restoration of Christian community or Comteans looking forward to an age of altruism. But except for the few content with enunciating an abstract ideal, there was a general agreement on the need for finding ways to bind the individual to the community that would be compatible with individualism. One approach was to deny that there was a problem, which was essentially the method of the laissez-faire economists who trusted in the invisible hand or, in his own way, the solution of Charles Fourier, who counted on the "law of attraction," his social equivalent of gravitation. A contrasting approach was that of the social scientists, who hoped by the empirical study of society to learn what "really" holds societies together as a prelude to showing how a society of individualists can be made to work.

Renouvier's was somewhere between these positions. Like the social scientists, he did not much fear the dissolution of the social order; if one should happen to collapse, it would be replaced by another. He was more worried by the tendency of the social order to crush the individual's freedom. But neither did he believe in the sort of spontaneous social order in the manner of the utopian Fourier or the laissez-faire economist Jean-Baptiste Say. For Renouvier, society was not an entity distinct from the individuals who composed it, nor did it have rights distinct from theirs. His approach to social questions was both a moral and a methodological individualism; a sociology built on his assumptions would be closer to that of Gabriel Tarde than that of Emile Durkheim.[75]

75. Or is it closer to that of Max Weber? See the recent defense of a Weberian methodological individualism in the works of the French sociologist Ray-

Social questions were essentially moral questions for Renouvier, but in his moral philosophy the isolated individual is only a convenient fiction necessary for the construction of the whole. Moral man is always part of a society, and morals essentially concern the relations among individuals. Society is thus an ethical necessity, but it is also a historical product. Men are born into a social context not of their choosing; every step in their experience adds to the network of connections involving them with other people, for good and for ill. The existence of social connections is both the prerequisite for any moral action and the reason why most of our actions tend to fall far short of the right, even when they are not positively evil.

The view of the relations of the individual and the community that emerges from Renouvier's philosophy is thus a complex one. It combines a recognition of what the individual owes to society—other people, living and dead—for both good and evil with an aspiration toward a better society, defined as one that promotes individual freedom and increases man's opportunities for moral behavior. For Renouvier, the reforms of institutions and individuals are so interconnected as nearly to form a vicious circle; indeed, they would form a vicious circle were it not for the free will of the individual.

He shows why we should be skeptical of all those reformers who propose to make a new man by the reform of institutions, for every such proposal assumes the existence of the kind of men it is supposed to produce. Obvious though this seems, it goes against a major part of the social thought of his century and ours, which, despairing of the possibility of reforming individuals—inevitably too corrupted by their social situation—has preferred to believe in the possibility of radically perfected institutions. The condition of the world is such that it is unreasonable to expect men to renounce the possibility of improving it, daunting though the prospect seems.

Renouvier was not so much a pessimist as Schopenhauer, though his hopes would rise and fall with circumstances. The improvement of indi-

---

mond Boudon. Renouvier did not go as far as Weber in finding the social world irrational.

viduals, despite the weight of social solidarity, is possible because man has free will, however rarely or badly he exercises it. Freer men can join together to create freer institutions, as history has demonstrated, but only if we believe in the primary value of individual freedom can we hope to make a better world. Renouvier's social philosophy, like his moral doctrine and his epistemology, rested on a *croyance:* the freely chosen belief in the reality of man's freedom. He shows us that though reason denies us exaggerated hopes for this world, it also protects us against exaggerated despair.

The denial of exaggerated hopes for this world leads us to the question of what we may hope for from another world, or even whether it is legitimate to believe in the possibility of another world. The rise of messianic reform movements in the nineteenth century was, in part at least, a counterpart to the decline in the Christian hope for immortality. This secularization of religious expectations was frequently expressed in an antireligious polemic, attacking the churches for offering the poor "pie in the sky, bye and bye" when what was needed was bread in the here and now. The need for bread was indeed often acute, but what the social reformers mostly offered was "pie in the here, but not now." As it became evident that the generation of those living was not likely to see the promised land, so it became necessary to make the promise more attractive.

To justify such views, Renouvier pointed out, is to sacrifice the individual utterly to the community. Individuals might choose to sacrifice themselves in the interest of generations to come, but he did not believe that this can be made a moral obligation, and Christian commentators often lamented Renouvier's lack of feeling for the self-sacrifice of the saints. He was, indeed, suspicious of saints (even more of secular ones), for they are only too ready to sacrifice other people to their visions. He clearly understood that the denial of a future life could serve to justify a vision of this world in which the individual would be ruthlessly crushed in the name of the moral reform of humanity, and he repeatedly warned against this danger, but I doubt that he anticipated the scale on which his fears would be so tragically realized.

While the logic of Renouvier's critique has been ratified by experience, can we say any more than that people who believe in the cause of freedom in this world should recognize that to believe in a future life is not, at least not automatically, to be an enemy of freedom in this one? Renouvier argued only that it was not against reason to believe in a future life; reasonable men might differ over its reality. As for him, a future life was a moral necessity, for without the existence of a future life, man's moral potential could not be fulfilled. Perfect moral community in this world is impossible because of the solidarity of evil, but Renouvier could not bring himself to renounce a hope that seemed necessary to give meaning to this life.

For more conventionally religious people, his line of argument was scarcely fulfilling, but Renouvier's appeal, like Kant's, was essentially addressed to the educated unbelievers of his day. The terms of the question do not seem much different in our time. The world still seems basically divided between those who adhere to a transcendental faith (whether supported by reason or not) and those who profess a purely immanent view of man (whether thought out or not). Both positions lend themselves to social doctrines hostile to individual freedom, but their rivalry is sometimes productive of practical freedom, each furnishing a counterweight in communities where the other is dominant. Is an intermediary position like Renouvier's—which might be called transcendence within immanence—ever likely to be accessible to other than an intellectual elite? It is especially the intellectual elite, with its proclivity for extremes that made it the architect of religious persecution in past centuries and materialist totalitarianism in ours, that most needs Renouvier's message. It would at least be a measure of protection against the "*trahison des clercs*" that Julien Benda denounced in the 1920s and that has been no less a danger to the West in subsequent decades. It was no accident that Benda cited Renouvier at the opening of his classic essay.[76]

Despite two brief incursions into the fringes of political activity, Renouvier's life was essentially that of an independent scholar devoted to the elaboration and perfection of his ideas through an intensive study combining the classics with the latest authors and a continuous rewriting of his ideas. Late in life he would lament having lived too much in an ivory tower, and there is little doubt he would have benefited personally and intellectually from having had to work with others more fre-

76. Exordium to Benda, *Trahison des clercs*.

quently.[77] But his thought was not the product of an ivory-tower mentality; it was his personality rather than his intellect that inclined Renouvier to solitude. He was always intensely interested in what was going on in the Western world, not just in philosophy but in science, religion, politics, and society. He would know as much about them as can be gained by reading, which is more than many unreflective people learn from direct experience. Nor can it be said that Renouvier's thought was lacking in realism. While not without his elements of naïveté, as demonstrated in his campaign to enroll free-thinkers as Protestants (see Chapter III), he was extremely lucid in his self-awareness and realist to the point of pessimism in social and political matters.

Renouvier was sensitive to the appeal of many of the ideological currents of his day and had to fight hard to liberate himself from some of them. He would thus not underestimate their potency, even when submitting them to the most relentless scrutiny. He was too imbued with the history of Western thought to be excessively optimistic about the impact of his critique on the holders of these ideas; demonstrable falsity had never prevented ideas from flourishing. But he had a strong sense of his vocation as a critic and a highly combative temperament that would keep him fighting to the end of his life against the illusions of his contemporaries. Despite his penetrating critique of the dominant doctrines of social reform, Renouvier never became an apologist for the existing order, whose immorality he condemned in the strongest terms. But he would not adopt a sociopolitical theory and preach its implementation in the name of either science or the philosophy of history. He would show how those who did take such positions were the enemies of freedom and thus the enemies of any real progress.

Renouvier's exemplary value for our time is thus that of an independent critique of ideas and institutions, an intellectual who did not subordinate his personal struggle for truth and wisdom to the exigencies of an ideological cause. His example shows that it is possible to reject the temptation to erect absolutes without giving up the pursuit of truth and justice. This was the aim that Renouvier attributed to his last philosophy, *personnalisme*, but was present throughout his thought: "We must not

77. *Derniers entretiens*, 88.

aim at absolute perfection, nor at absolute justice; we must fight with all our strength to bring a little more justice into the world. . . . Whether we are to be our own makers depends in part on our reason and on our reasonable use of our liberty." [78]

The *clerc* need not be a person indifferent to the issues of his day but must be one who knows how to put a critical distance between himself and the most seductive ideologies of his time. This is never an easy position to take—intelligence, even moral sensitivity, is not enough—but Renouvier showed how it can be achieved both in the example of his life and through the liberating thrust of his philosophy.[79] It seems important to show how these possibilities developed in the context of the intellectual struggles of the nineteenth century, for the problems Renouvier had to contend with do not seem fundamentally much different from those of today. Of course, it would be possible to write about Renouvier—not just possible but interesting—as if this connection with our time did not exist. Traditional ideals of scholarship and "objectivity" would seem to demand such an approach. But Renouvier is a subject who calls for a different treatment, not one that presents him uncritically on his own terms but one that shares his belief in the importance of ideas and the reality of free will.

78. *Ibid.*, 64.
79. For Renouvier, philosophy was and is always a struggle for truth against tradition and other views that imply truth is something already possessed (*Esquisse*, I, 326).

I

Moral Philosophy and Social Action

> Criticism aims at renewing political life by introducing a simple proposition which will be the salvation of all states, and our own: Judge honor in politics exactly on the same grounds as we judge it in private relations.
>
> —Renouvier, *Critique philosophique* (1872-I)

There is a remarkably broad agreement that Western society in the late twentieth century is undergoing a serious crisis in public and private morals. This agreement is to be found in virtually every part of the political spectrum and in the most divergent religious positions. Diagnoses may differ, but the sense that something is wrong is widespread.

For some, the principal symptom is sexual license; for others, it is the increase in crimes against persons and property; for still others, it is the decline of the work ethic. The list could be extended almost indefinitely. There are some areas of general agreement: For example, the rise in crimes against persons is a bad thing. There are other areas—sexual behavior, for one—where one person's sign of decay is another's sign of progress, as in today's conflict over legal abortion. Many issues are clouded by the habit, common in Western society, of regarding change as ipso facto progress, and especially regarding anything that can be labeled, however erroneously, an expansion of liberty as a sign of progress.

49

It has been a particularly twentieth-century tendency to deny that there can be any enduring standards of right and wrong and to redefine *moral* as "progressive." This is, as Renouvier pointed out, one of the distinctive symptoms of the characteristics of our moral crisis. Today's believers in the unlimited virtues of "freedom" and "progress" have merely carried to an extreme one of the central themes of modern thought.

Seldom has there been so much talk about freedom and so little understanding, or even serious consideration, about its meaning, especially in the context of morals. It requires some reflection to understand the possible, indeed the necessary coexistence of liberty and limits, and that reflection belongs in the domain of moral philosophy.[1] This is not an esoteric question but one of everyday importance, one accessible to us all. It does help, nonetheless, to have the assistance of a philosopher who is as deeply committed to the theoretical reality and practical importance of liberty as Renouvier. For Renouvier, liberty is the very foundation of morality, for liberty is self-government and not self-indulgence.

Since many intellectuals have come to conceive of freedom as an absolute good, they cannot admit that any evil can come from the freely chosen acts of individuals.[2] The very idea of evil has to be banished to make such a position plausible; in its place, contemporary society, building on ideas that became common in the nineteenth century, has put the idea of *deviance,* a mere departure from the common norms of one's society. From this position it is easy to blame society rather than the deviant for any behavior that the society somehow persists in disapproving. It has even become fashionable to castigate society for daring to disapprove.

The extremes to which this position can be pushed would defy belief in any era but our own: No century has seen more frequent and blatant apologies for murder, whether individual or on the scale of millions. In

1. See, *e.g., Critique philosophique* (1876-I), 265. This point is well understood in Judith N. Shklar's brilliant *Ordinary Vices* (Cambridge, Mass., 1984).

2. Fourier explicitly excluded the moral law from his phalanstery, but even he thought, as Renouvier (*Critique philosophique* [1873-I], 34–35) pointed out, that perfect sexual liberty would be possible only in the perfect world of the future, not among men as they are.

the sphere of sexual relations, even the dominant idea that anything is permissible between "consenting adults" has been taken as an infringement on their freedom by those incapable of drawing any intellectual or emotional distinction between children and adults. Any reaction against actions or advocacy of the most immoral behavior stirs hysterical fears that "freedom" is under attack.[3] The letters-to-the-editor pages, even the editorial columns, are swamped with cries to the effect that to allow the slightest repression of public vice would trigger a series of events leading inexorably to a society comparable to that of Nazi Germany. Our historically ignorant "intellectuals" seem unaware that freedom ever existed before their lifetimes, that it existed even when social constraints were much more extensive and powerful than today.

Being "progressive" has become synonymous with being an apologist for crime and vice in the eyes of many on the political right, and some on the left have not been able to resist the temptation to glorify both crime and vice. The political consequences of this conviction are just beginning to make themselves felt in such issues as abortion rights. Cleavages on moral issues are always dangerous to democratic societies, especially when they seem continually to be widening.

How could such a condition have come about? Crime and vice are, to some extent, socially defined and hence subject to alteration. They do have social as well as individual causes. As we shall see, one of the merits of Renouvier's individualistic morality is that it takes these social facts into account. What we are concerned with in this chapter is not crime and vice but moral ideas, including how people react to crime and vice. The crisis in our moral ideas is in large part of intellectual origin, and we have to turn to the nineteenth century to find where it has come from, for in this area as in so many others, the twentieth century has merely carried to extremes the ideas of an earlier age.

On the question of the relations between the sexes Renouvier was certainly not a "Victorian," but neither was he an apologist for self-

3. Many Western journalists seem totally unable to distinguish mountains from molehills or their ego gratification from the public interest. Not only do they lack philosophy and historical perspective, but they seem remarkably devoid of common sense.

indulgence disguised as freedom. What distressed him in the contemporary situation was the absence of justice, especially the inequality of rights and duties between men and women. While in any society there could be empirical justification for differences in applied morals, in pure morals there could be no distinction of the sexes. The institution of the family was the particular locus of difficulty in the nineteenth century. In the France of the Napoleonic code, the rights of women, married or unmarried, were drastically inferior to those of men, and Renouvier never ceased to complain about the inability of the French to liberate themselves from the morals of Napoléon's dictatorship. Beliefs had certainly changed, but the law seemed unreformable.[4]

This introduced an increasing hypocrisy into society as the legal institution of marriage differed from the beliefs and practices of much of bourgeois society. Renouvier himself must have felt the strain, because while conforming his actions to his moral doctrines, he still felt compelled to disguise publicly his departure from convention. Thus, even his closest friends appear to have been unaware that "Mme Renouvier" and the philosopher were not married. Though in conformity with his ideas on *"union libre,"* it would not meet today's ideals for "relationships," given the intellectual disparity between the partners—no Harriet Taylor and John Stuart Mill here, but a perfect harmony and enduring affection remarked by all the visitors to La Verdette, their home in the suburbs of Avignon.

Renouvier's combination of realism and idealism in morals perhaps reflected a sense of his own human limitations, for he also had an illegitimate son (known as Adrien Aucompte) by his cook. To preserve appearances, mother and child were sent away; Renouvier contributed to their support and to the boy's education. Taking responsibility for one's acts is perhaps the part of Renouvier's practical ethic most needed today. In this case it was an obligation he interpreted rather broadly, evidently motivated by affection as well as duty. After the death of both his "wife" and the boy's mother, Renouvier brought his illegitimate son to live with

4. For further reading on the status of women in France, see the extensive bibliography in Claire Goldberg Moses, *French Feminism in the Nineteenth Century* (Albany, N.Y., 1984).

him at La Verdette, entrusting him eventually with the management of the little estate and taking pride in his practical accomplishments. Renouvier also took under his wing Adrien Aucompte's legitimate half brother André, together with André's motherless children. The Aucomptes would in effect become Renouvier's family and eventually his heirs since he outlived all his family except his sister's children (who were otherwise well provided for).[5]

Clearly, Renouvier's acquaintance with the moral issues of his time was direct and personal. He sought to understand and interpret them in the light of universal values and the standard of rationality. He understood that it is not enough to denounce the injustice and hypocrisy of one's time while practicing self-indulgence. He also recognized that although marriage and the family might be divorced from religion, they could never be an entirely personal affair between partners, however equal, but were also relationships involving society. Responsibility for children was a primary consideration. It would seem obvious that we have today a desperate need for an ethic of obligation, not just to save our civilization from collapse but to promote the cultivation of those qualities that distinguish man from the lesser creatures: reason and liberty.

It has been common in conservative circles to trace the present crisis to the eighteenth-century idea that man is naturally good and society the cause of evil.[6] Modern scholarship has shown that eighteenth-century thinkers were far from unanimous in endorsing such an idea and that even those who leaned toward it were not inclined to draw many practical consequences.[7] There was certainly a reaction against the idea of Original Sin, whether presented in the mythological trappings of Catholic tradition or the harsher accents of German Protestantism. But more

5. These details on Renouvier's personal life are all taken from Méry, *Critique du christianisme.*

6. See, *e.g.,* the works of Thomas Molnar, such as *The Decline of the Intellectual* (New Rochelle, N.Y., 1961) or *The Counter-Revolution* (New York, 1969).

7. For examples, see Henry Vyverberg, *Historical Pessimism in the French Enlightenment* (Cambridge, Mass., 1958).

important was the reaction against the claim that Christian faith and doctrine were the essential foundations for both moral philosophy and actual public and private morality. One of the main ingredients of the philosophical movement was the conviction that morals could be given a secular foundation superior to the old religious one.

In the eighteenth century, this view was held by only a few, but they were spread over a broad front. The two main divisions that would battle each other as well as religious tradition in the nineteenth century were the philosophical and the scientific approaches. The moral philosophy of Kant was the outstanding monument of secular rationalism. On the scientific side, there was no comparable single figure but a powerful movement resting its arguments on an empiricist psychology. In France, this approach was most prominently embodied at the turn of the century in the so-called *idéologues*. The motives behind both approaches were of the highest; aside from extremists like the marquis de Sade (so much admired by some twentieth-century intellectuals) no one wanted to undermine contemporary moral standards or even to change them very much.[8] Rather, they wanted to ensure the survival of those standards in a world where, they thought, religion was going to count for less and less. As Western history demonstrated, religious sanctions had not proved all that efficacious in the past, and, what is worse, religious differences had often provided excuses for the most barbarous acts. Rational, scientific ethics would produce unanimity by removing any reason to differ and because they would proceed from the discovery of the real roots of morality, would be vastly more efficacious in practice.

On the whole, the moral philosophers were much less sure than the would-be moral scientists that they could produce a universally effective substitute for religiously sanctioned morality. After all, a tradition as old as Western philosophy held that only an enlightened minority would ever be capable of faithfully following the light of moral reason, while the masses would continue to need some superstition or other. Even the phil-

---

8. Sade offers a clear demonstration of what can happen if individual freedom is erected into the absolutely supreme value without any countervailing forces: Anything is permitted; the rights of the individual become the justification for murder and rape. See, for example, his *La Philosophie dans le boudoir* (London, 1795).

osophical deists of the eighteenth century preferred that their servants go to Mass and make confession. But there was no comparable tradition to restrain the ambitions of the scientists, and the growth of egalitarian sentiment increased the pressure for general solutions. The *idéologues* could see the mote of conflicting creeds in the eyes of the defenders of religious morals and believed that they could pluck it with the tools of psychological research and introduce the stability of experimentally demonstrated facts. They failed to see the beam of conflicting scientific theories where they thought they were establishing the serenity of universal agreement. Still less did these sincere humanitarians foresee that arguments ostensibly based on the natural sciences would be used in the nineteenth century to justify various assaults on Western ideas of right and wrong.[9]

The illegitimate use of the name of science was only one of the sources of the modern moral crisis, but it had a catalytic effect, multiplying the virulence of other strains of thought. This was particularly true in its interaction with the belief in individual freedom. As long as freedom was seen in the context of actual social experience, its qualified and conditional character was so evident as scarcely to arouse discussion. When it was taken up by people who thought social and moral questions could be answered with the same certainty and universality as questions in the physical sciences, the way was open to every extremism. If freedom is good, then absolute freedom is the absolute good—so runs the modern equation. If freedom is not total, it does not exist at all—this is the common corollary.

The failure of the popular ideologies of the past century—Marxism, Freudianism, and the lesser fry—has provoked a kind of anarchic skepticism that finds so much oppressive and professed to be unable to distinguish between Western democracy and Soviet totalitarianism.[10] For many intellectuals, the promise of Marxist science was a total liberation of man's potentialities (assumed to be good) in contrast to the innumer-

9. There has been a revived interest in the idéologues. See, for example, Cheryl B. Welch, *Liberty and Utility: The French Idéologues and the Transformation of Liberalism* (New York, 1984).

10. While popular Freudianism exalts libidinal freedom, Freud himself was far from believing in the virtues of absolute freedom; quite the contrary.

able restraints under which he labors in the present order of things. Their belated realization that socialism in practice leads to the contrary has not produced a greater realism but a kind of nihilism of resentment against the world.

The habits of our language incline almost irresistibly to the metaphor that would hold that our problems result from a tendency to take certain nineteenth-century ideas to their "logical" extremes, but we should resist such language because our present extremes are not logical but paralogical, just as "scientific" morality has proved to be just more scientism.

Among nineteenth-century philosophers, no one can help us better than Renouvier to understand why the dominant strains of thought leading to the present crisis are, and always were, intellectually unsound. It would be too much to hope that this would help to weaken adherence to them, especially among the intelligentsia. Today's intelligentsia seems less capable of reasoning than its nineteenth-century predecessors. Despite his pessimistic evaluation of humanity, Renouvier never abandoned hope that reason can sometimes have some influence. The philosopher owed it to himself to press on with the search for truth, and he went on trying to get others to listen rather than taking refuge in a Stoic or Epicurean resignation. Whether even Renouvier could make that choice today is hard to say.

There was a widespread tendency in the nineteenth century to regard traditional moral philosophy as a kind of *bavardage sentimental* (emotional idle chatter) that had little relation to the real world and still less efficacy in it. Whatever its methods, the search for a *morale indépendante* would have to provide itself with some of the trappings of science. Even Renouvier could not escape this necessity. More fundamentally, he believed his approach to *be* scientific, but not in the narrow sense that led the eighteenth-century empiricists astray. He would not make the mistake of trying to build a moral doctrine on the model of any of the natural sciences, whether mechanics, physiology, or whatever. He hoped to introduce into moral thinking standards of rational examination, hypothesis, and argument appropriate to the nature of the subject.

Of course, what was appropriate to this subject was an object of contention in the nineteenth century. The empiricist strain would continue and even become more sophisticated before giving way to the laboratory-oriented experimental psychology of the later nineteenth century. It would be the ancestor of the behaviorist moral doctrines of the twentieth century.[11] There would emerge out of the natural sciences another approach more characteristic of nineteenth-century attitudes, namely, that based on the idea of biological evolution.[12]

Despite its self-image of modernity, evolutionist ethics had difficulty rising above a position fully expressed in ancient Greece—the right of the strongest and the virtue of success. Efforts of evolutionists to qualify this outcome were purchased at a high price in self-contradiction. Later in the century, a distinctively new approach emerged that retained the drive to be scientific but severed the umbilical that linked these efforts to biology. This was the sociological, or social-science, approach, which would aim at not a moral science but a *science des moeurs*. The study of moral behavior as a social phenomenon had its roots in a more traditional ethnography; the new sociologists aimed to go beyond mere description to arrive at the foundations of morals. They expected this study to be eventually of immense practical benefit.[13] Though falling considerably short of its aims, the sociological approach often attained a more genuinely scientific character than the others mentioned, at least as long as it remained aware of its limitations.

The sociological approach introduced a powerful element of relativism into the study of morals that led many to fear that it was basically subversive of the whole idea of morals. The other self-styled scientific approaches had assumed that they at least eventually would be able to establish some eternal verities, verities of the same character as Newton's laws of motion and equally certain.

More traditional moral philosophy had always known something of the same split. The search for universal truths was regularly confronted with the diversity of human behavior. The purest standards elevated by

11. Behaviorist moral doctrine: Might equals right. The self-appointed "superiors" have a right to apply behavioral conditioning to the "inferiors." It is the Western version of Soviet "psychiatry."

12. See Linda L. Clark, *Social Darwinism in France* (University, Ala., 1984).

13. See what I say about sociology in *From Philosophy to Sociology* (DeKalb, Ill., 1983).

philosophy, like those of religion, seemed well beyond human capacity. Moral philosophy thus always had to be doubled by a casuistry that adapted its teachings to the conditions of particular societies. The linkage between the philosophy and the casuistry was always uncertain and inconsistent. The inevitable subjectivity of the casuistry clashed only too obviously with the claims to absolute certainty made on behalf of the philosophy (or the religion), and many philosophers simply pretended that the casuistry was beneath their concern.

Renouvier would not adopt any of these approaches. Traditional moral philosophy was either too dependent on religious sanctions or lacking in philosophic rigor. The would-be scientific approaches were all vitiated by their underlying determinist metaphysical assumptions. Fortunately, he thought, there was another approach, which had already been given a powerful expression in Kant's *Critique of Practical Reason* and *Introduction to the Metaphysics of Morals*.[14] It was true that there were some problems with Kant's ethical theory, but Renouvier thought they could be solved by remaining truer to Kant's method, to the insights of the critical philosophy, than Kant himself had been.

Renouvier would choose to call his approach neither moral philosophy nor *science des moeurs* but a *science de la morale*. This label may have been unfortunate insofar as it has misled people who have not read his treatise into thinking that his work was just another product of nineteenth-century scientism. On the other hand, it has the advantage of distinguishing, when properly understood, just what Renouvier thought he was aiming at. Both substantives are important: *science* because he was seeking to establish knowledge and not just opinion or traditional belief; *morale* because he was not going to describe or analyze existing or historical *moeurs* but establish the foundations of right and wrong and examine their applicability to the real world. The relations between the pure and the applied doctrine were of vital importance:

> To be properly called sciences, morals and mathematics must both be founded on pure concepts. Experience and history

14. Only critical philosophy, Renouvier insisted, can produce a truly independent ethic. See *Science de la morale* (Paris, 1869), I, 10.

are even farther from following the laws of morality than nature is from exactly fulfilling mathematical ideas; however, these laws and these ideas are equally necessary rational forms, the former necessary as a standard of measurement for our senses, the latter necessary to guide our lives and to provide a standard by which to judge them.

Just as there are pure mathematics and applied mathematics, so there ought to be a pure morals and an applied morals.[15]

Of course, there is room for debate whether this was a viable project, but it cannot be dismissed out of hand.[16] Science was so popular in the nineteenth century that the term was used to cover almost every intellectual activity. Renouvier was using it in a more rigorous though broad sense, at least as justified as the common term *social science*.

The term *science de la morale* also indicates that Renouvier was aiming at conclusions valid for the whole of mankind. He was perfectly willing to agree with the ethnologists that diverse civilizations have different moral codes, but he would not agree that we treat them as equally valid and incomparable from one civilization to another. The latter approach, much touted in our century by anthropologists feeling guilty about Western imperialism, is not the humanitarian generosity that its advocates believe.[17] It is in fact antihumanist because it denies the essential minimum of common humanity that Renouvier expressed in his idea of the person.

What is common to humanity is also the foundation of morals: freedom of the will and its corollary, moral responsibility. Without freedom and reason—however debased, corrupted, and suppressed—we cannot speak of men, and we in fact recognize as fellow men, however different,

---

15. *Ibid.*, v.

16. Octave Hamelin's paraphrase (*Le Système de Renouvier* [Paris, 1927], 356) is clearer than Renouvier's original (*n*15): "History is no doubt farther from realizing the prescriptions of morality than nature is from realizing the theorems of geometry and mechanics."

17. For an analysis of Western "guilt," see Pascal Bruckner, *Le Sanglot de l'homme blanc: tiers-monde, culpabilité, haine de soi* (Paris, 1983).

the members of all the world's cultures. Some cultures are so debased, Renouvier agreed, that it may be practically impossible for them even to recognize, let alone pursue, our common moral values, but this fact of experience does not negate the universality of values. This apparent contradiction presents problems to an empiricist, who believes values can be drawn simply from facts, but not to a critical philosopher.

In the critical philosophy, the universality of moral values is rooted in an understanding of what makes human beings different from other animals. Our presentation here thus goes somewhat in the reverse direction from Renouvier's, for his moral philosophy is the crown of his philosophical edifice. The main pillar, which he established earlier but I will deal with in the next chapter, is his concept of the freedom of the will. It is enough for the moment to be aware that the whole question of morals hinges on that of freedom: "Man is endowed with reason and believes himself free. . . . This is the double foundation, necessary and sufficient, of morality in mankind." [18] Without freedom there can be no sense in which an individual is responsible for his actions. Efforts to get around this by redefining *freedom* or *responsibility* have been at best clever sophistries.[19] Human freedom, however, is not something that can be proved to exist. It could be just an illusion perpetrated by a playfully malevolent deity. But we can treat it, as Renouvier does, as a *moral* certainty. There is no other solid foundation for our moral or intellectual life. Morality and liberty are thus mutually supporting concepts.

Following Kant rather closely, Renouvier began by establishing the terms of pure morals. His method was to proceed from the abstract to the concrete. The basic concept of moral obligation thus appears first as a form independent of any content, of the goods or aims of men. Reason shows us what justice is and establishes it in our consciences where it cannot be overthrown by the influence of the external world. Reason,

18. *Science de la morale*, I, 1.
19. Some of these efforts are described at length in Mortimer J. Adler, *The Idea of Freedom: A Dialectical Examination of the Conceptions of Freedom* (Garden City, N.Y., 1958). It should be noted, Renouvier argues, that the founders of the ethics of duty (the Stoics, Kant) did not believe in real free will (*Critique philosophique* [1879-I], 213).

not nature, can offer principles of conduct to man. We can know what is just through the use of our reason, while utilitarian morals lose us in uncertainty over what is useful.[20]

Pure morals must therefore be established without reference to utility. The centrality of liberty in the definition of man leads to the supreme value of the individual's moral autonomy. The value of moral autonomy is the postulate on which the different formulations of the *categorical imperative*—Kant's term for the regulating principle of moral obligation—are erected. They all hinge on the obligation to treat other men as ends in themselves, which we can do only if the maxims of our moral conduct can be universalized.[21] Only this humanist universalism stands in the way of our treating some humans as merely means to our ends, thus denying their humanity.

In order to establish the categorical imperatives, which he preferred to call *persuasifs morals* (convincing moral ideas), Renouvier elaborated the moral obligations of the individual by stages, beginning with deliberately chosen abstractions and moving toward the complexity of reality.[22] He starts with the individual as a moral entity taken in isolation, and the first foundation of obligation is obligation to oneself.[23] First "seek the rule [which ought] to govern actions" and then "generalize the person of the [moral] agent" is Renouvier's procedure.[24] Duty to others

20. *Science de la morale*, I, 116, 109, 140.

21. "It can thus be erected into a precept: Recognize the person of others as your equal by nature and in dignity, as being in itself an end, and as a consequence prohibit yourself from using that person as merely a means to attain your own ends." Kant's version (*Groundwork of the Metaphysic of Morals*, trans. H. J. Paton [1948; rpr. New York, 1964], 96) is essentially the same: "Act in such a way that you always treat humanity, whether in your own person or in the person of any other, never simply as a means, but always at the same time as an end."

22. *Science de la morale*, I, 1–28; for a one-paragraph summary of his method, see *ibid.*, 96.

23. See Hamelin, *Système de Renouvier*, 358–61. Renouvier explicitly recognized that the isolated individual is a fiction (*Science de la morale*, I, 12).

24. *Science de la morale*, I, 69. Renouvier insists that this process of abstraction followed by generalization is characteristic of all sciences.

is thus deduced from duty to oneself by (to use the Kantian terms) a "synthetic judgment." [25] This too is first considered at the most general possible level. Although these first steps are deliberately abstract, they indicate from the beginning that Renouvier's moral philosophy is concerned with the good of the individual.

When Renouvier moves to the level of the relationships of one man to another, the Kantian character of his moral philosophy becomes strikingly evident. Their common ethic is first formal: Its rules of conduct are independent of any content. When questions of content are introduced, as they must be in real life, error, difference, and misunderstanding creep in. At the level of pure morals, uniformity and agreement are both necessary and possible. Formal reciprocity—justice—is the rule: It exists when we treat each other as equals: "Recognize the human being in others as your equal by nature and in dignity, as being an end in itself and, in consequence, forbid yourself to use others as a simple means to achieve your ends." [26]

Kant's first "supreme principle of practical reason [*i.e.*, morals]" also establishes the unity of rights and duties: Each has the right to be treated in the way he has a duty to treat the other. This is not simply a case of desire or utility—"as you would have others do unto you"—but as you *ought* to be treated by others. Justice for Kant and Renouvier is a categorical imperative, that is, obligatory in its own right, for its own sake, not for any reason exterior to itself: "Duty is . . . a debt facing a credit. The two together make up *Justice:* it is just to fulfill one's duty and to claim one's rights." [27]

The rule of conduct is also general. It applies in all circumstances and to everyone, which gives the second form of the maxim: "Always act in such a manner that the maxim on which your conduct is based can

25. *Ibid.,* 59. In between these, Renouvier also discusses man's duty toward nature in terms that led some readers to the mistaken conclusion that he was a vegetarian (*ibid.,* I, 29–50). He found that nature sets man some bad examples, but he remained worried about the carryover from our treatment of animals to our treatment of each other.

26. Hamelin, *Système de Renouvier,* 364–65.

27. *Ibid.,* 365.

be made into a universal law by your conscience or formulated into an article of legislation that you could consider the will of all reasonable beings."[28] The emphasis on universality, much decried in our day of cultural relativism, is important for putting the question of right and wrong above the sphere of mere individual whim or personal opinion. It requires us to take a point of view not outside but more extensive than ourselves.

Renouvier's moral code is thus individualistic, or as he would later prefer to say, personalist, but it is not egoistic or hedonistic. Advocates of traditional moral doctrines, especially Catholics, have found that Renouvier's individualism neglects the collective dimension of moral conduct. It would be more accurate to say that they have different visions of this dimension: Renouvier considered Catholic ethical teaching in essence immoral because it subordinated the individual's conscience to something outside him; it promoted heteronomy instead of autonomy. Far from grounding morals in the community, the church had in effect handed the conscience of the individual over to the priest as confessor and spiritual director.

Any effort to found morals otherwise than on the individual conscience leads, in Renouvier's opinion, to a repudiation of morals.[29] Moral individualism does not separate the individual from the community but establishes the only universal basis for his obligations to it. The kind of communitarian sentiments advocated by religions have the effect of linking some groups together more strongly, but at the price of pitting them against other groups, those with different faiths. We cannot love all our fellow men, but we can recognize an obligation to act justly toward them.[30] Both anti-individualistic and individualistic morals have their

28. *Ibid.*, 367.
29. The foundation of morals outside of reason leads to the subordination of morals to other purposes (*Science de la morale*, I, 151–53).
30. Renouvier points out the dangers of an ethic of love on several occasions (*e.g.*, *Science de la morale*, I, 204–207) and rejects the ethic of sacrifice (*ibid.*, 211–12). He agreed that religious motives may impel men to moral acts but insisted that the definition of moral acts can be supplied only by reason (*ibid.*, 48).

risks in practice; it was thus all the more important to make the pure theory as sound as possible.

While no hedonist, Renouvier was hostile to any ascetic ethics or doctrine of self-sacrifice. Despite his pessimism about mankind, he was not attracted to the kind of negation of the world preached by Schopenhauer or Indian religion. He had a certain grudging admiration for people who were able to conform their lives to their nonrational opinions, since all moral behavior involves a conquest, an effort of self-control that men find very difficult. Christian advocates of self-sacrifice from love of God and one's fellow man caused him a considerable unease, however. Although he could recognize a certain beauty in self-sacrifice, he was also aware that believers in self-sacrifice had a penchant for sacrificing others to their personal convictions. Today's suicide-bombing Muslim fanatics are a perfect illustration of the type of behavior he found in many Christian zealots of an earlier age.[31]

Religious critics and secular metaphysical absolutists also find in Renouvier's Kantian approach an insufficiently sure foundation for morals. Indeed, Renouvier preferred to call a *"persuasif"* what Kant had labeled an "imperative," thus drawing attention to the relativism basic to his critical philosophy. Renouvier's relativism, however, does not detract from the certainty of our knowledge about morals any more than Einstein's relativity detracts from the certainty of our knowledge of the laws governing motion. In both, relativism has the function of defining the limits and character of our knowledge. Knowledge exists only in the human conscience; therefore, it cannot help being relative to the person. Moral knowledge, and the imperatives that express it, rests on postulates about man's freedom that cannot be scientifically demonstrated.

This does not prevent Renouvier from speaking of a science of morals, because the same can be said of all other sciences.[32] Our certainty of their validity rests on beliefs external to the system by which we under-

---

31. Fortunately, such extremists have always been a small minority among both Christians and Muslims.

32. This is far from the position of those current French philosophers who excuse their lack of rational argument by claiming that science too is a matter of imagination. See Jacques Bouveresse, *Philosophe autophages*, 48.

stand the phenomena studied in any field of rational enquiry. Renouvier's position is thus at an opposite pole from the historical, geographical, or cultural relativism of the social-scientific approach to morals. Our moral knowledge is relative to the conditions of our humanity—it cannot be otherwise—but it is not relative to our membership in this or that community in this or that time or place.

Religious absolutists were particularly worried by the absence of any divine sanction in Renouvier's system of morals. From his point of view, any presumed divine sanction could not add to or detract from the truth of his moral maxims. The divine promise of rewards or punishments, on the other hand, might serve as an incentive to practice these maxims, though the experience of some centuries showed only a limited effect, which should have made the believers in religious morals more modest, he thought, in their claims.[33] In any case, Renouvier was not convinced that the moralizing effect of Christianity had outweighed its immoral impact in giving a justification to men's conflicts and alienating their consciences.[34] He did think, however, that a promise of rewards in another life could help motivate people within the framework of his purely rational code. The threat of eternal punishment for transgressors of the moral code he found profoundly immoral—which appears to be the opinion of most Christians today. Renouvier would understand how the position of the religious absolutists was rooted in the traditions of their faith. He was inclined to find less excuse for the philosophical absolutists, who were bound only by their metaphysical doctrines.

Empiricist and hedonist opponents of the pure morals of obligation complain that it ignores the "fact" that men act only in the pursuit of ends and that the common end, the end sought by all men, is happiness. The exercise of one's duty may for some be a source of happiness, thus deriving its significance from this end and not in itself. The rational mor-

33. On sanctions, see Hamelin, *Système de Renouvier*, 379–80.

34. See his interesting demonstration of how the moral history of the West might have been better without the triumph of Christianity: *Uchronie: l'utopie dans l'histoire; esquisse historique du développement de la civilisation euro-péenne tel qu'il n'a pas été, tel qu'il aurait pu être* (Paris, 1876) [originally published as a series of articles in 1857].

als of Kant and Renouvier is open to such motivations but insists that they must have a secondary or subordinate role. Renouvier admitted the pursuit of happiness as a major motivation in morals. Against Kant, he insisted that we cannot exclude sympathy for other men from morality.[35] Renouvier also recognized a kind of "moral sense" that is a nonrational version of rational morals, "a combination of sympathy with justice, properly so-called."[36]

Renouvier also admitted utility as a secondary motive but insisted that it cannot be the basis of our moral rules because our calculations of utility are too difficult, too subject to ignorance and error. While moralists have wrongly rejected any involvement of pleasure, pleasure cannot furnish any consistent rule of conduct.[37]

Though Renouvier thus did not entirely exclude utility from the domain of pure morals, it is mainly a factor in the development of applied morals, where indeed it cannot be escaped. His critique of the English utilitarians was very thorough, but mainly at the level of pure theory, for he respected their personal rectitude and believed they had contributed to raising the moral tone of their country. What their philosophy inevitably failed to do was to establish any rule by which we can clearly and consistently distinguish right from wrong. Efforts to give utilitarianism a more scientific character have had the effect of exposing its weakness. Jeremy Bentham's felicific calculus foundered on the absurdity of his quantification of the unquantifiable and comparison of the incomparable. John Stuart Mill's effort to escape these absurdities by recognizing differences of kind and quality in our pleasures can finally do no more than propose his personal values as a universal standard for mankind. He could not say why mankind ought to accept that standard. Only a rational morals can justify the obligation that distinguishes moral action from empirical prudence.

Given the inclinations of contemporary thought, Renouvier saw a greater menace in the attitude of the social-scientific relativists than that

35. On the secondary principles, see Hamelin, *Système de Renouvier,* 372–78.

36. *Ibid.,* 374–75.

37. *Ibid.,* 375–76, 377.

of the absolutists. The social-scientific relativists saw themselves as on the cutting edge of progress and were inclined to class Renouvier with the philosophical absolutists as advocates of an intellectual effort that had had its day and failed to build any bridges between its ivory tower and the reality of human diversity.

While respecting their moral earnestness and sincerity, Renouvier was convinced that they were wrong and that their manner of being wrong had harmful consequences. Their position was wrong because it rested on deterministic postulates that were in his view incompatible with a scientific understanding. Their postulates were harmful, like all determinisms, because they destroyed the idea of pure morals, hence any possible general criterion of morality.[38] The historical form of relativism was the most dangerous because it provided support for immoral actions by retrospectively justifying the crimes of the past and by justifying the sacrifice of individuals in the present for the benefit, whether specious or real, of other individuals in the future. There was no crime that could not be held necessary or even good by such relativists. Renouvier would not have been surprised, though he would have been distressed, by the crimes that would be committed against humanity in the twentieth century and the readiness of intellectuals to apologize for them.

But what about the "ivory tower" charge? Is there not some truth to it? Kant has seemed especially vulnerable to this charge because of his insistence that the only moral acts are those committed solely out of duty, with no other motive. Renouvier agreed that duty had to be the main motive but denied it could ever be the sole motive. The pursuit of happiness cannot be excluded, though it must be kept subordinate.[39] In applying his doctrine, Kant also advocated, as moral, actions so out of touch with reality as to seem immoral to most people.[40]

38. "The historical school of progress has neglected or denied the idea of pure morals; it has destroyed their very foundation, by teaching that the good is relative to the times, that present evil is a past good, in a word, that no criteria for morality exist" (*Critique philosophique* [1872-I], 4).

39. *Science de la morale*, I, 119–24.

40. Everybody cites the famous argument about not lying to save a friend from a murderer. Renouvier did think society could stand more truth telling than was common, even though he rejected Kant's absolutism (*ibid.*, 247–60).

Renouvier agreed that most philosophers have not come out of their ivory towers. Usually content to act "as if it were sufficient to promulgate duty in the abstract," they have often been unwilling to dilute the moral purity of their positions by examining how they might be applied in the real world.[41] Though religions have also fallen short of what is needed, they have at least shown some concern for helping man in his moral misery.[42] Renouvier believed that it was part of the philosopher's job to grapple with this question, not merely to practice casuistry by explaining how to act in particular cases but to develop a *"science appliquée"* that would explain in general terms the principles for the application of moral ideas in an immoral society.[43]

The parallel Renouvier established between mathematics and morals does not fully cover the problem. There is a difficulty in morals that does not exist in mathematics—how to prevent the *morale appliquée* from obscuring and corrupting the *morale pure*. Renouvier's method called for adapting the principles of *morale pure* to the conditions of the real world while maintaining their distinction. The nature of the real world was not allowed to influence the formulation of the precepts of *morale pure;* empirical data would be considered only in connection with *morale appliquée*. On the other hand, the concepts of pure morality would be the polestar that would keep us from getting lost on the uncharted seas of applied morality.[44]

Where Kant had simply tried to evade the question by applying the unmodified principles of pure morals to real life, Renouvier would show how to modify those principles while protecting their purity, but without consigning them to uselessness.

Examining the problem of applying the critical imperatives in the real world, Renouvier came to the conclusion that they could be followed without risk only in a world in which everyone followed them and therefore in which we could trust everyone to behave according to the same moral norms. We can treat others as ends in themselves if we can expect

41. *Ibid.*, 231; *Critique philosophique* (1872-II), 274–75.
42. *Science de la morale*, I, 213–14.
43. *Ibid.*, v–vi.
44. *Ibid.*, vi–vii.

them to treat us as ends in ourselves. This observation seems enough to condemn the Kantian ethic because we cannot in any existing or known human society expect such treatment from others. Anyone who acted as if he did expect such treatment would soon be destroyed. A moral code, Renouvier insisted, is not a prescription for sainthood.[45]

But if the ideals of moral philosophy are not hard to reach, of what use are they? How do they differ from rules of prudence? The ideals expressed in the categorical imperative are simultaneously essential and unrealizable. Or rather, as Renouvier would say, they are realizable only in a "state of peace" where their reciprocity is assured. But even when unattainable these ideals serve as a standard to guide our acts in the real world, and we must keep them in mind even when we must also violate them:

A man with a strong and free conscience . . . wants to base his conduct on a moral maxim, as far as is compatible with the present state of human relations and without breaking his solidarity with his fellow men. And even when he finds himself forced to depart the farthest from the ideal, he likes very much to envision that ideal in all its purity, then to violate it knowingly, rather than to try to convince himself by means of unhealthy subtleties that he has not really left the domain of the true moral law.[46]

Renouvier is clearly far from the Socratic illusion, represented in his time and ours by those who think "education" is the answer to all social and moral problems, that if we know what is right, we must necessarily do it.

45. Renouvier made this clear in a long description of what a world in which man's reason truly reigned would be like (*ibid.*, I, 219–27). Christianity was faced with a similar problem in the inapplicability of many of the prescriptions of the Sermon on the Mount, but Christianity could at least call on some people to be saints, even if the mass of the faithful were not expected to reach such heights. Moral philosophy, on the other hand, cannot make such demands, in part because it cannot hold out the promise of comparable rewards.

46. *Critique philosophique* (1872-II), 277–78.

At first it may seem hard to understand how moral ideals can preserve their meaning, even in their necessary violation. Renouvier insisted that the real world is so far from being a state of peace that it can only be called a "state of war." [47] And in war no one expects all the rules of moral conduct to apply, and some even argue that the only measure of virtue is success.

Western history has been full of efforts to moralize war, to hedge it in with restrictions, and these efforts have occasionally had some limited successes. There has also been some reflection on the conditions under which war may be justified, and it has become widely accepted that self-defense is a legitimate rationale, though subject to abuse. Renouvier undertook to apply this concept from the law of nations to the problems of everyday moral conduct. The basic rational maxims of moral conduct are conceived in terms of a state of peace and must be modified when applied in a state of war. Renouvier proposed to make this adaptation an applied science instead of a traditional casuistry. [48]

Moral philosophy cannot content itself with assuming the existence of a state of peace: "We do not have peace; we have war. And we must ask a *law of war* to furnish, in part, the foundation for our concrete ethics, the reasons for the laws we need, and the practical moral precepts which take account of experience and of history." [49] Living in a state of war, we have the right—which comes close to an obligation—to practice the "right of defense," a concept that applies to individuals and to social groups. [50] Because others will seek to use us as means to their own ends,

47. Renouvier considered the distinction between the state of war and the state of peace the capital idea of his *morale appliquée* (Hamelin, *Système de Renouvier,* 400). Hamelin agrees that it is "of high value and remarkable effectiveness"; see also *ibid.,* 388–91.

48. Renouvier found that international law jurists have often committed the reverse error of regarding war as the natural state (*Science de la morale,* I, 232); *ibid.,* 250–52, 78.

49. *Ibid.,* 227.

50. Renouvier insisted that the idea of a social contract had to be understood in the context of the idea of the state of war (*ibid.,* 265). The right of defense is an extension of the right of self-preservation (Hamelin, *Système de Renouvier,* 391).

we may defend ourselves against being so used by using others as means to our ends, in the measure needful to defend ourselves and those dependent upon us. Renouvier distinguishes three basic categories in which the right of defense can be invoked: (1) protection against attack on the person, (2) protection of property, and (3) protection against the breach of contracts.[51] The moral exercise of the right of defense in these areas also requires us to avoid hatred in the exercise of our rights. Like any rule of conduct, this one presents difficulties in application, but they are difficulties of judgment rather than principle.[52]

In practice, people tend to resolve these difficulties by following the conduct customary in their society, assuming that experience has justified it. At best, we can exercise our moral free will and seek to conform our acts as closely to the ideal as the circumstances permit, knowing that we need not reproach ourselves for failing to go further.[53] Custom and reason may agree, for example, that it is permissible to lie to save a life, another's or one's own, but be less certain that it is also permissible to lie to save oneself or another from a social embarrassment. The philosopher will not automatically assume that the truth is always more important than the harmony of social relations. Its supremacy is rationally assumed only in the state of peace.

Renouvier's concern about political and social structures was closely connected to his thinking about the right of defense. He was an advocate of social reforms that would strengthen the ability of individuals and families to protect themselves against being used by others, individually or collectively. Therefore, he laid a strong stress on the value of property as one of the most effective means of protection against the encroach-

51. *Science de la morale*, I, 243–44.

52. *Ibid.*, 261–62, 330–31.

53. "It must be remembered that the individual is the first, unique thing for all morality and all law, . . . and conclude necessarily in favor of the right of the person against society, without any other conditions than the seriously interested defense and an enlightened conscience, sure of itself" (*ibid.*, 262). Our moral duty in politics is essentially similar. Where we are not acting alone but with others, our duty is "to make the fact conform to the ideal *as much as possible, that is to say, as much as we judge possible in good conscience*" (*Critique philosophique* [1876-II], 230; italics in the original).

ments of society and government.[54] Property, he remarked, has the curious quality of "owing its guarantee and defense to the social bond and of securing a guarantee and defense of the individual against the tyranny of that very bond." The main problem was that so far, it was a defense available only to a minority. This gave a special urgency to his interest in finding practical equivalents of property holding that would be accessible to the working classes of an increasingly urban society (see Chapter IV).

In politics, his republicanism was partly motivated by the same concern. Given the state of war, government would always be necessary. In the freest possible society there would still be a substantial element of constraint, hence the importance of a government that would be no more oppressive than necessary. The democratic republic was a means for society as a whole to protect its interests against domestic tyrants and against foreign enemies, who would seek to use it for their own ends, and it was also a means to maximize the possibilities of defense for individuals within the society.[55] Republican government would also serve as a barrier against the Saint-Simonian illusion that we can have a government by men who are enlightened and good, unlike the mass of society, thus justifying the most authoritarian regimes. The republic constitutes a recognition of the state of war, regulating the clash of opposing rights of defense instead of trying to abolish them.[56] It provides a mechanism for settling issues by majority vote rather than force of arms. Its decisions are always provisional, subject to future revision, and it provides legal means for the minority on any issue to continue to advocate a position that may someday be shared by the majority. The republic is thus the most moral form of political organization.[57]

The circumstances of the development of republicanism in France led many nineteenth-century republicans to believe in the moral role of the laic state. This may seem surprising, for it is the sort of attitude we would

54. *Critique philosophique* (1872-II), 293.

55. *Ibid.*, 294. Exclusion from self-government is servitude (*Science de la morale*, I, 370).

56. *Critique philosophique* (1881-I), 153, (1872-II), 294–95, (1873-II), 10. The state of war is the origin of duties as well as of rights, *e.g.*, a certain duty of minorities under the necessary conditions of majority rule (*ibid.* (1873-II), 7).

57. *Ibid.* (1873-II), 8, (1876-I), 266–67; on the limits and virtues of democracy, see *Science de la morale*, I, 240.

expect to find among authoritarians, as indeed we do. In the nineteenth century, none pushed this further than the Saint-Simonians, who invested the rulers of the country (not exactly the state in traditional terms) with a truly sacred authority and a sacerdotal function. Renouvier rightly described their ideal as a theocracy. The Saint-Simonians—and Comte in their wake—were proposing not merely a total restructuring of society but the establishment of a new religion in conformity with the needs of that new social order.

This was far from the ideal of Renouvier and the other republicans, so why did they too want the state to have a moral role? For politicians like Jules Ferry, the essential matter was undoubtedly the cement, the bond between the mass of the population and the republican form of government. But did this not risk creating the rationale for a more powerful and authoritarian state than they really desired? That was certainly a possibility, but it seemed a risk that had to be taken, and Renouvier's right of defense provided one rationale for taking it.[58] For the republican state could not hope to survive in a French society where Catholic values and traditions had been established for centuries unless it constituted itself as the defender of its own system of moral values.[59] Catholic values were demonstrably hostile to those of a free society, so a free government that did not establish itself as a moral authority would simply be committing suicide.[60] The attitudes inculcated by Catholic education permeated even those who turned against the church:

> In this sense, M. [Louis-Auguste] Blanqui, demagogue, is more profoundly catholic than M. A[lbert] de Broglie, aristocrat; likewise, Lamennais has never ceased to be a Catholic even when

58. Renouvier charged the French ruling classes with rejecting the moral role of the state for three bad reasons: fear, historical determinism, and "false liberalism" (*Critique philosophique* [1876-II], 100).

59. Not the Catholic faith but the theocratic ambitions of the church are the enemy of free government and individual rights (*ibid.* [1877-II], 265, 194). To be a "*morale publique*" and not a civil religion as in antiquity was the aim of Renouvier's program (*ibid.* [1877-I], 35).

60. The education question was for Renouvier literally a battle for the future of the French nation (*ibid.* [1877-II], 338. For his view on the unsuitability of Catholic education in the modern world, see *ibid.* (1874-I), 35.

his intolerance became the spokesman of the People and no longer of the Pope. Those who do not see that moral education in the public schools is a very urgently needed means of fighting this inescapable Catholicism and also of creating the true "education of universal suffrage" are failing to take into account the illness from which France suffers and the dangers which its republican institutions face.[61]

Was this situation the natural outcome of the process of secularization in Western society, or was it peculiar to the situation of a Catholic country?[62] Renouvier expressed himself on the moral role of the state in quite universal terms, but it is also clear that for him the problem was particularly acute in a country like France. This sense of crisis led him to insist in the early years of the Third Republic that there must be a rigorous exclusion of all churches from civic and political matters. One consequence of this separation is that the state must be the highest moral authority in the land, that its rights on moral questions are superior to those of all churches.[63] It should be evident, however, that there is no hint of state worship in his attitude, any more than there is worship of society in his religious thought.[64] The republican state exists to serve its individuals; to serve them and to preserve itself so that it can continue to serve them, it must assume a role of moral leadership.

There is a built-in guarantee against tyranny in Renouvier's conception of the state's role, at least in theory. Whether it would be an adequate barrier against the misuse of the moral powers of the state may be doubted, and he would see the domination of a socialist outlook in the

61. *Ibid.* (1880-II), 344.

62. Renouvier recognized a similar situation in Belgium (*ibid.* [1872-I], 279); he considered his message to be addressed to liberals in any "papist" country (*ibid.* [1877-I], 234–35). He attributed J. S. Mill's rejection of a state monopoly of elementary education to his not living in a Catholic country (*ibid.* [1877-I], 233–34).

63. See, *e.g., Critique philosophique* (1872-I), 279, (1877-I), 35, (1879-I), 123.

64. Nor is there any elitism, for he does not think the governors are capable of any greater virtue than those they govern (*Science de la morale*, II, 322–23).

moral instruction of today's French schools as a perversion of his ideal. For Renouvier, the state's moral role is defined by philosophical inquiry, which by explaining the moral nature of humanity indicates the path of the state's relation to society. In this conception the state's role is to promote the ends of the individual in the moral more than the material sphere, and these ends are identified by critical philosophy.[65]

The central objective is thus moral autonomy through the exercise of free will. Evidently man can go only so far in this direction under the state of war.[66] The republican state can enlarge the sphere of freedom through its political and social action, but nothing is more important than its role in the moral education of the citizenry: "It is, then, with great good sense that education has been regarded as the basis of practical politics. It is education's role to develop reason and to inculcate morality insofar as these are transmissible, and thus to enable men to exercise their autonomy and to respect the autonomy of others."[67] As long as the state's moral activity is confined to this liberating function, it is less dangerous than a failure to act:

> Finally, if there is ever a need to seek the right way of applying the laws of reason to society . . . if ever there is a case where the *state of war* calls for the use of compulsion—within the limits I have indicated—this is the case with education. [This is so because education] forms the unique and radical means of achiev-

65. On the need to keep state education within its proper limits to avoid despotism, see *Critique philosophique* (1877-I), 235–36. Renouvier's position is distinct from the utopianism of the socialists, who expect to radically cure humanity of its vices by constructing a new milieu for man (*Science de la morale*, I, 217–18). Renouvier insists that only the critical morality can be truly independent: "Thus morals require critical philosophy. No other philosophy can logically establish them independently of religions and their particular beliefs, of transcendental doctrines, or systems and hypotheses" (*ibid.*, 10).

66. "Absolute" liberty in the sphere of education, as in any other, is hostile to any social order (*Critique philosophique* [1876-I], 246). "There is no particular difficulty in reconciling personal autonomy with the exigencies of the moral concept of the state" (*ibid.*, 246–47).

67. *Science de la morale*, II, 224.

ing the reform of unjust customs and of making men free and worthy of freedom.[68]

There can be little doubt that the main reason Renouvier invested the state with a moral character was to establish its independence from the church. If the church has a monopoly on moral guidance in a society, it would be impossible to deny it rights of intervention in the state, for it would be a higher authority than the state. One of the goals of Renouvier's effort to establish a *"morale indépendante"* was thus to legitimize the separation of the church from the state.[69] But he also required the state to undertake a positive role in the moralization of society. Democracy required a reform of primary education based on the three principles of *"gratuité, obligation, laïcité"* (*i.e.*, it should be free, obligatory, and secular) that would be necessary if the state was to carry out its principal moral role, the moral education of youth.[70] Even a state monopoly in moral instruction would not be contrary to freedom under the state of war, and one of Renouvier's main points in the campaign to establish laic moral instruction was to convince other liberals of the legitimacy, even the necessity, of such a monopoly. "Toleration of the intolerant cannot be a precept for us, since their attacks put us on the defensive." This state moral education would be an important part of "an organization of the conditions needed to assure the exercise of [all our] liberties."[71]

68. *Ibid.*, I, 415; see also *ibid.*, II, 137, on the difficulty of confining the state to its proper role.

69. Such a monopoly thus creates a de facto theocracy (*Critique philosophique* [1876-I], 243). While supporting absolute separation in principle, Renouvier believed that existing circumstances required the state to retain some power to defend itself against political activity by the church (*ibid.* [1873-II], 406). Separation did not mean that the Bible should be excluded from state schools; it was a question of how it was to be used (*ibid.* [1873-I], 167).

70. *Ibid.* (1872-II), 161. On the urgent need for laic moral education, see *ibid.* (1874-I), 37.

71. *Ibid.* (1878-II), 307–308. Catholics tried to give the liberals a bad conscience by claiming liberty for their teaching, but they intended to use it, he believed, to gain the power to exercise their continuing, unrepudiated, unrepu-

The program of moral education established by the Third Republic was something of a disappointment to Renouvier, who wished for a bolder break with the past.[72] But despite the efforts of republican political leaders to avoid conflict by stressing continuity with moral traditions, the education of teachers and the drafting of programs of instruction were open to a considerable influence of a Kantian ethics.[73] Because he remained outside the educational establishment, Renouvier's influence was only indirect in this process, but it was substantial. His articles in *Critique philosophique* were read by influential educators, and he had personal or epistolary contact with several.[74] The objection of Catholics to what they saw as a Protestant direction in moral education had only a limited political effect as long as the Catholic church appeared to be an enemy of the Republic.

More dangerous for the substance of the laic *morale* was the social pressure to use it as a weapon for conformity and social peace (if not inner harmony). Concerned with the Catholic danger, Renouvier probably did not give enough attention to the danger of this subtle corruption within republican ranks. The moral programs of the early Third Republic in the primary-school system, aimed at the majority and essentially terminal, contained a strong element of social control. The purpose of moral education, as he saw it, was not to teach the poor to be content with their place in society any more than it was to teach them hatred of the rich. All classes deserved and could make use of an inculcation in the moral values of individual freedom and personal responsibility.[75]

---

diatable intolerance (*ibid.* [1873-I], 149). The quotation about tolerance is from *ibid.* (1873-II), 150; see also *ibid.* (1875-II), 49, 51, (1877-II), 302. *Ibid.* (1876-I), 161. He also defended the right of the state to regulate private secondary schools to ensure against any teaching "hostile to the principles of natural morals and of civil and political law as universally recognized by the Western nations" (*ibid.* [1872-II], 166).

72. Waelti, *Morale kantienne*, 102–104.

73. Lucien Roure, *Doctrines et problèmes* (Paris, 1900), 147–49.

74. Waelti, *Morale kantienne*, 91–100.

75. There has been much work on education recently; see, *e.g.,* Stock-Morton, *Moral Education*. Renouvier blamed the education received by the

Renouvier's moral philosophy was most at one with Kant in its devotion to the goal of the autonomy of the will. To obey the moral law the individual gives himself (rather than receives from outside) is the practical meaning of freedom.[76] This self-imposed duty is not arbitrary or even subjective since it can take place only in conformity with the categorical imperative in which men discover what they ought to do through reason. The rule of reason is not tyranny or even heteronomy, as some have advanced in recent years under the influence of an otherwise salutary reaction against totalitarianism. It is the liberation of what is most human in us because it involves overcoming not merely the pressures of society in their various forms but also the dictates of our animal nature (which are often confused with freedom by today's irrationalists).

In the Kantian philosophy, a moral act is one performed because we perceive it as a duty. As we have seen, Renouvier was not willing to follow Kant in ascribing moral value only to acts performed solely out of duty. The sense of duty has to be present, but Renouvier admitted the legitimacy, even the practical necessity, of an admixture of other motives.[77] He did not think these others detracted from the moral autonomy expressed in a moral act, and in any case, they are inescapable in the real world. It is gravely important, however, that the passions remain in a supporting role, for altruism or Christian love for one's fellow man can offer no stable rules for moral conduct. Renouvier showed that a morale of love was a morale that easily adopted the maxim that the ends justify the means and thus becomes a rationalization for deceiving people "for their own good," as parents do their children when, for example, they refrain from telling them they are adopted, or even as the Inquisition did when it sent relapsed heretics to the stake because it would improve their

French bourgeoisie for its record of weakness as a ruling class (*Critique philosophique* [1878-I], 68).

76. This explains his objections to Catholic ethics (*ibid.* [1873-II], 146). Renouvier associated this view with the Enlightenment as opposed to the theocratic spirit (*ibid.* [1877-I], 39–40).

77. Here he opposes Kant (*ibid.* [1872-II], 403, [1873-I], 217, [1878-I], 33, 36). The passions may support, but they may also oppose, just action (*Science de la morale*, I, 287).

chances of eternal life by preventing them from further offending God. To his Christian critics, Renouvier responded that "the age of [morals based on] charity in theory was, in practice, an age of blood." [78]

The drive for moral autonomy supposes free will in the moral subject.[79] Renouvier insisted again and again that we cannot meaningfully talk about morals unless we believe that men are responsible for their acts and that we cannot hold men responsible for their acts unless we believe they possess a free will.

The logic of this equation has caused a lot of perturbation in Western thought. Few have tried to break it directly, so strongly does it appeal to both common sense and reflection, but there have been many efforts to get around it. The growing strength of deterministic convictions made it a problem for many. If, as determinists hold, men cannot act otherwise than they do, what sense does it make to hold them responsible? How can one justify either sanctions or rewards? Few have been prepared to follow the reforming British industrialist and social theorist Robert Owen in concluding that rewards and punishments should indeed be eliminated from society, a proper education making them unnecessary. Others have tried to redefine responsibility so that it could be applied even to wholly determined acts, but this has seemed self-contradictory to most people.

Social scientists, seeing the individual as determined by the collective, have transferred the idea of responsibility to the society as a whole. But this has had the effect of vacating the concept of morality, since no one can explain what this collective responsibility means without resort to theological realism of the kind used to support the Catholic doctrine of Original Sin or the organicist metaphors that treat society as an individual, thus merely displacing the problem. The only consistent determinism would be one that held that we cannot help hanging the murderer, who could not help committing the murder, and that our indignation against him is as inescapable as his feeling of having been justified (at least at the time; he may be determined to feel remorse

78. *Critique philosophique* (1873-I), 213, (1878-I), 37, (1873-I), 216.
79. As we shall see in the next chapter, free will is something we choose freely to affirm. In a sense, morals come first for Renouvier: There is free will because there is a moral law (*ibid.* [1872-I], 70).

later).[80] A few people have managed to believe this, at least part of the time, but very few have dared express what they know will seem absurd or a cruel joke.

Because of his concept of the *solidarité du mal* (the solidarity that binds men together in the evil they do, like the *solidarité du bien,* which connects them in the good they achieve), Renouvier cannot help recognizing that society does bear a responsibility for criminal acts, a responsibility that attenuates that of the individual, and he agrees that we must try to take this into account in our practice of criminal justice.[81] But free will suffices to show that individual responsibility still exists. Even in cases where the individual responsibility of the criminal is clearly diminished, the right of defense allows society to protect itself against him.

Renouvier was already concerned in the 1860s that the direction of "positivist politics" was leading toward the idea that we should treat criminals as sick and should therefore prescribe treatment rather than punishment. He brilliantly described why this would not be an advance in humanity but a dangerous path to follow.[82] In 1888 he pointed out that the same danger was hidden in the principles of utilitarianism:

> The notion of the right and the just [is] basically preserved within the utilitarian schools . . . by the force of both classical and religious traditions, which preserve a principle of *obligation* of conscience (or of autonomous virtue, or the Decalogue), [but it logically] ought to give way—following the same path as doctrines and opinions—to the principle of the *purge of the social body* by the verdict of competent judges called to pronounce on the state of physical and moral health, that is of *adaptation*— possible or impossible—of the individuals whose criminal acts point them out as chargeable with a more or less great *harmfulness* or *dangerousness* to a well-ordered society.[83]

80. Insofar as crime is simply natural, so is punishment (*ibid.* [1888-II], 207).

81. *Ibid.* (1873-I), 104, (1888-II), 209–15.

82. *Science de la morale*, II, 196–98.

83. *Critique philosophique* (1888-II), 206.

A similar danger for any conception of moral responsibility was to be found in evolutionism:

> The system of evolution tends to destroy the juridical spirit by replacing the ideas of merit, culpability, and punishment by the single conception of a psycho-physiological state of the individual, to which, in good logic, one can only apply a medical treatment when that individual is found to deviate considerably from the normal type, or, to phrase it differently, from the current average in opinions, inclinations, or manners.[84]

The application of such views would inevitably give the self-designated experts an enormous, uncontrollable power over their fellow men.

The predominance of deterministic philosophies in his century, Renouvier thought, was beginning to have a demoralizing effect on society that risked catastrophe.[85] This was a tendency that made a mockery of the optimistic determinists' belief in progress, for Renouvier could not conceive of a progress that did not involve the growth of the ability and willingness of men to assume moral responsibility for their acts.[86] This was another way of saying that the growth of freedom is the only measure of progress.

We will look into Renouvier's defense of free will more deeply in the next chapter, but it is important to stress here that his belief in its reality was particularly, but by no means exclusively, motivated by moral considerations. Moral autonomy was an aspiration that Renouvier thought intrinsic to man, and free will was necessary for its achievement. However, he was a long way from thinking that all our acts, or all our acts involving moral issues, display an exercise of free will. On the contrary, he saw that exercise as an ideal rarely achieved by most people, perhaps never achieved by many. He readily acknowledged that our acts are sub-

84. *Ibid.* (1880-I), 377.
85. *Ibid.* (1883-I), 333.
86. The exercise of freedom is the only means of moral improvement. As most people are always satisfied with custom, such improvement can only be the work of a small but active minority (*Science de la morale*, II, 133–34).

81

ject to a host of determinations, both physical and psychological. Our choices at any moment are circumscribed by the state of our health, our emotional involvement with the other people concerned, the influences of our upbringing, the common values of our milieu, our concern for our job, and so on. It is easy to extend the list, indeed so easy that it produces some difficulty for determinists to explain how the resultant of so many vectors is itself determined, given what Renouvier called the law of large numbers. However, as long as we do not apply moral reflection to our decisions, we may consider them determined rather than free.

It is the possibility of this free decision, however rarely it is exercised, that is vital to Renouvier's moral philosophy. We do have, he insisted, a capacity of meaningful choice; alternative outcomes are possible. However much an act seems to have been determined by various factors when we look at it in retrospect, our decision, our choice, can have been the factor that turned the result in one direction instead of another. Renouvier likened this act of freedom to an act of creation. Our intrusion into the multiple series of causal chains initiates a new chain of causality. This possibility, whether we exercise it or not, is sufficient to give meaning to the concept of moral responsibility and therefore to serve as a foundation for Renouvier's moral philosophy.

I started this chapter with a condemnation of our current moral anarchy and especially the effort to justify it in terms of individual rights and liberty. Moralists have always had to accept the risk—the certainty—of being laughed at by the objects of their criticism. To become too indignant about the behavior of mankind is indeed ridiculous. Given its record, we should know enough not to expect much better. The world has worse problems than drug abuse or disordered sexual relations, and what I am attacking here is mainly the intellectual disorder, the confusion of ideas about morality and freedom. If I am indignant, it is against the intelligensia that instead of providing a standard against which to judge our moral disorder has often reduced itself to cheering it on, whether sincerely or cynically. For the future of Western civilization, this unprecedented indigence of the intellectuals is one of the gravest symptoms of decline.

An ethic of freedom and responsibility seems the only way out of the intellectual crisis of Western morals. Practical improvement, on the other hand, seems more likely to come from movements of religious inspiration, basically dogmatic and unlikely to be liberal. The problem is not to construct a new moral code or to find new moral ideas. As Renouvier remarked, all moral codes are better than man's behavior. He was convinced that man's behavior was worse in his time than in most, and he thought it likely to become worse in the next century. Whether his evaluation of the nineteenth century was right or not—I think he was too harsh on his contemporaries—his forecast for the next century has certainly come true.

The tragedy of the nineteenth century was that some of its noblest ambitions were flawed. The tragedy of the twentieth century has been that the Western intelligentsia is so disoriented by the overwhelming evidence of the failure of their predecessors and idols that it has been unable to make a rational diagnosis of the situation. In morals as in other areas, Renouvier offers a starting point for this necessary reflection.

II

The Philosophical Defense of Liberty

The primary merit of man is to be free.
—Renouvier, *Deuxième essai*

There was a general feeling in the nineteenth century of being present at, or part of, the greatest expansion of liberty in the history of the human race. Some saw this development in essentially negative terms as the destruction of an ordered and time-tested society, likely to end in anarchy and chaos. At the other extreme, many of those who welcomed it saw the process as not proceeding rapidly enough, hobbled by prejudices, vested interests, and ignorance. Whether fearful or hopeful, few doubted that the triumphant progress of liberty would continue.

In this atmosphere, it is not surprising that the question of liberty attracted much serious thought. The history of its development was examined, its sociological foundations analyzed, the political conditions of its growth debated. What was curiously lacking was attention to the relations between these historical, sociological, and political inquiries and the more obscure trends of Western philosophical thought. If anyone had cared to look, he could have found plenty of evidence that these trends were fundamentally hostile to the idea of liberty and that they threatened to undermine its intellectual foundations.

The discussion of political freedom and human rights had become a major theme in Western thought only beginning in the seventeenth century, while the theological and philosophical problem of the freedom of the will, whether limited to the question of salvation or more generally understood, had a long history in Western thought, had indeed been one of the perennial big questions of philosophy.[1] The question of the relations between this freedom of the will and the more concrete issues of political freedom and individual rights had rarely been examined, if only because political and individual freedom were rarely issues before modern times. But even when they became issues, few saw any need to connect these practical questions with the abstruse debates of philosophy.

Unreflective opinion had two choices: Either there was no connection between free will and public freedom, or there was some direct but not very clear connection between the two. The former attitude, common from the beginning of the nineteenth century, enabled thinkers to be simultaneously defenders of political freedom and exponents of deterministic and materialistic philosophies that denied free will.[2] This was a secular counterpart of the traditional Christian attitude that emphasized free will for reasons of practical morality but could not reconcile it with the theological determinism of an all-powerful, all-knowing God.[3] Few thought that there was any serious conflict, and still fewer imagined that the diffusion of deterministic philosophies would serve to undermine the cause of political and individual liberty.

Renouvier was, I think, the first, at least the first major philosopher, to see clearly into this danger and to devote himself to drawing attention

1. *Deuxième essai,* xiv–xv. Free will was a problem in religion before becoming one in philosophy but a problem most Christians avoided simply by believing in free will and predestination simultaneously. Greek philosophy, the first to give this question nonreligious consideration, was inclined to psychological determinism, though there were, Renouvier believed, some defenders of freedom—Aristotle, Pyrrhus, Epicurus (*Esquisse,* I, 227–28, 238, 240–43).

2. See Karl Popper, *The High Tide of Prophecy: Hegel, Marx, and the Aftermath* (London, 1945), 197, Vol. II of Popper, *The Open Society and Its Enemies.*

3. *Esquisse,* I, 249–50; see also I, 248–51.

to it while proposing a remedy. The development of his neocriticist philosophy was itself a response to what he had come to see as the anti-liberty forces dominant in nineteenth-century thought. Under the influences of discussions with his friend Jules Lequier, he became convinced of the reality of human free will and its central importance for the understanding of everything else.[4] This conviction came to Renouvier while he was still deeply under the influence of his first contact with the Saint-Simonians. He experienced, not an overnight liberation from their deterministic viewpoint, but a more gradual readjustment of his views, which became a complete detachment from them only after 1851. Perhaps the failure of the socialist movements in 1848, rooted as they were in the would-be scientific philosophies of the preceding three decades, finally persuaded him of the dangers of rejecting free will.[5] Alienated from political life during the Second Empire, he would spend nearly two decades in the construction and elaboration of his philosophy of liberty, establishing its foundations and exploring its consequences.

Renouvier was aware that for a long time the question had been of mainly religious significance: whether man's salvation depended on free will or on predestination.[6] This debate had reached its peak, in both vehemence and subtlety, in the famous exchange between Erasmus and Luther in the sixteenth century. The emergence of a secular debate over free will was a result of the rise of the scientific worldview in the seventeenth century. The ascendancy of the idea that the world was governed by invariable laws, taking the role previously occupied by an all-

4. Renouvier's account of his "conversion" to free will is in the last part of Vol. II of the *Esquisse*. Lionel Dauriac ("Les Moments de la philosophie de Charles Renouvier," *Bulletin de la société française de philosophie*, IV [1904], 23) defined the high point of Lequier's influence—the writing of the *Deuxième essai*—as one of four "moments" in Renouvier's philosophical development.

5. Mouy (*Idée de progrès*, 43) argues that the disappointments of 1848 played a key role in shaping Renouvier's idea of liberty. For Renouvier, free will came to be seen as the ultimate basis of political liberty (*Deuxième essai*, 551). See *Histoire*, IV, 431, and especially *Esquisse*, II, 382, and *Deuxième essai*, 371*n*1.

6. Renouvier saw free will as one of the basic concepts of both philosophy and Christian doctrine (*Histoire*, IV, 277).

powerful, all-knowing God, seemed to leave less and less room for the view that man was somehow an exception to the general rule. The most heroic task for the modern philosopher was to find a means of validating science *and* free will simultaneously, and the most heroic effort of the eighteenth century was that of Immanuel Kant. But for many in the next century, it seemed that Kant had saved free will only at the cost of making it irrelevant.[7] Fichte tried to rescue Kantian philosophy from this unhappy outcome, but in the general opinion (only recently challenged by Alexis Philonenko, Luc Ferry, and Alain Renaut) his effort led to the fairyland of absolute idealism, denying reality to the material world.[8]

Against the rising tide of determinism, Renouvier would try to show that Kant could be the launching pad for a defense of free will that would maintain its practical relevance and demonstrate its compatibility with natural science, properly understood. He did not claim to be presenting any new arguments in favor of free will; he felt they were in any case unnecessary.[9] Renouvier's reasons for coming to the defense of free will were partly shared with Kant and partly his own. As we have seen in the previous chapter, the shared part was the most familiar: a concern for the connection between free will and moral behavior. Free will was for Kant the essential basis of *practical reason;* without it, the whole idea of moral obligation ceased to have meaning. For Renouvier, this consideration remained central. Without moral responsibility, man would not be

---

7. What does it matter to man if he has freedom in the world of the noumena if his world of phenomena is entirely determined? Renouvier later felt that Kant held on to free will solely for the sake of morals while not really believing in it (*Quatrième essai,* 35–36).

8. Renouvier praised Fichte as a defender of freedom and criticized him as a mystic (*Quatrième essai,* 46). See Alain Renaut, *Le Système de droit: philosophie et droit dans la pensée de Fichte* (Paris, 1986); Luc Ferry, *Le Système des philosophies de l'histoire* (Paris, 1984), Vol. II of Ferry and Renaut, *Philosophie politique;* Alexis Philonenko, *La Liberté humaine dans la philosophie de Fichte* (Paris, 1966).

9. Renouvier was concerned to establish a rationalist and not an empiricist view of science. He saw free will as perhaps the main issue dividing the rationalists and empiricists (*Histoire,* IV, 262). He indicated that there had been no new arguments in favor of free will since Kant and Rousseau (*Esquisse,* I, 280).

distinct from the rest of the animal kingdom, and the whole of civilization would be meaningless. But this was not the sole basis for his concern
with free will, and this additional concern moved Renouvier beyond
Kant and Fichte, bringing him closer to our own time.[10]

It is not just the moral aspect of civilization that hangs on the reality
of free will, in Renouvier's opinion, but the whole of our intellectual life.
Free will is also the foundation on which philosophy and the natural
sciences rest.[11] Without free will, our ability to know anything, whether
about man or about nature, is fatally undermined. Scientists do not need
to believe in free will, and as he knew, they prefer to avoid this sort of
question. In practice, they can legitimately do so because in their narrow
spheres of inquiry they have developed techniques of investigation that
work even when the scientist is unconscious of the fundamental assumptions on which his method rests. But without free will, the certainty of
scientific truths becomes illusory; a consistent determinism must lead to
a profound skepticism.[12] Renouvier would never despair of convincing
the scientists that just as our concepts of right and wrong depend on free
will, so do our concepts of true and false. Indeed, without free will, we
could not even talk sensibly about things being true or false.

If, as he pointed out, I hold such and such a view to be true and I am
determined by forces outside my control to hold this view, the person
who disagrees with me is equally determined by outside forces in his
position. If these mutually contradictory positions are equally necessary,
what grounds can we have for the certainty that either view is the correct
one?[13] If our belief that our ideas are determined is itself determined, so
is the other person's belief in free will determined. Under these conditions

10. Renouvier saw Kant's German disciples as having abandoned liberty for
determinism, optimism, and pantheism (*Histoire*, IV, 467).

11. See *Deuxième essai*, 227.

12. *Histoire*, IV, 399; *Deuxième essai*, 327.

13. *Histoire*, IV, 399; *Deuxième essai*, 306–307 (according to Hamelin,
Système de Renouvier, 242). Necessity destroys truth: "If everything is necessary,
error is necessary just as much as truth is, and their claims to validity are comparable" (*Deuxième essai*, 327). For a restatement of his argument that freedom
is essential to the certainty of our knowledge, see *Esquisse*, II, 270–74; see also,
Science de la morale, II, 377.

how could it make any sense to speak of one view as "right" and the other as "wrong"? If, on the other hand, our choices are free, I may freely choose to believe in free will or in spite of the apparent contradiction, to believe in universal determinism. Of the four possible positions revealed by this analysis, the only one that can serve as a foundation for a rational certainty in the truth of our beliefs is to freely believe in freedom.[14] But as Renouvier insists, this means that we must give up any pretension to the absolute certainty of our beliefs.[15] The truth of free will cannot be proved so that no rational person can doubt it. It is a relative truth, like all our other truths, but more important because it plants a relativism at the very core of our thought.[16]

Scientists, Renouvier thought, should have no difficulty understanding and accepting this because science is built on an awareness of the conditional character of our knowledge, an openness to the discovery of new truths and the abandonment of old ones.[17] In fact, he had to admit, many scientists were still under the sway of older metaphysical concep-

14. The four are (1) we are determined to believe in freedom; (2) we are determined to believe in determinism; (3) we freely believe in determinism; (4) we freely believe in freedom. See *Deuxième essai*, 478; *Histoire*, IV, 399; Hamelin, *Système de Renouvier*, 273–74.

15. "Certitude is not and cannot be an absolute. It is, as is too often forgotten, a condition and an action of man: not an action or a condition where he grasps directly that which cannot be directly grasped—that is to say, facts and laws which are outside or higher than present experience—but rather where he places his conscience such as it is and as he supports it. Properly speaking, there is no certitude; there are only men who are certain" (*Deuxième essai*, 390). For Renouvier's battle against the idea of evident truths, see *Histoire*, IV, 75, 261; certitude is a sort of "personal contract," "a real contract that a man makes with himself" (Lacroix, *Vocation personnelle*, 114).

16. *Deuxième essai*, 309–10 (according to Hamelin, *Système de Renouvier*, 242). There were, however, "great probabilities in its [free will's] favor" (*Deuxième essai*, 475). "It ought to be a universally accepted maxim that *everything that is in the mind is relative to the mind*" (*Deuxième essai*, 390). Philosophy needs to take into account the existence of disagreement among philosophers (*ibid.*, 414). Renouvier's approach to the existence of these disagreements is one of the distinctive features of his philosophy.

17. On the use of hypotheses in science, see *Premier essai*, 200.

tions of truth, except in the conduct of their personal research, and were unaware of any inconsistency in their position.[18] Some who were aware were evidently afraid that to admit that an act of belief was at the base of scientific knowledge would risk undermining the claim of science to objectivity and, even worse, open the way to the proliferation of pseudoscientific beliefs.[19] In reality, pseudoscientific beliefs were already proliferating under the aegis of the belief in determinism. Without a critical analysis of the nature and limits of scientific knowledge, however, our intellectual life is subject to a constant abuse of the name and prestige of science.

The abuse of science takes many forms: the application of research methods to fields where they do not apply, the application of particular concepts to areas other than those where they originated, the confusion of "Science" with the operations of particular sciences. One of the main intellectual trends of the nineteenth century, which Renouvier called *scientisme*, usually rendered as "scientism" in English, was the product of this abuse. Renouvier's relativism does not justify believing in whatever we want to believe.[20] It insists on submitting our opinions to every possible test of logic, experiment, and experience. But we have to admit that our logic, the hypotheses on which our experiments are based, the schemas of thought by which we interpret our experience, all rest ultimately on acts of belief and not on absolute certainties.[21]

If free will is thus essential to both morals and science, just what does he mean by it? Over the centuries, most of the debate over free will

18. Renouvier credited the English empiricists, following Hume, with freeing science from the metaphysical concept of cause (*Histoire*, IV, 273).

19. This is the concern of Parodi (*Du positivisme à l'idéalisme*, 184–85), who finds in Renouvier a dangerous fideism. So does Brunschwicg (*Progrès de la conscience*, 625). For Renouvier's praise of Boutroux's argument that the contingency of the laws of nature is not a threat to science, see *Histoire*, IV, 673–74.

20. Dauriac ("Moments de la philosophie," 30–32) strongly makes this point. It would be interesting to compare Renouvier's conclusion on this point with the similar view expressed by Richard Rorty, coming from a rather different direction.

21. *Histoire*, IV, 692; on the need for faith in reason, even though such faith is in itself not a rational act, see Popper, *High Tide of Prophecy*, 218–19.

has failed to advance our understanding because of the lack of agreement about what is meant by the term.[22] I cannot solve that problem, but I think we will see that Renouvier's view makes the issue more comprehensible.

Free will, for Renouvier, is a capacity possessed by human beings, and only by human beings, that enables them to choose whether to accept one idea or another, whether to perform one act or a different one. It is thus a rejection of the doctrine that holds that all events, mental or physical, are absolutely determined and cannot be other than what they are.[23] Free will is also a rejection of the doctrine of chance, for it is an active power and not the "liberty of indifference" so belabored by determinists.[24] Chance is also hostile to liberty, since it denies man a real power of decision.

The existence of free will requires a measure of indetermination in the universe but could not exist if nature were essentially indeterminate.[25] Our acts of free will are the beginnings of chains of consequences and would have no meaning if their consequences were not subject to cause and effect. "Free acts are not effects without causes; their cause is man, the ensemble and fullness of his functions. They are not isolated, but are always closely attached to the preceding condition of the passions and of knowledge. *A posteriori* they seem henceforth indissoluble parts of an order of facts, although a different order was possible *a priori*." [26] The laws that permit us to say this is followed by that do not admit of an infinite regression into the past, according to Renouvier. Therefore, every series of phenomena—and indeed the existence of any phen-

22. Adler, *Idea of Freedom.*

23. See definition of free will in *Histoire,* IV, 337; on liberty as choice, see *Deuxième essai,* 466; on real alternatives, see *ibid.,* 339. Renouvier is rejecting a causal necessity, not analytic necessity, as in the syllogisms of logical operations (*Premier essai,* 232–36).

24. *Deuxième essai,* 330–34, 336, 337; Hamelin, *Systeme de Renouvier,* 242–43, 249.

25. "Liberty does not require the complete indetermination of particular future events, even of those that are directly connected to it" (*Deuxième essai,* 459); see also *ibid.,* 357; Hamelin, *Système de Renouvier,* 244.

26. *Deuxième essai,* 359; see also *Science de la morale,* II, 361–62.

omena—must have a beginning that we cannot explain in terms of antecedents.[27]

The act of creation of the universe is thus replicated (in a much smaller way!) in every act of free will. Every act of free will is the creation of a new series of phenomena, a series that would not otherwise have existed.[28] These new chains of cause and effect are not simply the product of the intersection of existing but independent series, as A.-A. Cournot argued, for such intersections, though they appear random from the point of view of any one of the colliding series, would be necessary from a higher viewpoint.[29] They must be new beginnings, arising from a conjuncture in which, given the antecedents, more than one consequence was possible: "ambiguous futures," Renouvier called them.[30] Free will is the capacity to opt for one or another of those futures.

Philosophies of determinism can operate at different levels. Everybody agrees that at the phenomenological level we experience the feeling of freely making decisions.[31] And some philosophers, like Alfred Fouillée, argue that this "apparent freedom" is not only all there is but that it is

27. *Premier essai,* 237; *Science de la morale,* II, 360–61. Most scientists today reject the idea that infinite regression is an absurdity; *Esquisse,* II, 378–79. We cannot explain beginnings because they are by definition at the limits of our possible knowledge.

28. *Esquisse,* II, 196–97.

29. A. -A. Cournot, *Considérations sur la marche des idées et des événements dans le temps modernes* (Paris, 1973), 9–10, Vol. IV of Cournot, *Oeuvres complètes,* ed. André Robinet.

30. *Deuxième essai,* 210. "The real indetermination of various phenomena envisaged in the future" (*Premier essai,* 240). "[A determinist] would renounce everything called reflection and reason, for these functions do not work without the consciousness of a *representative self-motivation,* which is itself linked to an awareness of the *real ambiguity of future conditions* before it takes action" (*Histoire,* IV, 769). See also *Troisième essai,* xlvii; Hamelin, *Système de Renouvier,* 230.

31. Renouvier freely admitted that the feeling of freedom is not proof of its reality (*Deuxième essai,* 289–90, 329–30). See the interesting passage on the "illusion du possible" (*Premier essai,* 240–41). Some have argued that statistical regularities show that even apparently free acts are really determined. Renouvier refutes this argument and turns the Law of Large Numbers against determinism

sufficient to enable us to call man free. More common is a psychological determinism arguing that while man possesses an apparent freedom of action in the sense that he is directed by his own decisions and his own ideas, those ideas are entirely determined and could not be other than what they are. Some have argued that this "freedom" is sufficient to justify holding men morally responsible for their actions.[32] Others, more consistently, recognize that this view is incompatible with the idea of responsibility and are ready to give up responsibility. More vaguely, one can believe in a determinism at the level of molecules and atoms, but virtually nobody believes it will ever be possible to demonstrate any connection between determinism at this level and man's mental processes.[33] Likewise, it does not seem possible to see any relationship between the indeterminism that some physicists recognize at the subatomic level and what the philosopher understands by free will.

Renouvier recognized an element of dependence of our minds on physical processes but insisted that mental processes are radically different from physical ones and cannot be explained by them.[34] He also recognized the existence of psychological determinisms—existence would hardly be possible without them—but insisted that free will requires only that their sway not be absolute and universal. Psychological determinists argue that there is a real struggle of alternatives in our minds but that the outcomes, whether ideas or actions, are always decided by the "strongest motive" and are thus effectively determined. Renouvier exposed the circular reasoning of this argument, which succeeds simply by

---

(*Premier essai*, 245, 247; *Deuxième essai*, 344–51; *Science de la morale*, II, 362–73).

32. This includes Renouvier, in the sense that freedom cannot be proved (*Science de la morale*, I, 5–6). Some have called acts "free" when the contrary act was not possible, a view Renouvier rejects (*Histoire*, IV, 673).

33. See Richard Rorty, *Philosophy and the Mirror of Nature* (Princeton, N.J., 1979).

34. Freedom is not a biological fact (*Deuxième essai*, 285–86; see also 250–52). Biology cannot explain consciousness, even if some day it succeeds in demonstrating the organic seats of the passions (*Deuxième essai*, 255, 257–58). On the impact of chemicals on our minds, see *Troisième essai*, 112.

baptizing whatever motive appears to have been decisive as the "strongest" without being able to explain why except by ex post facto rationalization.[35] Still, Renouvier concedes that most of our thoughts and actions may be considered determined, in the sense that they are unreflective. He was particularly interested in studies of the formation and persistence of habits.[36]

Free will involves—is—an effort not simply to submit to the forces that tend to shape our thoughts. It is an effort of decision based on reflection, a choice.[37] Thus while it is a universal capacity of man as man, free will is practiced quite variably. No one uses it more than a fraction of the time; many have lost even the desire. It is a capacity that can be strengthened by exercise; we can, so to speak, make a habit of the exercise of our will, just as we can make a habit of letting things be decided for us.[38]

35. On Herbert Spencer's effort to get around this, see *Histoire*, IV, 336: "The equivocal [character of the question]: *is it the determining factor because it is the strongest, or do we call it the strongest because we determine ourselves on the basis of it?* is lifted by a theory which sees nothing in the will which either determines or is determined. It is the act, it is the *motor change*, which is the passage from the idea to the act that is determined. . . . The will is only the concomitant and the sign of this determination, *when the determination is made and in the sense that it is made.*" For Renouvier, on the other hand, the will is already present in the motives (Hamelin, *Système de Renouvier*, 243).

36. *Deuxième essai*, 88, 196–203. Renouvier was an admirer of Félix Ravaisson's *De l'habitude* (Paris, 1838).

37. The will "is produced in all these higher states of consciousness that are called attention, systematic abstraction, sustained and varied reflection, states which are genuine 'self-motivated analyses'" (Hamelin, *Système de Renouvier*, 228). For Renouvier, reflection requires free will, which is why men, but not animals, have it (*Deuxième essai*, 68). Conscience itself is a voluntary function for Renouvier (*ibid.*, 219). "A motivated action is a free action" (Hamelin, *Système de Renouvier*, 281).

38. *Science de la morale*, II, 385–86; but even the slightest use of free will establishes its reality (*ibid.*, 371). "This one precept, *use your freedom*, if it is followed, founds the morality of action, . . . [and] in many cases can assure the preponderance of reason" (*Deuxième essai*, 340). See also *Premier essai*, 346–47.

Free will is thus obviously connected with rationalism for Renouvier. It consists, not of following our sentiments or our desires, but of controlling them through the use of our reason. The will is a regulating rather than a generating force for Renouvier; presented with choices, it can decide which to adopt. Far from yielding to the strongest motives, it decides which are the strongest.

The conditions with which Renouvier surrounded the exercise of free will have seemed to weaken it in the eyes of some who saw themselves as radical defenders of liberty, such as Pierre-Joseph Proudhon.[39] But one of the weaknesses of more traditional defenses of free will has been to claim too much for it. By being realistic, Renouvier strengthened the case. His concept of free will is not simple or easily conveyed in an aphorism, but it is strong. It is also important to note that for Renouvier, free will was a postulate rather than an apodictic certainty.[40] It would be a contradiction in terms to claim to have made a case for free will that all thinking men would have to accept.

Free will is, he believed, a difficult concept, less easy to grasp, and appearing later in history, than the idea of determinism.[41] Free will is a reality and not just an appearance, and he believed he had demonstrated that reality as far as humanly possible. The objections that have been raised to belief in free will were taken seriously by Renouvier, which has rarely been so for other defenders. The easy and deceptive solutions—those that define freedom in ways that make it a euphemism for determinism or those that, like the Stoic, define freedom as acceptance of determinism—were exposed and set aside. Having clarified our understanding of what free will is in the process of defending its reality, Renouvier would also devote great effort to showing what it meant for human experience in the past and in the future. Perhaps more important, he would be concerned to show the consequences of rejecting the belief in free will.

39. Even Hamelin (*Système de Renouvier,* 246) thinks Renouvier restricts psychic liberty too much.

40. It was not logically provable, but neither is necessity (*Deuxième essai,* 365).

41. *Ibid.,* 472–73.

We can see that Renouvier's defense of free will against universal determinism was not a defense of metaphysics against science. He attempted to defend free will from a phenomenist point of view compatible with science. He was campaigning against the abuse of the name of science to promote certain metaphysical views, commonly unacknowledged to be such. Determinism, materialism, and positivism were, for him, overlapping, if not quite identical, enemies. Positivism was the only one to be able to claim some novelty. Determinism and materialism, far from being outcomes of modern science, were metaphysical conceptions that had made their appearance in Greek antiquity.[42] To refute them was in no way to attack modern science. Positivism, on the other hand, had some claim to modernity and was sufficiently related to the development of modern science to have been imaginable only at the beginning of the nineteenth century.

Unfortunately, positivists from Saint-Simon and Auguste Comte on seemed unable to confine themselves to the legitimate domain of science. Comte presented his positivism as a comprehensive philosophy of science, explaining its nature, history, and future.[43] Or rather, it was the science of sciences, since it purported to rest on no metaphysical assumptions but to establish the "auto-foundation" of science on itself. Despite Comte's efforts to tightly delimit the area of what is and is not scientific thinking, positivism readily became the basis for much pseudoscientific development. Renouvier attributed this to its lack of critical self-reflection, and his criticism of positivism was also a defense of the permanent relevance of philosophy.

There are aspects of positivism that Renouvier accepted as in accord

42. Science is a legitimate source of metaphysical intuitions, but it is important to maintain a sense of the distinction between science and metaphysics, and especially not to accept claims of metaphysical doctrines to be scientifically demonstrated (*Esquisse*, I, 286–87). Renouvier was glad that science had become more aware that getting to "the bottom of things" was not its mission (*Histoire*, IV, 715–16). Modern debate, he argued, has simply given determinism a more scientific appearance than it had in antiquity, but not made it a scientific position (*Esquisse*, I, 295).

43. But Comte's philosophy of history was not only utterly unhistorical (*Quatrième essai*, 165–68); it was also not compatible with his view of science (*Esquisse*, II, 235).

with science.[44] But even as a doctrine of science it was too narrowly conceived. Comte's construction of the hierarchy of sciences was untenable, his version of their historical development inconsistent with the data. Comte cut himself off from important aspects of scientific inquiry by such attitudes as, for example, his rejection of the calculus of probabilities.[45] He had one of the qualities Renouvier thought essential in a philosopher, a solid knowledge of mathematics.[46] But he had, even in mathematics, too fixed a conception of science, one that could not adapt to its inevitable changes.

As a result, by the end of the century, Comte's views would be badly outmoded in several areas. What was worse, from Renouvier's point of view, was that Comte arbitrarily excluded from the domain of legitimate inquiry many topics that had been of perennial concern to man and would continue to be so. By excessively circumscribing the exercise of reason, he invited an extension of the domain of unreason. For example, Comte's rejection of psychology (he considered that only the physiology of the brain could be a positive science) made him fall for the pseudo-physiology of Gall's phrenology.[47] And when Comte in later life became aware of what had been left out of his philosophy, he proceeded to fill the void with a number of his own dubious hypotheses.

The peculiarities of Auguste Comte's Religion of Humanity were not what menaced liberty in his thought, and Renouvier found that among the invented religions of the nineteenth century Comte's had a more genuinely religious character than most.[48] What was menacing was Comte's application of positivism to support authoritarian government. In this Comte was following his mentor Saint-Simon, a vigorous advocate of the rule of specialized elites (though he varied in his opinion of which

44. For example, "the reduction of knowledge to the laws governing phenomena" (*Premier essai*, xi).

45. *Deuxième essai*, 524–29; *Histoire*, IV, 227–28. Renouvier rejected efforts to use the calculus of probabilities to refute free will; he found on the contrary that it lends support to his view (*Esquisse*, I, 291–95).

46. Renouvier notes that this quality is curiously lacking in the English empiricists since Locke (*Histoire*, IV, 43).

47. Many of his views were outmoded by the time Comte adopted them (*Histoire*, IV, 228); *ibid.*, IV, 227–28, IV, 240.

48. *Ibid.*, IV, 245.

elite should be at the top of the social pyramid). For both men, this elite dictatorship was justified by the possession of certain knowledge. Their philosophical views about knowledge were therefore of direct political and social significance.[49]

Since Comte's positivism restricted the domain of genuine knowledge to the narrowest concept of what constituted science, his ideal was a world in which everything knowable was known with the unchallenged authority of science and nobody paid attention to the things that were not knowable on these terms. Freedom in such a context could be only a freedom to be wrong, to have false ideas, meaningless ones. Freedom was thus a meaningless idea. As Renouvier observed, the only thing strange about J. S. Mill's description of Comte's as the most complete system of tyranny ever devised was how long it had taken the English defender of liberty to discover what Comte had never attempted to disguise.[50]

The abuse of scientific thought, or more commonly the abuse of the name of science, for the promotion of social and political doctrines hostile to freedom was thus one of the basic reasons why a continuing philosophical critique of science was necessary in the nineteenth century and remains necessary today.[51] Only if we have an accurate idea of what science is, what it can and cannot do, can we evaluate the legitimacy of the inevitable efforts to draw sociopolitical conclusions from science. Science cannot supply this critique.

Indeed, as Renouvier pointed out, there is no such thing as "Science."[52] There are sciences, more or less unified or interrelated, depend-

49. *Premier essai,* xi. This connection has recently been argued with much force by Spragens, *Irony of Liberal Reason.*

50. For J. S. Mill's comment, see *Auguste Comte and Positivism* (London, 1866), 74. The Saint-Simonians saw liberty as destructive and therefore useful only in "critical" periods of history (*Quatrième essai,* 153–58). Renouvier admitted that Littré and his group of positivists had often defended liberal sociopolitical positions (*Histoire,* IV, 550). *Ibid.,* IV, 246–48.

51. On the need for that critique today, see Bouveresse, *Philosophe autophages.*

52. The title "Science" could only be claimed by the *"critique générale,"* which seeks, not universal knowledge, but the most general possible view (*Premier essai,* 85–96).

ing on the state of current knowledge, and there is the scientific method, drawn from the practice of specific sciences. But when an author hypostasizes Science, you can be almost sure he is going to advance some views not scientifically justified.

Much of the weakness of positivism came from the fact that Comte saw no need for a critique of knowledge and thus failed to understand the character of his main assumptions.[53] The abuse of science for sociopolitical purposes in the nineteenth century was often rooted in the uncritical assumption that certain doctrines were fully demonstrated by science. This was particularly true of the doctrines of universal determinism and materialism. Both ideas have their origins in pre-Socratic philosophy, but it was widely assumed that they had been verified by modern science. Renouvier was determined to show that they remained metaphysical concepts that although widely shared by scientists, had no necessary part in the actual working of scientific investigation.

Scientists study the phenomena accessible to their techniques and through the use of hypotheses tested against the phenomena develop laws describing the patterns of behavior of these phenomena. It is not necessary for them to postulate that these phenomena are the outward signs of some reality called *matter.* Scientific research is compatible with both materialistic and idealistic philosophical assumptions. Renouvier would not have been surprised, and would probably have been pleased, by what twentieth-century physics has done to the concept of matter.

The general idea of determinism is necessary to the functioning of science, and scientists are prone to assume its universality, though such an assumption is not necessary to their work. The assumption of universality generally derives from a metaphysical conception of "cause" that is not validated by science. The idea of cause-and-effect has prescientific origins, and indeed "cause" had developed such a metaphysical weight that one of the features of the scientific revolution, as Renouvier saw it,

---

53. Emile Boutroux, "La Philosophie d'A. Comte et la métaphysique," *Revue des cours et conférences,* XI (1902/1903-I), 63; according to Renouvier, Comte accepted Condillac's associationist psychology without examination (*Histoire,* IV, 227).

had been to eliminate concern for "causes." [54] Scientists sought to establish relationships between phenomena and to develop in mathematical form the laws expressing those relationships. What "caused" these relations was not of concern. Gravitation, as Newton explained it, is not the cause of the attraction of bodies for one another but a description of the laws of the relationships of physical bodies considered from a certain point of view. In general, Renouvier accepted Hume's critique of the idea of causality and thus accepted the adequacy of a purely phenomenological approach to science.

The opposite of universal determinism is thus not chance or hazard but a world governed by laws. A world of chance would be as hostile to freedom as a world of universal determinism, and equally void of human meaning.[55] But does a world of laws leave more room for freedom than either of these? In Renouvier's conception, it certainly does. By helping us to liberate ourselves from the mistaken conviction that science considers everything that happens as determined by its antecedents from all eternity—for universal determinism cannot admit a beginning—Renouvier's philosophy helps us avoid being duped by the social and political doctrines claiming to explain how things had to be and especially how they must be in the future.[56]

The Illusions of Progress

The most common form such doctrines took in the nineteenth century was historical determinism. Historical determinism is compatible with

54. Renouvier was also concerned to show that belief in causality is distinct from belief in absolute determinism (*Esquisse*, II, 14–15).

55. Nonetheless, a "certain indeterminism in the application of natural laws is doubtless a condition for free will" (*Histoire*, IV, 349). "The postulate of freedom presupposes a given order of relations and of laws whose necessary empire it only partially limits" (*Esquisse*, II, 394).

56. Renouvier suggested that the generation of Saint-Simon and Comte caught the "fever of universal explanation" from Laplace's success in unifying astronomy (*Quatrième essai*, 174).

philosophies of decadence or cyclical recurrence, but in the nineteenth century it led overwhelmingly to the doctrine of necessary progress.[57] Seeing the advance of liberty in Western society in the nineteenth century, optimists proclaimed its *necessary* expansion in the future without reflecting on the contradiction between the very idea of liberty and the idea of any necessary development. Necessary progress, Renouvier observed, is a secularized version of religious fatalism or predestination.[58] A prop, in other words, for people who do not have confidence in freedom. "Progress" served as a kind of deus ex machina for J. S. Mill and Auguste Comte to rescue them from the vicious circle of utilitarian morals, bridging the gap from egoism to altruism. So strong were the appeals of determinism and progress in the nineteenth century that they could inflect the sense of a social movement contrary to the intention of its founder or leader. Thus Fourier's most devoted disciples would display attitudes contrary to his belief in free will and his rejection of automatic progress. One of the reasons liberty would be shown to be so fragile in the twentieth century was the welcome given in the nineteenth century to doctrines of necessary progress.[59]

It has become fashionable today to denigrate the optimistic faith of the nineteenth century in progress, but most people continue to believe that there was progress in the nineteenth century. Despite the hammering that faith in progress has taken from the realities of the twentieth century,

57. Renouvier remarked that Vico's *corsi e ricorsi* were closer to the facts of history than the dominant contemporary themes of linear progress (*Histoire*, IV, 475).

58. This is a secularized providentialism, according to Emile Faguet (quoted by Mouy, *Idée de progrès*, 15). This was Renouvier's view too: "the public's passion for any great illusion which will replace the absent gods for it" (*Quatrième essai*, 145). "Just as formerly men asked divine grace to justify events and to make men reach their goals, so today men ask the same of history and of progress" (*Science de la morale*, II, 380).

59. *Histoire*, IV, 364. Spragens (*Irony of Liberal Reason*, 132–37) has an interesting discussion on Comte's merger of historicism and empiricism; *Histoire*, IV, 201, regarding Fourier. Philosophies of history would menace liberty if they were true (*Deuxième essai*, 257); on the demoralizing effect of the belief in necessary progress, see *Quatrième essai*, 699.

most intellectuals, I suspect, continue to hold it dear. It is not so much the reality of progress that is defended today as the moral virtues of believing in it. Even the conservative sociologist Robert Nisbet has defended a continued belief in progress as necessary if we are to make any progress.[60] However much ironic detachment intellectuals try to maintain toward that sacred relic, they know that to abandon it would force them also to abandon too many other idols of the tribe.

It may be more accurate to say that the dominant French intelligentsia today has replaced progress, as the nineteenth century understood it, with "novelty." This neophilia has had the disastrous effect of rejecting all standards of judgment based on reason or experience. To a certain extent, it involves a cynical play on the continued popular belief in progress to promote the material and ego interests of the intellectuals. This puts the average late-twentieth-century intellectual in a position that one might call *false consciousness*. Can this situation long endure, or will we see a return of historical optimism? We should not be too surprised by the latter, for it offers an easy explanation of experience, though at the expense of the realities of that experience: One of the dogmas of the religion of progress is that whatever happens is "really" progress if we properly interpret it, and it gives meaning to what might otherwise be obscure and hope to what might otherwise be discouraging.[61]

Renouvier saw as the classic example of this distortion of experience the nineteenth century's rehabilitation of the Middle Ages. Perhaps we shall live to hear that Nazi Germany and Stalinist Russia were "necessary" stages in the emergence of an earthly paradise (which is not here

60. Robert Nisbet, *History of the Idea of Progress* (New York, 1980), esp. Chap. 9, "Progress at Bay," and the epilogue. Mouy (*Idée de progrès,* 161) agrees with Hamelin that there is a moral need to believe in progress if we are in fact to make progress.

61. Renouvier cites as an example the historical writing of P. -J. -B. Buchez: "The consequence of these theories founded on the principle of the *sovereignty of the end* is a systematic rehabilitation of both the policy that led to the Saint Bartholomew's Day Massacre and the dragonnades and the politics of the *Montagnards* of 1793. The unity of religion and the unity of the nation were the sovereign ends. Christianity and terror thus formed an alliance, for the benefit of the Catholic idea and of reason of state" (*Histoire,* IV, 89).

yet, to be sure, but just around the corner). Faith in progress has performed miracles of this kind before.

If we really want to come to grips with the catastrophes of the twentieth century and to understand why the idea of progress has been called into question, we can do no better than to consider the criticism of the idea of progress advanced by Renouvier in the nineteenth century. For what Renouvier argued was that the idea of progress (as understood by most in his century) was not validated by science and reason.[62] As we have already seen, he argued that universal determinism is not supported by science, but there are more, and more important, lessons to be found in his critique of necessary progress.

Renouvier shows why his contemporaries' belief in progress would not lead us to the "broad sun-lit uplands" of our dreams but would contribute to the loss of political freedom and to intellectual stultification.[63] "Progress, as determinism views it, is authoritarian in principle, revolutionary if need be, . . . to give birth to a new authority; and the end justifies the means, without [the end] having to be moral, for it suffices for it to be determined, and that we can tell by what happens."[64] What has happened in the twentieth century has been in its main outlines what Renouvier feared it would be. Examination of his reasons will take us into the heart of the political and social tragedy of our time.

62. Renouvier thus opposed traditionalists, Saint-Simonians, positivists, and Marxists (Lacroix, *Vocation personnelle*, 142). Renouvier did, however, believe that Europe had made some progress (*Quatrième essai*, 701–702).

63. Belief in progress sacrifices the individual (*Esquisse*, I, 179). "This universal optimism, applied to an historic future, but with a short-range goal, an end that is near, interpreted by a popular millenarianism, joined with a simplistic socialism and a feeling for current and pressing needs which cannot be easily satisfied by adopting a taste for sacrifice, should lead one day to unexpected results, contrary to its true spirit and its hopes" (*Histoire*, IV, 14–15).

Belief in automatic progress undercuts our ideas of good and evil (*Histoire*, IV, 710–11). It renders liberty superfluous: "It is independent of liberty and of merit, in the past and in the future. Properly understood, the system should lead to considering liberty as no more than a remora, if it's possible at all. Happiness should produce itself" (*Histoire*, IV, 351).

64. *Science de la morale*, II, 385.

Renouvier's assault on the optimistic doctrine of inevitable progress was carried out with both philosophical and historical arguments. The philosophical arguments were probably the most conclusive for him, but he understood that it is possible to differ over philosophical positions.[65] What he found especially difficult to understand was how anyone could look at human history and still believe in continuous and automatic progress.[66] The great system builders were also great oversimplifiers: "Hegel and Comte, as well as Bossuet and Vico, treat history the way Eudoxus and Ptolemy treated astronomy, with their ideal spheres."[67] Rather than looking at all of history, most empirical arguments for progress lean heavily on the history of Western science or in more recent years the advance of material comforts or life expectancy. The progress of the sciences in the past has also favored growth of the illusion that science will in the future be able to solve all our problems.[68]

In the nineteenth century there were also some who argued the reality of moral improvement as well as an intellectual advance, and especially the superiority of the nineteenth century over its predecessors. Renouvier's measure of progress was the level of individual freedom, certainly a good measure from which to criticize the belief in inevitable progress but not an easy one to apply in any precise way.[69] Unlike many of his contemporaries, Renouvier was not convinced that individual freedom had made great strides in the nineteenth century, but what worried him most was the illusion that the gains made were secure and that further expansion was certain.

The principal reason why there could be (and had been occasionally) progress was the same reason there could be no inevitable, necessary

65. This was so especially in the light of his own early belief in progress, which began to wane in 1843–47 (Mouy, *Idée de progrès*, 34–36).

66. See *Esquisse*, II, 228; the idea of progress is a philosophy imposed on history, not something that grows out of historical experience (Mouy, *Idée de progrès*, 10–11).

67. *Quatrième essai*, 694.

68. *Histoire*, IV, 713.

69. Renouvier made liberty the measure of progress (*Science de la morale*, II, 329). Hence his preference for Fourier over Hegel (*Troisième essai*, 183–87).

progress: free will.[70] Even if, as Renouvier admitted, most of the decisions men make are psychologically, socially, or otherwise determined, the presence of even a few free acts prevents any long-term necessary process of development.[71] Free will also makes possible not just failure to progress but also regression, and he found enough historical examples to support his conclusion. Modern optimism about progress, he observed, took root in the eighteenth century, but its most celebrated advocate, Condorcet, did not consider it absolutely inevitable, nor did he hold regression impossible.[72] The domination of historical determinist views in the nineteenth century seemed to Renouvier an abusive extension or corruption of more realistic eighteenth-century views. In philosophy, the main culprit was Hegel, though most of the main schools were also guilty.[73]

Renouvier was familiar with Hegel only in translation and through the influence he had on several French thinkers.[74] No one would claim that Renouvier was among the more profound exegetes of the Berlin philosopher, but he clearly understood something vital about the influence Hegelianism was to have on nineteenth-century thought. While also

70. *Quatrième essai*, 701–702; *Esquisse*, II, 237; *cf.* Mouy, *Idée de progrès*, 38–39. Renouvier quotes Spencer to the effect that if there were such a thing as free will, it would interfere with progress (*Histoire*, IV, 353).

71. See *Esquisse*, II, 335.

72. "Good faith can ask itself whether the exploitation of man by man (or what is called such) is not something more essential to our great urban agglomerations and better entrenched there than in the simpler societies of antiquity, whether it's quite true that the military spirit and institutions are weakened in a century which has seen Bonaparte's wars or in a country which has spent a third of its revenues and a large part of its able-bodied youth on the army" (*Quatrième essai*, 162). Condorcet, like Renouvier, saw the Middle Ages as a regression (Lacroix, *Vocation personnelle*, 146).

73. See Mouy, *Idée de progrès*, 80. Renouvier considered Leibniz the founder of modern evolutionism (*Esquisse*, I, 142, II, 235–36). He was particularly hard on Schelling (for example, *Histoire*, IV, 14). He discusses Hegel in *Histoire*, IV, 15–20.

74. This included Renouvier, by way of Victor Cousin, in his early career (Mouy, *Idée de progrès*, 21–22).

taking issue with Hegel's logic, Renouvier was more concerned with his philosophy of history.[75] In logic, his reproach was related to his criticism of Kant: Where Kant found it impossible to choose between what seemed to Renouvier two mutually contradictory positions, Hegel positively relished contradictions so that he could subsume them in some higher synthesis. Both positions were offensive to Renouvier's devotion to the principle of contradiction.[76] It was not the threefold dialectic Renouvier objected to, for he used it himself in the construction of the categories, but the way Hegel used it to justify his historical determinism and undermine the idea of permanent values.

Hegel's theory of progress essentially concerned Western thought. Like most philosophers of progress, he ignored those parts of the world that did not fit into his schemata. Even as a history of thought, Hegel's theory had to torture the historical record to produce the desired results: "Every man with common sense who is confronted by the spectacle offered by the history of philosophy will at once form a singularly different idea than that desired by the sophistry of Hegelian philosophy."[77] Even worse from Renouvier's point of view, the Hegelian view had to justify the dominant thought of every period as the best possible for that period, contributing to the upward march of Western ideas. It can offer no basis for deciding what is right or wrong in a given time.[78] The minority thinkers in every period are always wrong, even if their ideas are taken up by the majority of thinkers in some later period. The working of progress justifies the persecution they may have suffered for being out of time and place. This was the intellectual-history equivalent of the justification, common in political histories, of all the crimes of governments and peoples as necessary for progress.[79] Indeed, Hegel did not stop short of that, arguing the progressive virtues of war and that those who are in the

75. Renouvier was also critical of Hegel's contribution to the rise of German *Naturphilosophie* (*Troisième essai*, 146–48).

76. Renouvier described Hegel's philosophy as "pantheistic Catholic realism" (*Troisième essai*, 182).

77. *Esquisse*, I, 2; see also *Quatrième essai*, 146–52. Renouvier did admit the existence of periods of progress in philosophy, for example, from Malebranche to Kant (*Histoire*, IV, 658–59).

78. *Deuxième essai*, 471–72.

79. See *Troisième essai*, 183.

right always win (the fact of winning demonstrating that they were moving in the direction laid down by history). It may be, as has recently been argued, that Hegel was a liberal in his time and place, but Renouvier was right in seeing Hegelian philosophy and its influences as profoundly antiliberal.[80] Even those who rejected Hegel's version of historical determinism—even standing it on its head, like Marx—would display a similar spirit, with similar moral consequences, in their schemes of things.

As for historical argument, Renouvier was especially offended by the fact that all these determinisms of progress had to consider classical antiquity—thought, religion, and society—inferior to the European Middle Ages.[81] Renouvier's attachment to antiquity was still in the spirit of the Renaissance, and his attitude toward the Middle Ages was that of the eighteenth-century philosophes. His knowledge of both periods was largely confined to intellectual history, though it was extensive within this area.[82] He therefore minimizes some of the problems of the ancient world and exaggerates the defects of the medieval.

A century of historical scholarship has made possible a more nuanced or more just appreciation of them, but belief in progress continues to have its impact on historians' interpretations, and we would do well to admit with Renouvier periods of regression and decline. In their aspirations to objectivity, modern historians have thought that excluding moral judgment would make history more scientific, and they have therefore confused historical relativism with moral relativism.[83] By itself, his-

80. Renouvier also considered Victor Cousin an advocate of the doctrine that winners are always right (*Histoire*, IV, 81), on the anti-individualist impact of Hegel's idealism, see *Troisième essai*, 13; on its antimoral character, see *Quatrième essai*, 143–44.

81. On the positivist view, see *Histoire*, IV, 647–48, and Lacroix, *Vocation personnelle*, 146. Man can progress even though the truth does not change (*Deuxième essai*, 469–70).

82. The four large volumes of his *Histoire* constitute a religious and intellectual history of mankind (non-Western thought is included) based on the best scholarship of the day. It is not just an astonishing performance for a man past retirement age but, as Hamelin remarks, would be a lifetime of work for a less gifted mind.

83. On Quinet as a rare historian to criticize this tendency, see *Histoire*, IV, 482.

tory cannot develop any standards beyond whatever appears to be dominant in a particular age. In practice, this relativism readily reduces itself to a justification of success, a worship of winners.[84] This is why Renouvier found most historical study in his time demoralizing.[85] Consciously or unconsciously, it tended to express the values of historical determinism, whether Hegelian or other.

It is likely that twentieth-century historians have been pushed in this direction more by the influence of the social sciences than by that of philosophy. The social sciences, as Paul Mouy has observed, seem by their very nature inclined to belief in progress.[86] Many historians have feared that adopting any moral, philosophical, or political perspective would distort their understanding of the past. But the rejection of such standards has made way for a determinism that itself stands as a screen between the historian and the realities of the past. The subject matter of history, if it is not to be confined to abstractions, must deal with men who have moral, philosophical, and political perspectives, and who cannot be understood without reference to those perspectives.

Renouvier's antiquity was the world that saw the birth of the idea of freedom, the experiment with democratic government, the free competition of ideas, religious pluralism, and high ideals of civic virtue.[87] His Middle Ages was a period of religious and intellectual oppression, regression from the scientific thought of antiquity, the dominance of church over state, the blight of superstition.[88] He undoubtedly minimized the blot of slavery on the ancient world, but in his philosophy slavery was never justified, as it inescapably is in deterministic views. At the

84. Joseph Ferrari (*Philosophes salariés* [Paris, 1980], 90) tried to distinguish: "Democracy invoked the theory of progress, and M. Cousin developed the theory of success."

85. *Histoire*, IV, 468–84; on Guizot, Michelet, Quinet, and the apologists for the Terror, see also *ibid.*, 81–82, 468–69; on historians as apologists for crime, see Popper, *High Tide of Prophecy*, 257.

86. Mouy, *Idée de progrès*, 160, 205–206.

87. *Quatrième essai*, 435–37; *Science de la morale*, II, 330–31, 345; *Quatrième essai*, 433. Secrétan chided Renouvier for exaggerating the virtues of the Greeks (Secrétan to Renouvier, August 4, 1873, in *Correspondance de Renouvier et Secrétan*, 92).

88. *Science de la morale*, II, 333–45.

same time, determinists have to hold that medieval serfdom was an advance over classical slavery, but we should not be convinced by the different resonances of the two terms that this was necessarily so.

A more clear-cut case of the errors into which a deterministic view of progress leads, in Renouvier's opinion, was that it requires thinkers like the Saint-Simonians to consider Scholastic philosophy superior to that of ancient Greece. For that matter, he did not see any pattern of progress within ancient philosophy: The Alexandrian and Neoplatonist schools were not an advance over Plato and Aristotle.[89] In his view, the Scholastic metaphysics was an evident regression, even aside from its involvement in the religious orthodoxy of its time. Far from making progress, it continued to have harmful repercussions on philosophy to his day.[90] His hostility was so great that he was unwilling to find any merits in medieval thought, even where there were possible affinities with his. He would thus dismiss scholastic defenses of free will as weak and inconsistent with the moral practices of the Church.[91] It is evident that Renouvier's hostility to the Middle Ages was of a piece with his hostility to Catholicism and that what he found bad in the Middle Ages he found to be essentially a result of the influence of the Church.[92] If this blinded

89. *Histoire,* IV, 652.

90. So strong was its influence that although Kant launched the overthrow of scholasticism, he was held back by an inability to shed all of its concepts. Thus Renouvier can think that he is more "critical" than Kant, more faithful to Kant's method. This concept of relations to one's predecessors is common modern philosophy, as Richard Rorty shows in his filiation of Hegel, Nietzsche, Heidegger, and Derrida (Rorty, *Contingency, Irony, and Solidarity* [Cambridge, Mass., 1989]).

91. See Mouy's effort (*Idée de progrès,* 48–50, 54) to explain the strength of Renouvier's hostility to the Middle Ages. Renouvier considered both Thomism and Neo-Thomism to be forms of apologetics and not really philosophies (*Histoire,* IV, 665).

92. Secrétan took Renouvier to task for injustice and incompleteness in this analysis (Secrétan to Renouvier, August 29, 1869, in *Correspondance de Renouvier et Secrétan,* 39).

On the contrary, the modern peoples who have come out of the sad school of the Middle Ages have been inculcated with timid manners which do not basically modify the passions and do not moderate them

him to the role of the Church in the preservation and transmission of Western, and indeed classical civilization, it did not undermine the force of his argument against optimistic historical determinism.[93]

Hegel's historicism was philosophical and idealist, perhaps one should say intellectualistic. History was presented as the unfolding of the "world spirit," and the actions of men, however superficially free in appearance, were always manipulated by the "cunning of reason" to serve its progressive goals.[94] No underlying physical or biological forces were needed to explain the working of this spirit. Thus while Hegel's historicism was to become the dominant attitude of the nineteenth century, most historicists would feel the need for a more scientific explanation of the mechanisms of necessary progress. Taking Hegel at his own appreciation as the culmination and end of Western philosophy, they would feel the need for an explanatory mechanism capable of predicting the future as well as explaining the past.

Some would seek this mechanism at the sociological level (Marx, for example); others, more numerous in the nineteenth century, I think, would be satisfied with a foundation in biology and the idea of evolu-

---

at all when they burst forth. The ideals of false humility and of peace at any price, the hypocrisy which follows from them, the appearances of constant acceptance and obedience, the servile forms of behavior that come from a long oppression of the conscience, the imitation of the sugary methods of the Church. . . . Finally, the long-established habit of simulated agreement in all thoughts, have so directed education and shaped souls that nature itself is spoiled, particularly among those nations that have remained Catholic, and it will not be restored, perhaps, till after many generations and in better circumstances. (*Science de la morale,* I, 357–60; II, 256–57)

For an imaginative construction of what the moral development of Europe would have been like had Christianity not triumphed, see *Uchronie.*

93. Unfair though Renouvier may have been, apologists for the medieval church should consider whether it was not responsible for destroying as much of the heritage of antiquity as it saved.

94. For a recent critique of the cunning of reason as it reappears in the hyperliberalism of Friedrich Hayek, see Ferry and Renaut, *Des droits de l'homme,* 150–55.

tion.[95] Biological evolutionism was an increasingly popular view before Darwin gave what would become the orthodox explanation of how it worked, even though, as Renouvier pointed out, Darwinian biology did not rule out retrogradation and stagnation.[96] The development of a full-blown evolutionist philosophy of history would be the work of Herbert Spencer, who had become an evolutionist even before the publication of Darwin's *Origin of Species*. Renouvier found Spencer a worthy adversary—"the philosopher of our century who has produced the most powerful constructions attempted since the principle of evolution has captured men's minds"—whom he particularly delighted to attack.[97]

Never afraid to attack the dominant ideas of his age, Renouvier would appear to have been wrong (and not just on the losing side) in his rejection (or at least highly qualified acceptance) of evolution, but the case against him is not so clear-cut as it may seem at first.[98] Given the state of knowledge at the time, his reservations about the biological argument were not unscientific, and indeed he pointed to some of the problems with the Darwinian concept of natural selection that have continued to bedevil biologists to this day.[99] But he did not pretend to be an expert

95. Renouvier saw Marx as following the Hegelian model: a process of evolution proceeding by revolutionary means (*Histoire*, IV, 568). On Marx as an evolutionist, see *ibid.*, 559–60. Renouvier saw Hegelianism as by nature vulnerable to a materialist reinterpretation (*ibid.*, 19).

96. "The [Darwinian] system ought then to admit, and it does admit, that *regression is possible*, and also that the vast majority of lower forms of life do not progress at all, *having no need to progress in order to survive*. But then why speak of a *continual progress toward perfection?*" (*Troisième essai*, 155). See also *Histoire*, IV, 380.

97. *Histoire*, IV, 315.

98. A certain acceptance of evolution appears in the *Deuxième essai*, 579, and later in his career Renouvier was prepared to admit a multilinear evolution of species, but not a single origin for all living things (*Histoire*, IV, 288–89). He doubted the dictum that phylogeny recapitulates ontogeny (*Esquisse*, I, 204–206; *Troisième essai*, 136). Perhaps he anticipated the use Oswald Spengler would make of it in his philosophy of history.

99. See, for example, *Histoire*, IV, 296–97, 342; *Esquisse*, I, 190–92; *Troisième essai*, 149–55. Darwinism has great problems with the evolution of

on biological questions, relying on contemporary experts. His real concern was the philosophical assumptions he saw underlying evolutionism and the way evolutionary doctrine was used as the basis for more wide-sweeping social and political theories. *Evolutionnisme* in his vocabulary was another form of "scientism," an abusive use of genuine, if debatable, scientific ideas. Spencer furnished a comprehensive example of this abuse.[100]

For all its scientific pretension, Spencer's evolutionism was as metaphysical as Hegel's historicism.[101] In place of the world spirit was a no-

---

man (*Troisième essai*, 198–210); see also *Histoire*, IV, 387. The insecurity of evolutionary theory is evident in the touchiness of its defenders today. See also Renouvier to Secrétan, November 14, 1875, in *Correspondance de Renouvier et Secrétan*, 126.

100. Evolutionism in the natural sciences and evolutionism as philosophy are often confused, even by scientists, including Lamarck and Darwin (*Esquisse*, I, 184–90). On the reluctance of many Darwinists to stick to facts, see *ibid.*, 203–204. Like many French, Renouvier was more Larmarckian than Darwinian; Yvette Conry (*L'Introduction du darwinisme en France au XIXe siècle* [Paris, 1974], 27) attributes this to post-1870 nationalism. Renouvier was always on the lookout for a genetic theory that would preserve the continuity of the human person (*Histoire*, IV, 294). "We are only fighting that evolutionism which claims to decide the transcendental problems of the supreme essence and of necessary and universal cause, and not the method—if it can be called that—that applies to the study of series of facts and events and to the laws of the generation and transformation of beings, within a given order of phenomena" (*Histoire*, IV, 279). The problem of the origins of existence is not accessible to science (*Histoire*, IV, 341–42); see *n*98, above. On the example of Schelling, see *Histoire*, IV, 14. Regarding Spencer, see *Histoire*, IV, 316–37; *Esquisse*, I, 213–20. Brunschwicg and Halévy ("L'Année philosophique en 1893," 478–80) think that the influence of evolution on philosophy had already begun to wane; Renouvier wondered if it would not prove ephemeral (*Histoire*, IV, 398).

101. Renouvier and other French thinkers were particularly concerned with the philosophical origins of Darwinism (Conry, *Introduction du darwinisme*, 76); see Mouy, *Idée de progrès*, 72–73. Biological facts were as little decisive for Spencer as for Comte (*Histoire*, IV, 385). Renouvier considered Spencer to be unfaithful to the British scientific tradition (*Histoire*, IV, 681–82).

less-inscrutable "force" constructing the world and then shaping human history to its own purposes and with its own method, which happened to guarantee progress through the survival of the fittest.[102] Thus, like Hegelianism, evolutionism furnished an apology for everything that has happened, indeed for every crime likely to be committed in the future. Renouvier repeatedly warned Christians against being overeager to accommodate themselves to it. Spencer was not entirely consistent when it came to drawing sociopolitical consequences from his grand historic doctrine.[103] His ultra-laissez-faire program tried to appear as the counterpart of the biological struggle for existence, and he condemned anything likely to interfere with the workings of nature, such as private or public charity, as leading to the survival of the unfit.

At the same time, he condemned war and predicted its disappearance, in defiance of both his idea of nature's processes and any more objective reading of modern history.[104] For Spencer, like Comte, had a metaphysical vision of historical development as passing through certain necessary stages, each of which would have the institutions and ideas appropriate to it.[105] Avoiding the mysticism of the number 3 that has afflicted so many philosophers of history, Spencer saw history as divided into two ages, the military and the industrial. Like all good prophets, he saw himself at the entry to the new age and announced that progress had reached the point where war among the civilized nations was no longer conceivable.[106] One of the dangers of believing in necessary progress, as Renouvier would point out, is that it encourages us not to analyze seriously what is happening or what has happened. The power of Spencer's intellect, the depth of his scientific learning, could not protect him against the greatest errors inevitable with a historical determinism because, like

102. *Histoire,* IV, 319, 355.

103. *Ibid.,* 18, 339–40, 343–51; Renouvier to Secrétan, January 4, 1887, in *Correspondance de Renouvier et Secrétan,* 157; *Histoire,* IV, 387.

104. *Histoire,* IV, 392–93.

105. Spencer was misconstrued as a positivist in France (*ibid.,* 250–52).

106. The war of 1870–71 surprised a lot of philosophers, but not Renouvier (Mouy, *Idée de progrès,* 200). Renouvier does credit Spencer with seeing that complete laissez-faire would work only in a totally pacific industrial society (*Histoire,* IV, 391).

Comte, he treated the critique of knowledge as a vestige of the unscientific past, no longer relevant.

There remains the question of how Spencer's doctrine is hostile to practical liberty. Was he not an extreme liberal, what would today be called a libertarian? Did he not consider this position the logical outcome of his determinist philosophy? Did he not present some of the strongest arguments produced in the nineteenth century against all government? The answer to all these questions is yes, but only at the price of a severe incoherence not uncommon among historical determinists.[107] If the unfettered competition of individuals for survival is nature's law, why has it never existed in civilized or any other society? There are obviously many reasons, including the refusal of human beings to accept this as an ideal and their support for institutions and practices that counteract the workings of nature.[108] But if nature was what Spencer and other determinists thought it was, it would be utterly contradictory to speak of resisting it, as he frequently did. A consistent evolutionism can say only that whatever is, is right.[109]

In practice, Spencer's doctrine appealed to the dominant social groups of his time; it was, as Renouvier said, an evolutionism of the satisfied that served them mainly as a weapon against any social activity

107. For Spencer's politics, see his essay "The Man *Versus* the State," in Spencer, *The Man Versus the State*, ed. Donald Macrae (Baltimore, 1969), 57–191. "The dogma of necessity can therefore generate, in the man who practices it seriously, either inaction or furor, resignation or enthusiasm, indifference or fanaticism, but, in all cases, it throws him from the paths of our natural and common morality. The existence of the most ordinary moral code is an anomaly in the determinist system" (*Troisième essai*, 455). Renouvier thought that any consistent evolutionist would be a pessimist (*Histoire*, IV, 746). He believed that J. S. Mill's liberalism was in contradiction with his philosophy (*Histoire*, IV, 366).

108. *Histoire*, IV, 388–89. Nature, as Renouvier pointed out, is a school of immorality. The study of the evolutionists heightened his awareness of this and thus contributed, in Mouy's opinion, to the increasing pessimism of Renouvier's later years. Renouvier certainly thought that nature was a school of pessimism (*ibid.*, 313).

109. See Mouy, *Idée de progrès*, 99.

that would threaten their comfortable positions. He feared that because it did not recognize any legitimacy in the claims that the working classes were making against society, Spencer's doctrine would only strengthen the growth of socialism and thus increase the threat to individual freedom posed by the socialist movement.[110] And if socialist collectivism were to be established by whatever means, evolutionism would offer no consistent grounds on which to criticize it. Nature would have spoken.

Historical determinisms, whether biologically inspired or not, carry with them not only a claim to make sense of the whole of the past but also a claim to be able to predict the course of future development. Hegel, it is true, tried to resist this tendency but could do so only by concluding that the course of intellectual development had reached its predestined conclusion. These philosophies of history also demonstrate—though unlike Hegel, projecting this conclusion into the future—a tendency to postulate some perfect future state where the mechanisms of historical struggle they have discovered will cease to function. Having rejected the Christian vision of a paradise in another world at the end of history, they insist on transporting that paradise to this world, which also involves the end of history (as, for example, Marx's classless society).

This claim on the future makes determinisms even more dangerous than their retrospective visions do. The paradise to be inevitably reached justifies everything done in its name in the present, especially the sacrifice of present freedoms in the name of a hypothetical higher freedom, "real freedom," to come. Renouvier feared what Karl Popper would call "moral futurism"—the doctrine that "future might is right."[111] This is no imaginary danger, as the innumerable Western apologists for Stalin's Russia or Mao's China have demonstrated. Of course, individuals may believe in historical determinism and its necessarily happy outcome for

110. *Histoire*, IV, 390–91.

111. Lacroix, *Vocation personnelle*, 149, 151; Renouvier observed that "great men" are usually fatalists (*Deuxième essai*, 468). "The theory that God reveals Himself and His judgment in history is indistinguishable from the theory that worldly success is the ultimate judge and justification of our actions; it comes to the same thing as the doctrine that history will judge, that is to say, that future might is right; it is the same as what I have called 'moral futurism'" (Popper, *High Tide of Prophecy,* 258).

the human race without on that account committing crimes or even "treating others solely as means" (to use Kant's and Renouvier's terms) any more often than we all do.[112] But a society in which this optimistic determinism reigns is terribly vulnerable to what J. F. Revel has called "the totalitarian temptation."[113] But that optimism in our historical outlook has prevented us from recognizing that Renouvier had pointed this out repeatedly over a hundred years ago.

The Pantheist Temptation

It seemed to Renouvier that the spread of historical determinisms was accompanied by the diffusion of a modern pantheism. The rejection of Christianity, or at least some of its salient historical characteristics, that marked the modern intelligentsia did not as a rule destroy all sense of an unknown, something that transcended man's knowledge or even his possibilities of knowledge. The idea of a personal God or any anthropomorphic divinity, it is true, seemed to belong to the superstitions of the past. The only outlet for this irrepressible sentiment seemed to be to call God the whole vastness of the universe—God is everything, and vice versa. This might be expressed in different ways, but the very diffuseness of such views tends to render them equivalent.

The first modern Western pantheist to have much influence was Spinoza, who demonstrated, in Renouvier's opinion, the close connection between determinism in philosophy and pantheism in religion.[114] The real upsurge of pantheism among Western philosophers he located in post-Kantian Germany, a development he attributed in part to their having failed to grasp the significance of Kant's achievement. Renouvier also saw this as a faltering of the Western philosophic tradition, which left an

112. Determinism logically supports conservative views, but it is often adopted by activist reformers, as in the case of Marx (Popper, *High Tide of Prophecy*, 199).

113. Jean-François Revel, *La Tentation totalitaire* (Paris, 1976).

114. Renouvier also considered Spencer's evolutionism a pantheism (*Histoire*, IV, 325).

opening for a reflux of orientalism.[115] The West had withstood a challenge from Oriental religion in Greek antiquity; he was afraid that the danger had returned and often referred to the German pantheists as "our Brahmans" or European Buddhists.[116]

Renouvier found manifestations of pantheism virtually everywhere in nineteenth-century thought, even in the liberal Christianity of his friend the Swiss Protestant philosopher Charles Secrétan. He once admitted to Secrétan that he had become so obsessed with the question that he was afraid he automatically suspected pantheism everywhere.[117] In his philosophical religion, as we shall see in the next chapter, he kept as far away from it as possible and did not hesitate to proclaim the superiority of anthropomorphic visions of God. However, the main reason that he became so preoccupied with the struggle against pantheism was the reason for his struggle against scientism and determinism: It posed a threat to reason, freedom, and individuality.

In any pantheism the only reality is the whole. Individuals are mere appearances, temporarily distinguishable; they come out of the whole and are reabsorbed into it. In Hindu and Buddhist tradition (at least as it was understood in nineteenth-century Europe), that reabsorption is presented as the highest good for man. It is, so to speak, the reward of man at the end of his cycles of reincarnation. In this view, individual existence is per se an evil, one very hard to get rid of. Renouvier admitted a certain internal consistency in the Indian view and even agreed that in its purer forms it was a moralizing religion, though he thought modern Indian religion largely degenerate superstition. But it was a threat to the

115. *Esquisse,* II, 330; on its German origins, see *Histoire,* IV, 5.

116. *Histoire,* IV, 420–21; Renouvier to Secrétan, April 26, 1872, in *Correspondance de Renouvier et Secrétan,* 72. Roger-Pol Droit ("Le Spectre du bouddhisme," *Magazine littéraire,* No. 279 [July–August, 1990], 45–47) cites Renouvier among many other nineteenth-century thinkers (Cousin, Quinet, Barthélemy Saint-Hilaire, in France; Hegel, Schopenhauer, Nietzsche, Hartmann, in Germany) who interpreted Buddhism as posing a threat of nihilism to Western thought.

117. Renouvier considered irreligion, historicism, and pantheism to be dominant at the end of the nineteenth century (*Histoire,* IV, 4–5). Renouvier to Secrétan, February 21, 1869, in *Correspondance de Renouvier et Secrétan,* 14.

Western philosophical tradition that had come to place a supreme value on the individual, and it was a threat to political and social freedom in Western societies, which rested on this value. Pantheism was thus a kind of indirect intellectual danger. It could lead to the corruption of rationality and an indulgence in fanciful mysticism. Politically, it could lead to the quietism and withdrawal that always tempt thinkers in times of prolonged social upheaval and a crisis of values.[118] Politically and socially, it could, in alliance with determinism, lead to the acceptance of the sacrifice of present generations in the name of some philosophy of history.[119] What can those generations matter if individuals are not ultimately real?

Many people, it is true, and Renouvier readily admitted it, who held pantheist positions also supported liberal-democratic politics. He conceded that the connections between our expressed opinions and our practical behavior are often tenuous. Individuals are too complex and inconsistent (and operate in an environment too hostile to consistency) for us to say that adherence, even sincere, to any particular idea will result in any particular behavior.[120] Even philosophers do not reach the level of predictable behavior, the famous regularity of Kant's daily life notwithstanding. Any view like Renouvier's (and ours) that stresses the importance of ideas in real life must take this into account.

It remains legitimate to argue nonetheless that the general diffusion of a basic attitude like pantheism can have social consequences that depend on its character as an idea. Certain things do tend to hang together: "Let us consider the theories which spread under the reign of the determinist spirit. These are: in religion, systems of divine grace; in morals, utilitarian systems; in politics, authoritarian systems."[121] Renouvier was not especially concerned that some pantheist would draw from the con-

118. In Spencer's case, quietism resulted from his thinking men mainly capable of slowing down the beneficent process of evolution (*Histoire*, IV, 394–96).

119. See *Quatrième essai*, 18; Renouvier found this tendency in the Saint-Simonians (*Histoire*, IV, 190–92).

120. See *Science de la morale*, II, 383; *Deuxième essai*, 455.

121. *Science de la morale*, II, 379.

sequences of his religious position an argument in favor of political tyranny, as some metaphysical determinists had done. What he did fear was that the diffusion of pantheism would weaken intellectual resistance to the forces against freedom in the world by undermining the importance of the individual.

It is a historical commonplace for philosophers to lament the immorality of their times, the lack of serious critical thought, the intellectual confusion of their contemporaries. This would seem almost a natural function of the philosopher as outsider, and every philosopher who aspires to think about some things more deeply than most people is to some extent an outsider. With human history as full of instances of miserable behavior as it is, there is always something to complain about. Moreover, any philosopher worthy of the name is going to believe that he has understood certain things better than anybody before him and hence will also be critical of the thinking of his contemporaries. This can be a futile game, but Renouvier's example shows that it need not be.

Not content to denounce the evils of his day, he made a determined effort to show *why* certain ideas like determinism and pantheism do not have the rational validity claimed by their adherents and why these wrong ideas are likely to have undesirable consequences.[122] By compar-

122. The Eclectic philosopher Adolphe Franck welcomed Renouvier as an effective critic of pantheism (Franck, *Moralistes et philosophes* [Paris, 1872], 483). Renouvier compared the determinist syntheses of the nineteenth century to medieval Summae:

At bottom, what is thus desired is a false and chimerical synthesis in the manner of these *summae* of the Middle Ages where the ability of the philosopher and the vanity of his knowledge shine equally. But there is, it is said, a relative truth for each epoch. It would be better to say that there had been appearances of truth on which mind and faith were exercised, but that science only recognizes truth and falsehood and does not leave any room for a false truth. Is it then a new falsehood that people want to set up under the banner of truth? Do they want to replace the political and religious hierarchies with a priesthood of false scientists, the old superstitions with faulty demonstrations, the fanaticism of an openly avowed faith with that which has usurped the name of science, finally, the modest, partial truth that liberty accompanies

ing Renouvier's arguments with the experience we have had in the twentieth century, we cannot help but be struck by the degree to which his anticipations—let us say his fears—have been confirmed by that experience. This should be enough to convince us of the value of philosophic reflection on issues that appear to most people rather remote from concerns of everyday life.

To be sure, there is a temptation to exaggerate the intellectual character of the disasters of the twentieth century, but it would also be a mistake to believe that they can be explained wholly in socioeconomic or even political terms. What Renouvier saw most clearly in the intellectual currents of his time was a threat to sustained critical thought, an impatience with the effort it requires and its residual uncertainties. The deterministic philosophies of the day, whether historical or evolutionist, not only were false sciences but offered easy answers that gave emotional satisfaction but cut short philosophical reflection.

The mind that becomes absorbed in these ideologies loses the capacity to see anything but what they present to it—in the manner they present it—and what is worse, loses all taste for independent and critical reflection. It risks losing that capacity to doubt that is essential to our humanity: "As long as any amount whatever of doubt is possible, if you never lose it, however small you may make it, we have wisdom, we have toleration and forgiveness, in a word, because of that apparent imperfection in humanity, we are *human*. On the contrary path, where doubt has been so thoroughly set aside that it cannot return, the absolute, when invoked, gives birth only to systematizing, mania, madness, intolerance, fanaticism, inhumanity."[123]

The decline of intellectual depth and seriousness in the twentieth century—evident to anybody who reads much nineteenth-century work, even of middling level—is usually traced to the effect of mass literacy, the mass media, the democratization of education; in other words, to social origins. Renouvier's critique shows that the intellectual currents

---

with a system of intolerant errors, a hybrid composition where science and religion pervert each other simultaneously in a revolting melange? (*Deuxième essai*, 523–24)

123. *Deuxième essai*, 479–80.

dominant in the century were themselves a force, however unintentionally, for the debasement of thought. Considerations that any sociologist
can point out will make unlikely a revival in our time of the high seriousness of intellectual debate that characterized the nineteenth century.
Most contemporary philosophers will ridicule anyone rash enough to
suggest the desirability of such a project. The very modest effort in that
direction of which we are capable today can start only through a reflection on the issues debated in the nineteenth century, issues we are far
from having transcended, and Renouvier's work offers us a powerful
starting point for that reflection.

III

The Religious Crisis of the Nineteenth Century

> The world is suffering from the lack of faith
> in a transcendent truth.
>
> —Renouvier, *Histoire*

The nineteenth century was one of the most interesting periods in the long history of Western religion. That history seems to have been telescoped into a few decades. Every form of Christian orthodoxy and heresy was flourishing; atheism was widespread and gaining adherents for perhaps the first time; pagan antiquity was openly presented as a model for modern man; new religions were being founded, some mystical and transcendental, others rational and secular. Some believers were uplifted by a sense of taking part in the founding of a new age of true faith, others depressed by a sense of witnessing the twilight of Western Christianity. The lifting of the weight of Christian tradition made possible the open expression of the most contradictory positions. The century that would pride itself on the triumph of reason over ancient superstitions also saw spiritualism and phrenology sweep through the educated classes.

Efforts to make sense of this chaos and these contradictions also appeared in great number and in mutual conflict. About the only position missing was doubt that sense could be made of it. Most popular were variations of the providential model, but French intellectual circles found these palatable only when suitably secularized. To see God's handiwork directly in all this turmoil was to place oneself uncomfortably close to Joseph de Maistre's view of the French Revolution as God's punishment of the French for their impiety and was therefore seen as a politically and socially reactionary stand.

Providence was more commonly secularized in philosophies of history, most systematically presented in France by Comte (building on the ideas of Henri de Saint-Simon) and in Germany by Hegel. But it was also an idea more generally "in the air," a popular version of the idea of progress, increasingly interpreted as a necessary progress. The secularized idea of providence had in some ways the same function as the religious: It offered a comfort to those whose peace of mind was disturbed by the evident disorder of the age. Providentialism could also relieve one of the need to think too deeply about the sensitive issues of faith and reason.

The question of the proper relation between faith and reason has been present throughout the history of Christianity. Most Christian thinkers have seen no great difficulty in reconciling the demands of faith and reason, and have insisted that they were fully compatible: Revealed truth held the place of primacy, but right reason must always find a way of being in accord with it. Few took the extreme mystical or rationalist positions. But in the eighteenth century doubts about this compatibility began to become more widespread, the key force for this change undoubtedly the rise of modern science.

While Christian faith showed itself quite capable of assimilating the scientific picture of the physical universe and relegating the "science" of the Old Testament to the status of myth, there were greater trials in store. The emergence of modern biblical criticism, shaped by the methods of historical research, threatened one of the foundations of revelation (the sole foundation for Protestants) and seemed to demonstrate the growing incompatibility of reason and faith. But the greater danger came from the secularized idea of progress, for this presented a view of man's history that seemed to allow no future for religion. When people begin to use terms like Comte's "metaphysical age" or to contrast an "Age of Reason" with an "Age of Faith," religious faith no longer seems a universal and eternal part of man's existence, and progress can easily be defined as the triumph of reason over faith.

Some intellectuals resolved their personal problems by an arbitrary compartmentalization, putting their faith and traditional attitudes in one part of the mind and their rational convictions in another, taking care to avoid any possibly embarrassing confrontation. This was especially popular among practicing scientists. Others, unable thus to hide the problem or adopt the secular historicist position that promised that the problem would soon go away, often found themselves without easy solutions. If one rejected the historicist schema and insisted on looking around at the world, it was, even in the late nineteenth century, harder to believe in the progressive triumph of reason and the disappearance of faith. It was (at least in part) out of an effort to reconcile the progressive ideas he was exposed to as a young man with the experience of the world around him that Renouvier came to reflect on this key issue of his century.

Renouvier's Search for a Rational Faith

In one way or another, religion was a part of Renouvier's entire life. He was born into a Catholic family with a strong Jansenist tradition, particularly embodied in his highly devout mother. His father, on the other hand, had largely secularized the Jansenist values of strict moral living and public service but did not consider his indifference to the formal cult to imply any fundamental disrespect for religion.[1]

From the beginning, Charles was closer to his father than his mother. As a result, he would never have to go through the crisis of faith so typical of nineteenth-century intellectuals. "From the age of the so-called 'first communion' and even before," he later confessed to his Protestant friend Charles Secrétan, "I was a little pagan."[2] The "myths" of the

1. On Renouvier's family, see Foucher, *Jeunesse de Renouvier*, 4–11; Méry, *Critique du christianisme*, I, 30–39.
2. Renouvier to Secrétan, January 11, 1875, in *Correspondance de Renouvier et Secrétan*, 109.

Christian tradition had no grip on his imagination. He would, with some difficulty, one suspects, learn to recognize that Christianity had been the source of much poetic and artistic inspiration, but he always remained closed to those aesthetic aspects of Christianity that had so enchanted Chateaubriand.[3] Renouvier's initial indifference was succeeded in his teens by a lifelong hostility to the Catholic church, which would not, however, alienate him from religion.[4]

Too young to have been directly affected, he was nonetheless aware of the atmosphere of religious strife that had followed the Restoration in southern France, especially the "missions" sent to restore this area to the Catholic fold.[5] To some extent, Catholicism would always remain associated in his mind with civil strife and the war of the political power situated far away in Paris against the nonconformity of the southern provinces. (Small wonder that this feeling would later form part of his hatred of the Second Empire, which violently crushed southern republicanism as it came to power.) Renouvier's education sealed his break with the church. Sent to the Catholic *collège* in Montpellier in 1825, he reacted much as the young Auguste Comte had ten years earlier in the same establishment.[6] Horrified by what seemed to him the stultifying obscurantism of his teachers and their authoritarian modes of instruction, Renouvier demanded to be removed. In 1829, his sympathetic father, then serving as a deputy, took the young man to Paris, where he completed his secondary education at the Collège Rollin in an atmosphere as secular as any tolerated under the July Monarchy.[7]

While still a secondary-school student and in his subsequent study at

3. See *Uchronie*, xi.

4. Renouvier later wrote of the advantages of never having had a faith to lose; he thought that it favored an independence of judgment in religious matters (*Histoire*, IV, 249–50).

5. See Méry, *Critique du christianisme*, I, 39, 43, 47; he refers us to *Histoire*, IV, *livre* xv. See Guillaume de Bertier de Sauvigny, *The Bourbon Restoration* (Philadelphia, 1966), 320–22.

6. Méry *Critique du christianisme*, I, 38; Foucher, *Jeunesse de Renouvier*, 11.

7. Foucher, *Jeunesse de Renouvier*, 11–13. Of course, Renouvier began here in the last year of the Restoration.

the Ecole polytechnique, Renouvier moved in circles that had consigned Catholicism to the dustbin of history but were by no means antireligious. On the contrary, they were seeking to create a new religion that would be adapted to the rise of scientific thought and to the emergence of an increasingly industrialized society. Renouvier was thus introduced to one of the major intellectual trends in post-Revolutionary France, a movement whose founding father was the late (d. 1825) Henri de Saint-Simon.[8]

Renouvier's elder brother Jules was already an ardent Saint-Simonian, and he introduced the timid Charles into the heady atmosphere of a group of (mostly) young men who really thought they were about to bring off a spiritual revolution of an importance equal to or greater than the political revolution. While Renouvier would later be embarrassed by and say little about his naïve youthful enthusiasm for the Saint-Simonians, their contact would leave a lasting mark on his religious inclinations, a mark that would not be entirely effaced by the domination Kant would exercise over his mature religious doctrine.[9] While repelled by the excesses of the Saint-Simonian cult, such as their search for a female messiah, Renouvier would never repudiate the Saint-Simonian commitment to the "rehabilitation of matter," though he was less happy with Enfantin's conversion of this to a "rehabilitation of the flesh."[10] In politics, he would not repudiate their concern for the material and spiritual welfare of the "poorest and most numerous classes."

His break with the Saint-Simonians was to come when he realized how much they reproduced the authoritarian character of Catholicism, expressed, for example, in a common enthusiasm for the ideas of Joseph de Maistre. Many disenchanted Saint-Simonians were to convert to Rome during the July Monarchy, but Renouvier took a different direction.[11]

8. On Renouvier's introduction to Saint-Simonianism, see Foucher, *Jeunesse de Renouvier*, 13–28; Méry, *Critique du christianisme*, I, 51–53.

9. On the Saint-Simonians, Méry (*Critique du christianisme*, I, 52) quotes Renouvier. Méry (*ibid.*, I, 123, 131–32), argues that Kant's influence was decisive as early as Renouvier's second *Manuel*.

10. Méry, *Critique du christianisme*, I, 119; *Histoire*, IV, 199.

11. *Histoire*, IV, 126–27.

Contact with the Saint-Simonians taught Renouvier that faith and reason might still work together outside the framework of traditional religion, but it also left him with a desire for a more precise understanding of the relations between the two than had been demonstrated by the enthusiastic apostles of the *Nouvelle Christianisme*.[12] Here again, it was the study of Kant that brought Renouvier to the position he would hold throughout his maturity and old age. One of the main functions of the critique of knowledge, as Renouvier understood it, was to establish the limits of scientific reason. Unlike positivism, Kantian criticism did not teach that everything not susceptible to scientific reason was either unknowable or not worth knowing. Like Kant, Renouvier would always be committed to the reconciliation of science and religion.[13] In this effort, an appeal to Kant enabled him to repair the weakness of eclecticism, which seemed to Renouvier too ready to sacrifice philosophy to religion. Renouvier would be concerned to demonstrate that there were certain questions essential to man—for which man had and would always seek answers—that science by its very nature could not answer. The essence of religion had to lie not in those domains where scientific research might one day show religious tradition to have been in error (and most of the possible demolitions seem to have been carried out by the end of the nineteenth century; only biology would reserve some surprises for the twentieth). Those domains might seem excessively narrow to any Christian, but Renouvier was convinced they were enough.[14]

12. Méry (*Critique du christianisme*, I, 120–22) cites Renouvier's first publication on religion: "Quelques mots sur le retour des idées religieuses en France" (*Revue indépendante*, July 25, 1843); see also Méry, *Critique du christianisme*, I, 485. Renouvier was influenced by Victor Cousin on the question of the relations of religion and philosophy (Méry, *Critique du christianisme*, I, 64, 66, 68, 72). Later in life Renouvier described the Saint-Simonians as propagating an intellectual conviction with the trappings of religion, but without its inner spirit (*Histoire*, IV, 198). As Kaufmann (*Goethe, Kant, and Hegel*, 210) points out, the only philosopher of the nineteenth century to succeed in creating a new religion did so unintentionally: Karl Marx.

13. On Kant, see Kaufmann, *Goethe, Kant, and Hegel*, 86.

14. Renouvier considered religion as natural to man as man, not as something he would "outgrow" (see Méry, *Critique du christianisme*, II, 36). The

Renouvier, like Kant, did not consider that questions outside the grasp of science automatically fell into the domain of unreason. The absence of proof meeting scientific standards did not mean that all beliefs were of equal validity. Renouvier had no intention of giving the sanction of philosophy to the multitude of religious vagaries of his day; he hoped to determine what a reasonable man might believe if he was inclined to religious belief. At first, he was content to list what he considered the three basic dogmas of a rational faith: the creation of the world, the existence of God, a future life for the individual.[15] Later in life he would

question of whether Renouvier's philosophy provided a defense of religion split both Catholic and Protestant observers: Yes, say Arnal (*Hypothèse suprême*, 85), Méry (*Critique du christianisme*, II, 498 and *passim*), Miéville (*Philosophie de M. Renouvier*, 178–79), Xavier Moisant (*Psychologie de l'incroyant* [Paris, 1908], 293–96), and most strongly Armand Schloesing ("Le Criticisme de M. Renouvier," *Revue chrétienne* [1882], 216). No, say Franck (*Moralistes*, 477–78), Lucien Laberthonnière (*Esquisse d'une philosophie personnaliste* [Paris, 1942], 156–57, Vol. VIII of Laberthonnière, *Oeuvres*), Ollé-Laprune (*Certitude morale*, 333–34), Waelti (*Morale kantienne*, 132). There had been a similar controversy over whether Kant promoted religion (Vallois, *Formation de l'influence kantienne*, 211).

15. Initially, Renouvier had a problem with creation, but when his application of the principle of contradiction led him to reject the possibility of an infinite past, he had logically to accept a beginning of the world. His phenomenology of conscience then led to the requirement for a creator. God as conceived by the metaphysicians did not fit this role (*Premier essai*, 342–48). Creation remained for him an incomprehensible reality, but a reality nonetheless. In the period of his *Essais*, Renouvier's reaction against Catholicism brought him close to the Hellenic ideal, and he made an intellectual case for preferring polytheism. Not until the 1880s did he definitively accept the unity of God (*Esquisse*, II, 351–52, 399–400). Parodi (in Dauriac, "Moments de la philosophie," 43–44) holds Renouvier's adoption of monotheism to be one of the two major changes in the history of his thought. Renouvier always insisted that he was an agnostic with respect to polytheism, even when presenting its advantages as a philosophical hypothesis (Renouvier to Secrétan, July 1, 1874, in *Correspondance de Renouvier et Secrétan*, 104); see *Deuxième essai*, 677, as example of his argument. His later monotheism was also presented as a personal conviction, not as a certainty (Méry, *Critique du christianisme*, I, 644). Renouvier's early polytheism was also a product of his conviction that true religions are always anthropomorphic

seek to explore just what these general concepts meant for him. Despite what most people would take as some rather bizarre cosmological speculations in his last years, he would always try not to overstep the boundaries established by his neocritical philosophy.

During the period of his *Essais*, Renouvier asserted the existence of divinity but professed openness on the question of whether there was one or more gods. He insisted that there was no philosophical objection to polytheism and indeed seems to have found it easier to conceive the origins of the world from a phenomenological viewpoint if they could be located in a plurality of consciences.[16] At the same time, he found greater freedom, toleration, rational enquiry, and morality in the polytheistic societies of ancient Greece and Rome than in those of medieval Christianity or Islam. It would be going too far, however, to assert that Renouvier was ever a polytheist.[17] He was aware of a certain ancient monotheism and the polytheism surviving in Christianity, but for intellectual reasons he declined to close the door on polytheism until around 1882. In particular, he was disturbed by the affinity of monotheism for absolutes in philosophy and its opening toward pantheism.[18]

As a theist, Renouvier had two distinct concepts of God, one religious, one philosophic, that were imperfectly reconciled. Religiously, he favored an anthropomorphic concept of God as the only kind that responded to man's authentic religious needs:

The serious notion of God as a person is accused of anthropomorphism, but this is the only idea of God which is compatible

---

(*Quatrième essai*, 395–96, 400, 767), but he also found an example of monotheistic anthropomorphism in the early Hebrews (*Quatrième essai*, 396; see Méry, *Critique du christianisme*, I, 137). See this chapter, below, for further considerations on immortality.

16. *Premier essai*, 369, regarding polytheism. *Ibid.*, 357; this is a key point on which he changed his mind (Hamelin, in Dauriac, "Moments de la philosophie," 44).

17. This was much to Prat's regret (*Charles Renouvier*, 149–55).

18. *Quatrième essai*, 764–65; Méry, *Critique du christianisme*, I, 206–207; Méry, *Critique du christianisme*, I, 208; *Histoire*, I, 294; Beurier, "Renouvier et le criticisme français," 489.

with the moral attributes of divinity. However, this label, taken in the simple etymological sense, is even less to be rejected by the doctrine of Conscience since, according to that doctrine, we have no other givens available to us besides those of the human conscience, its properties and its laws, on which to base, by means of generalizations and inductions, an idea of that which is first, sovereign or perfect. Those philosophers from Xenophanes to Feuerbach who have condemned man's penchant for representing God in his own image have protested in vain against one of the basic conditions of our intelligence. And have they not submitted to that same condition in forging gods with abstract ideas from their own understanding? The whole difference between them and the others consists in their preference for realist fictions . . . over the generalization of the idea of the person.[19]

Philosophically, he tended to identify God with the moral character of the universe, a rather abstract conception.

Renouvier's personalism aimed at bringing these two aspects together in the conception of God as a person, but that person tended to become nebulous as a result of Renouvier's effort to limit himself to rational considerations.[20] God remained an anthropomorphic concept only in the sense that our knowledge of him could only be relative, relative to our world and our lives. Christian theologians reproached Renouvier with failing to make enough distinction between man and God, bringing God down to man's level by denying him infinite qualities such as omniscience and omnipotence.[21] Renouvier considered those qualities as theo-

---

19. *Esquisse,* II, 204. Roure (*Doctrines et problèmes,* 144–47) is thus wrong in stating that Renouvier found Kant's idea of God too anthropomorphic. Méry (*Critique du christianisme,* I, 169) considers that Renouvier's anthropomorphism made him open to the appeal of Christianity.

20. Méry (*Critique du christianisme,* II, 371–72) states that only a person, with intelligence and will, could be the creator; see Miéville (*Philosophie de Renouvier,* 226, 229) for a Christian critique.

21. Octave Hamelin, "La Philosophie analytique de l'histoire de M. Renouvier," *Année philosophique* (1898), 37. Méry (*Critique du christianisme,* II, 382–83) points out that for Renouvier, the tendency of Western philosophy was

logical corruptions of authentic religion, which could admit for God only a *moral* perfection. At bottom, God was for Renouvier the guarantee of the reality of the *règne des fins* (reign of ends) for which man was destined.[22]

While Renouvier's idea of a rational faith was integrated into the whole of his philosophy, it was especially shaped by his idea of freedom. The contents of a faith had not only to avoid conflict with the demonstrations of science but also to support the aspiration for moral autonomy that we have seen was the central pivot of his philosophy. The center of Renouvier's religion, as of his ethics, was the concept of justice as defined by Kant's categorical imperative. It was a dilemma for Renouvier that man needs religion to support his thirst for justice in a hostile world, but in practice most religions have been hostile to justice in the name of love and charity.[23] Hence, despite the profound study of Christianity in his later years, Renouvier remained attached to Greek and Hebraic religions for their devotion to a justice which is conceived in human terms.[24]

In his personal life, religious feeling seems mainly to have served the role of ratifying his philosophical decisions, helping him to believe that his opinion was not merely a personal option but was somehow in tune with the universe: "An irresistible instinct leads us, then a free and reflective will confirms us in the belief that our truth is the truth, our good, the good."[25] Still, the individual believer's choice was paramount. Religion was at bottom a private matter.[26] To make religion a private matter

not to see God as a person and thus to fall into pantheism; see also Renouvier to Charles Secrétan, January 21, 1869, in *Correspondance de Renouvier et Secrétan*, 16–17.

22. See *Dilemmes*, 237; *Deuxième essai*, 676; *Histoire*, IV, 440. Miéville, *Philosophie de Renouvier*, 170.

23. Renouvier to Secrétan, August 14, 1869, May 2, 1875, in *Correspondance de Renouvier et Secrétan*, 30, 113.

24. See, for example, *Quatrième essai*, 617. Méry (*Critique du christianisme*, II, 499) attributes Renouvier's anthropomorphism to his assiduous reading of the Old Testament and finds an affinity for Judaism in his inability to accept Jesus as the Messiah.

25. *Deuxième essai*, 542.

26. On the necessity of choosing to believe or not in "the existence of a moral order in the universe," see *Esquisse*, II, 243; see also Verneux, *Idéalisme*

has certainly been one of the trends of at least the last two centuries, and not even Catholicism has escaped its influence in the twentieth century.[27] But in nineteenth-century France it was still a very contentious issue. Religion was part of the public sphere, and the public role of the Church was a profoundly political issue.

Renouvier and Anticlericalism

The interrelation of church and state was one of the oldest constants in French history; indeed, it was one of the distinctive characteristics of the French state. France had been baptized the "Eldest Daughter of the Church," and one of her kings had been canonized. Opposition to this alliance had been gradually developing since the Reformation and especially since the Revocation of the Edict of Nantes in the seventeenth century, but it could be effectively challenged only after the Revolution of 1789 had replaced the old divine foundation of government with the concept of the sovereignty of the people.

Opposition to the political power of the Church and to the monarchy would become largely inseparable in the nineteenth century.[28] It would also acquire a broad popular basis that affected the tone of the debate. Republican intellectuals would continue to denounce "*l'union du throne et de l'autel*" (the union of throne and altar), but by the Second Empire, when the throne had lost much of its majesty, popular writers were denouncing the alliance of "*le sabre et le goupillon*" (the sabre and

---

de Renouvier, 314–15. Renouvier's rapprochement with Christianity was essentially a product of his study of the period from Jesus to Paul, where he found an essential individualism, lost in later organized churches, and an absence of the metaphysical complications introduced by the construction of a philosophic theology; see, for example, *Histoire*, II, 481–42, on Saint Paul; elsewhere in this volume he argues that Jesus offered salvation to individuals, not groups.

27. See Georges Weill, *Histoire de l'idée laïque en France au XIXe siècle* (2nd ed.; Paris, 1929), 360.

28. On Renouvier's connection of Catholicism with monarchy, see Méry, *Critique du christianisme*, I, 466. On the general history of laicism, nothing has replaced the lofty dispassion of Weill's *Idée laïque*.

the censer) against the public liberties. However, it was during the First Empire that the identification of republicanism and anticlericalism was solidly established, a result of Napoléon's Concordat.[29]

Despite its traditional elements, the signing of the Concordat shed a new light on the political position of the Church in France. Napoléon did not belong to the long line of Catholic kings. Indeed, he was able to come to power only because that long line had been overthrown, and to the clergy he must have at first looked like a crowned *philosophe*. Napoléon, however, wanted not just to rule France (or even Europe) but to found a dynasty, and this meant reconciliation with the forces of social order and stability. The readiness of the Church to come to terms with the usurper dismayed the monarchists but confirmed the fears of the republicans. The Church was shown to favor authoritarian government, whatever its origins—as long as that government did not make war on the Church.[30] And was it not only natural that a Church whose internal structure was that of an elective monarchy should feel at home only with regimes of authority, especially with regimes that would put that secular arm in the service of the interests of the church? Did not the Church preach humility and submission to established authority and ridicule the idea that the people should have a voice in government (except where the ruler was not a Catholic)?[31]

Critics of republican anticlericalism have often forgotten that it was a real enemy the republicans were fighting in the nineteenth century. The

29. See Renouvier, *Le Personnalisme* (Paris, 1903), 191–92.

30. "Since the Revolution christianity no longer represents justice; it represents the Old Regime" (Pierre-Joseph Proudhon, *De la justice dans la Révolution et dans l'Eglise* [Paris, 1932], 642, Vol. VIII of Proudhon, *Oeuvres complètes,* ed. Bouglé and Moysset). On the natural tendency of church and state to ally, but also their inevitable rivalry, see *Personnalisme,* 150–51; see also Herbert Tint, "The Search for a Laic Morality under the French Third Republic: Renouvier and the 'Critique philosophique,'" *Sociological Review,* V (1957), 9. On the apparent irreconcilability of the Catholic church and the modern state, see *Histoire,* IV, 140.

31. For Renouvier's critique of absolutist, monarchical religion, see *Deuxième essai,* 682–84. Despite his hostility to the new German Empire, Renouvier approved of Bismarck's *Kulturkampf* while noting its failure (*Histoire,* IV, 135–36).

Second Empire and the pontificate of Pius IX were periods of intensified conflict between the Church and modern thought. It was the age of the encyclical *Quanta cura* and the *Syllabus of Errors,* of a reinvigorated superstition, as evidenced by the new cults centered on La Salette and Lourdes or the doctrine of the Immaculate Conception.[32] And all of this was crowned by the proclamation of papal infallibility by the First Vatican Council. Anticlericalism might become a mere reflex or a convenient tool, hypocritically utilized.[33] It would certainly outlive its *raison d'être* in the twentieth century, but it was an essential and inescapable part of republicanism in the nineteenth century.[34]

It is in this political context that we have to understand Renouvier's anticlericalism.[35] His youthful religious experience might have produced merely a Voltairian intellectual, content to make fun of the pretensions of the Church and the naïvetés of the faithful. It was his political experience and his philosophical reflection on that experience that would make him one of the intellectual leaders of French anticlericalism in the first decades of the Third Republic.[36] He would regret that the necessities of the anticlerical struggle would lead many to positions hostile to religion in general; he would try to show how one could be anticlerical without being unjust toward religion.[37] Anticlericalism was directed

32. These are Renouvier's examples (*Histoire,* IV, 128–30).

33. *Ibid.,* 131–32; Renouvier noted that infallibility might open the way for a reforming pope and could thus be a way to free the Church from some of its traditions. Moisant (*Psychologie,* 266) was a Catholic critic who credited Renouvier with condemning those politicians who use anticlericalism simply as a means to win elections.

34. Roger Picard (*Les Idées sociales de Renouvier* [Paris, 1908], 279–81) agrees.

35. Waelti (*Morale kantienne,* 82–83) recognizes the importance of the political circumstances even while regretting that Renouvier should have spent so much of his life at war with the majority of his compatriots. Renouvier would have replied that such is the philosopher's duty.

36. "One of the traits which makes Renouvier one of the great builders of democratic France, especially odious to those who detest it, is his doctrine with respect to the relations of the State and Catholicism" (Benda, "Idées d'un républicain," 30).

37. For example, *Histoire,,* III, 586–87.

against the political ambition and power of the Church that he feared had come to supplant the spiritual mission of the clergy.[38]

The disastrous consequences of the Second Empire's foreign policy were no surprise to Renouvier, but the resulting collapse of the regime was an unexpected blessing. Like many republicans, he saw Catholic influence as important in the confrontation with Protestant Prussia and felt that clerical pressure had contributed to shaping a policy harmful to French national interests.[39] Naturally, he was distressed by the violence with which the Communards expressed their hatred of the church and the state, but I doubt that he could help thinking the fault lay basically with Rome and the Tuileries. His main concern, however, was not with the past but the future and how to rebuild. In that process of reconstruction nothing seemed more important than to counter the influence of the Church. At first he seems to have had little hope, fearing a monarchist restoration and having little confidence in the political acumen of the republican Left. But, as he observed to Secrétan, things do not always turn out as badly as they might.[40]

Religion and Education

Even in the darkest days, Renouvier had been among those determined to build for the future. With his friend and disciple François Pillon, he conceived a philosophico-political weekly that began to appear in 1872,

38. Renouvier to Secrétan, December 7, 1873, in *Correspondance de Renouvier et Secrétan*, 99: "In France religion is dead, and that's the source of the strength *of these rascally priests.*" The emphasized passage is in Italian: "*di questi pretri scellerati.*"

39. Renouvier had not forgotten that Louis Napoléon's coup d'état of December 2, 1851, had been sanctified by a Te Deum on January 1, 1852. In general, he held the Church responsible for the ills of France under the Second Empire (Tint, "Search for a Laic Morality," 8; see *Histoire*, IV, 135). The war and the commune moved Renouvier closer to the Protestants (Méry, *Critique du christianisme*, I, 352–56, 489–94).

40. Renouvier to Secrétan, December 7, 1873, in *Correspondance de Renouvier et Secrétan*, 99.

La critique philosophique. The anticlerical struggle would be a central part of this effort to contribute to the intellectual and moral rebuilding of France. Here more than anywhere else Renouvier would develop the full force and breadth of his anticlericalism, in both his advocacy of specific political programs and his philosophical arguments. It seemed to him that if France was to have any chance of breaking out of the vicious circle of political conflicts that had made every regime since 1789 short-lived, that fundamental reform must be undertaken at the very base of society. The future of the republic, of any republic, must depend upon the people. An enlightened leadership was not enough.

This conviction had made its appearance among the republicans of 1848, and the failure of that revolution had convinced Renouvier more than ever that the establishment of political freedom in France could be achieved through a republican education of the people. The weakness of France for monarchical or despotic regimes seemed to him primarily a product of its Catholic education. This was a matter not just of schooling but of the general permeation of society by Catholic values and habits of mind.[41] Renouvier frequently remarked on the penchant among anticlerical and even atheist political and intellectual leaders for authoritarian solutions, and he attributed this to the influence of Catholic upbringing or education or more generally Catholic influence on the intellectual and moral atmosphere.[42]

His main concern, then, was to campaign for a laic and republican education reaching all the classes of society. He did not underestimate the difficulties:

41. This was one of the reasons why Catholic schooling was allowed to continue (*Histoire*, IV, 120).

42. On this view as represented in the *Critique philosophique,* see Tint, "Search for a Laic Morality," 11, who quotes from an article by J. Milsand. Renouvier did not think much of the intellectual quality of nineteenth-century *libre-pensée* in France, finding only two anti-Catholic works worth noting: Renan's *Vie de Jesus* and Proudhon's *De la justice dans la Révolution* (*Histoire*, IV, 133–34). His arguments for the disjunction of religion and the state, or more generally against the concept of a "spiritual power," were also directed against the Saint-Simonians and the positivist heirs of Joseph de Maistre (Méry, *Critique du christianisme*, I, 236).

It is necessary for the philosopher and the historian to recognize that the force of the Catholic Church's resistance to legislative action has become so great that it can defy all measures capable of bringing about a rapid and durable change in the state of affairs. If the liberal impulse is lively, without being pushed to extreme violence against clerical institutions, the force of inertia is always enough for the Church to preserve its main fortresses, as long as ideas and moeurs have not undergone major modifications in the depth and mass of the nation. These modifications will take a long time.[43]

He wondered if the republican state was capable of such a long-term effort.

Renouvier's contribution as a philosopher to this political struggle had several aspects. One was his effort to convince other republicans of the centrality of the educational issue, another to make proposals about the content of a republican education, and a third to persuade the hesitant that drastic measures were not merely politically necessary but morally justified.

It may be useful to take the latter point first, since it may be less familiar, though the issues raised have surfaced more recently and in different contexts. The defenders of a Church-dominated education had long contented themselves with the assertion that their monopoly of revealed truth entitled the Church to a monopoly on popular education. But when they ceased to be politically strong enough to preserve that monopoly, they had eventually evolved a new tactic: to appeal to the principles of their enemies and demand freedom of education. The use of this argument grew in frequency and force in proportion to the growth of the republican demand for a system of laic, free, and compulsory education. Under the educational banner of the right of parents to decide what sort of education their children were to have and who was to give it to them, the Church leaders fought to limit the growth of public education, and the republican extremists began to counterclaim a state mo-

43. *Histoire,* IV, 139.

nopoly of education. Renouvier saw any monopoly as harmful to freedom, but he considered the Church position hypocritical, and argued that all children should be obliged to attend public primary schools and that all members of religious orders—priests, monks, and nuns—should be prohibited from teaching children, that is, those whose education choices were made for them.[44]

But how could liberals take such a position? How could Renouvier, the champion of moral autonomy, sanction such an intrusion of state power into the lives of citizens? For many liberals, this was a problem, a problem whose analogy in our time has been the right of Communists to teach in tax-supported schools. Renouvier's position would be similar to that of Sidney Hook in the latter struggle—to show that liberal principles do not require a surrender of power to those who would destroy liberty. To those tender consciences who feared, like the anti-anti-Communists of our day, that to fight the enemy was to become like him and thus to betray one's principles, Renouvier offered his doctrine of the right of defense, first worked out in his *Science de la morale*.

The tender-minded were committing an intellectual error, the error of confusing the state of war with the state of peace. In the real world—that is, the state of war—we are obliged to work for the advance of freedom and moral autonomy, always the highest goals, but we can do this effectively only if we recognize the conditions imposed by the state of war. In his last days, Renouvier still vehemently insisted that "the war against fanaticism, intolerance and injustice is a holy war."[45] In his time, freedom for the individual, freedom for the community as a whole, could be advanced only by infringing on the freedom of the Catholic church and its believers who followed it. Unfortunately, we cannot avoid treating people as means, and to protect ourselves from being used as means

44. Renouvier to Rev. Hyacinthe Loyson, April 1, 1903, quoted by Méry, *Critique du christianisme*, II, 512. Adults, on the other hand, should be free to choose their own teachers.

45. Méry (*Critique du christianisme*, I, 442–43) is right in saying that Renouvier took a pragmatic position on church-state relations, but this does not justify calling him a "*Maurras de gauche*" who considered religion as only "*ancilla regiminis*" (*Derniers entretiens*, 99–100).

by others, we have a right of defense.[46] One can argue whether the danger was so great as to justify the means Renouvier advocated, but the principle he was acting on has retained its validity.[47]

Renouvier's position was also consistent with his idea of the moral role of the state, for the state could be substituted for the Church in the moral education of the people only if it had a legitimate moral mission. Renouvier, despite his admiration for the ancient city-states, was far from making a religion of the state, and indeed the state could have a moral role only because morals in his view were basically independent of religion. The state could—must, Renouvier insisted—teach a moral doctrine that did not infringe on the religious liberty of any of its citizens, and fortunately such a doctrine existed, for he (and others) had developed it in the midcentury.

Renouvier's intellectual support was welcomed by the makers of the educational policy of the Third Republic, but he also had serious differences with them. The politicians were professionally inclined to play down the novelty of what they were proposing for civic moral instruction, and he feared that they might as a result fail to make their teaching different from that of the Catholics. For Renouvier, the legitimacy of the moral role of the state in education hinged on its commitment to freedom for its citizens. That commitment was essential to the functioning, even the survival, of a democratic republic, and the republic was thus perfectly justified in insisting that its citizens receive a moral education appropriate to free men and women. His support for state education was thus conditional, though in the political circumstances of the 1870s and 1880s in France it could hardly have been stronger.

The main concern of Renouvier's campaign in the *Critique philosophique* was to communicate the moral outlook he had already developed elsewhere. This involved both the exposition of his own doctrine and the critique of Catholic education. Renouvier was generally a respecter of persons in his polemics, but his assault on the doctrine and teaching of

46. He criticized Taine for failing to recognize this (*Histoire*, IV, 540).

47. Laberthonnière (*Critique du laïcisme*, 36–38) is wrong in arguing that for Renouvier the state of war justified any means of attacking the Church or that he was seeking to create a *"théocratie renversée* [upside-down theocracy]." Renouvier was critical of that kind of anticlerical too.

the Church in this period earned him the reputation among Catholics as a prominent member of the Voltairian Left.[48] A few who read him more closely developed a more nuanced picture, for they saw he was not a mocker of religion. Though Renouvier was fully on the side of the advocates of a *morale indépendante,* he did not favor the total exclusion of the mention of God from the state's moral instruction. This and other divergences from some of the framers of republican educational policy led him to develop his own version of primary moral instruction.

He published a long series of articles in the *Critique philosophique* under the title "Petit traité de morale à l'usage des écoles laïques" (A Little Treatise on Morals for the Use of Secular Schools), which was meant to be read by the teachers, not the pupils.[49] Cast in the form of a catechism—inescapable, he would say, in a Catholic country—Renouvier's primer of moral instruction did not perhaps differ a great deal from most of the similar works inspired by the educational program of the early Third Republic except by the solidity of the philosophical base on which it rested, so different from the sentimental humanitarianism of many liberals.

How much influence did Renouvier have on the educational program of the early Third Republic? The only answer we can give with much confidence is: more than some have thought and less than others have claimed.[50] The existence of many parallels between his proposals and the program of the Ministry of Public Instruction cannot be used to

48. See, for example, Laberthonnière, *Critique du laïcisme,* 36*n*1; he saw Renouvier as not just anticlerical but a systematic enemy of religion (*ibid.,* 33, 28) and indeed an atheist from beginning to end (*Esquisse d'une philosophie,* 154). Not all Catholics shared Father Laberthonnière's conviction that outside the Church of Rome all is irreligion.

49. In 1875–77. Collected as *Petit Traité de morale a l'usage des écoles primaires laïques* (Paris, 1879). (There was a second edition in 1882, published jointly with the Protestant publishing house of Fischbacher.)

50. A fairly strong claim for Renouvier's influence is made by Julien Benda ("Idées d'un républicain," 36); the most thorough discussion is Tint, "Search for a Laic Morality," 6–7; see also Stock-Morton, *Moral Education.* This subject deserves more study than I have given it here.

demonstrate more than a common fund of ideas and attitudes shared widely among republicans.[51] Most of the political leaders of the educational reform proclaimed their allegiance to one of Renouvier's bêtes noires, positivism, as popularized by Emile Littré, and they adopted positions Renouvier did not approve.[52] In the politics of the Third Republic, this positivism bore little resemblance to the ideological totalitarianism espoused by Auguste Comte.

Jules Ferry, the parliamentary architect of the republic's educational reform, shared many of Renouvier's political attitudes—a somewhat conservative republicanism, hostility to clericalism and reaction, hostility to Jacobinism and socialism.[53] Renouvier always recognized that men with wrong ideas might act rightly, and vice versa, but he doubted that a lasting reform could be built on an unsound foundation. Although he was not in direct contact with the leading political figures, there is at least some reason to think that Renouvier exercised a less often avowed but not less real influence on the professional leaders of educational reform. In addition to his publications, which attracted a group of readers influential out of proportion to their numbers, he was in personal contact with some of the real architects of the education programs, men such as Félix Pécaut and Louis Liard.[54]

As is (and was then) well known, a disproportionate number of the educational reformers of the early Third Republic were Protestants.[55] This gave the struggle to establish a state program of moral instruction

51. This is a weakness of some Catholic critics of Renouvier; for example, Roure (*Doctrines et problèmes,* 147–49).

52. Littré agreed that anticlericalism was necessary for the defense of the republic ("Education politique," 426).

53. See Claude Nicolet, "Jules Ferry et la tradition positiviste," in *Jules Ferry, fondateur de la république,* ed. François Furet (Paris, 1985), 23–48.

54. See Waelti, *Morale kantienne,* 91–104.

55. For a very sketchy account of the situation of Protestants in France in the early Third Republic, see Douglas Johnson, "Jules Ferry et les protestants," in *Jules Ferry, fondateur de la république,* ed. François Furet (Paris, 1985), 73–77. For a more thoughtful look, see Barnett Singer, *Modern France: Mind, Politics, Society* (Seattle, 1980), Chap. 2, "Minority Religion and the Creation of a Secular School in France."

an air of religious conflict in the eyes of many Catholics, who were understandably outraged that such a tiny minority was apparently able to wield the power of the state against the religion of the vast majority. And the Protestant reformers would not have been human had they not occasionally savored the irony of the situation. Renouvier appeared so often in alliance with the Protestants during the educational struggle and wrote so approvingly of Protestant ethics that many Catholics appear to have assumed that he was of Protestant origins.[56] His relations with Protestantism would indeed become very close during this period, but there was always an ambiguity in that relationship that not every observer noted.

The Campaign for Protestant Registration

Renouvier's greatest moment of public notoriety came as a result of his most curious initiative in religious affairs.[57] This was his campaign of "Protestant registration" waged in the pages of the *Critique philosophique* and its short-lived companion, the *Critique religieuse* in 1877 to 1879. His proposal was simple enough, so simple as to appear ingenuous—"an enterprise in which Renouvier revealed himself as ingenious, but even more as ingenuous," as Albert Thibaudet remarked.[58] He called for all Frenchmen who were disaffected from the Catholic church to enroll themselves and if possible their families on the *état civil* as Protestants. He had done so in 1873.[59] By all accounts, these disaffected Cath-

56. For example, Moisant, *Psychologie de l'incroyant,* 274, 279.

57. See, for example, Archambault, *Renouvier,* 52: "It made quite a stir in its time."

58. On the *Critique religieuse,* see Méry, *Critique du christianisme,* I, 514–23; on Renouvier's campaign more generally, see Prat, *Charles Renouvier,* 267–72. Méry (*Critique du christianisme,* I, 488) noted that Renouvier had previously respected religious faith, but not until this campaign had he openly supported a positive religion. Thibaudet, "Réflexions," 548.

59. Renouvier to Ernest Havet, April 24, 1879, in Méry, *Critique du christianisme,* I, 511–12: "I am not and . . . I have never been, even when a child, personally open to the christian faith. I *enrolled* in the Reformed Church, as you perhaps are aware, in order to take a public position which I consider useful in

olics were much more numerous than actual Protestants, and their inscription on the *état civil* as Catholics gave a distorted picture of the religious convictions of the population as a whole. Their registration as Protestants would hardly give an accurate picture either, but it would promote one goal Renouvier thought highly important: It would weaken the image of the Catholic church as the religion of the vast majority of Frenchmen. This, he thought, would have a salutary effect on public policy and, perhaps, even on the policies of the Church.[60]

In Renouvier's eyes there was no serious hypocrisy in changing registrations, certainly no more than in remaining inscribed as a Catholic when one never went to Mass, rejected the dogmas of the Church, and detested the influence of the priests. Perhaps even less hypocrisy, since Renouvier was not calling for people to join or attend the Reformed church unless they wanted to, though he thought the experience would be beneficial for many and would help cement a family unity badly damaged by the different proportions of religious practice among French Catholic men and women. The main purpose of the campaign remained political, however, and was conceived as an exercise of the right of defense. No one was required to pretend he believed anything he did not believe.

One part of this campaign was aimed at encouraging Protestant congregations to welcome, if not actually to seek, newcomers on their rolls. Renouvier especially urged them not to make difficulties for free thinkers and others whose convictions were hardly orthodox. Naturally this generated some controversy, but by and large its reception among the Protestant pastors was surprisingly favorable.[61] Perhaps the greatest obstacle was the almost closed character of French Protestantism.[62] Obliged by

---

the present state of our customs and political parties. . . . I believed that I could do this with a sound conscience and without deceiving anybody, and without making any [doctrinal] commitment whatsoever."

60. See Méry, *Critique du christianisme*, I, 498; Méry (*ibid.*, 461) found this an effort at a political reformation along lines suggested in the eighteenth century by Turgot.

61. *Ibid.*, 506.

62. On French Protestantism in the 1870s, see *ibid.*, 485–88, and Prat, *Charles Renouvier*, 280–81.

decades of persecution to turn in on itself and discouraged from any effort at proselytism, the Eglise réformée was unused to dealing with people whose families had not been Protestant for generations. The fact that Renouvier was an outsider raised suspicions, but the advantages of his proposal were sufficiently evident to shake the torpor of many church leaders. Not surprisingly, the number of registrations was not large, and Renouvier soon came to recognize the naïveté of his hopes and let the whole thing drop, though in his personal life he still counseled people to become Protestants.[63]

Renouvier had contented himself with inscription on the *état civil* as a Protestant and did not until 1884 join the Protestant congregation near his home in the suburbs of Avignon. He successfully fought off an effort to expel him mounted by some conservatives who doubted the sincerity of his convictions. Otherwise, he seems to have taken only an occasional part in church affairs, though he maintained an active correspondence, personally and in his role as editor, with many pastors. He would count a number of them as friends for the rest of his life.[64] On the whole, he

63. See Prat, *Charles Renouvier,* 275–77; Schloesing ("Le Criticisme de M. Renouvier," 391–92) thought that neocriticism could help shake Protestant evangelism into greater activity. Renouvier (Renouvier to Secrétan, February 23, 1873, in *Correspondance de Renouvier et Secrétan,* 88), noted with pride that he helped arrange a Protestant wedding for two registered Catholics. On Renouvier's reflection on the reasons for the failure of the campaign, see *Histoire,* IV, 481, and Prat, *Charles Renouvier,* 278–80.

64. Renouvier joined this congregation along with his natural son Adrien Aucompte (Méry, *Critique du christianisme,* I, 577–84). The children of Adrien's legitimate half brother André Aucompte were all raised as Protestants at Renouvier's suggestion (*ibid.,* II, 10–11). Many orthodox pastors accepted his sincerity (*ibid.,* 492–94). Waelti (*Morale kantienne,* 116–17) credits Renouvier with good faith despite his not really being a Christian. I think Méry (*Critique du christianisme,* I, 355) goes too far in calling Renouvier a "political director of consciences" for Protestant pastors. Renouvier was not reluctant to give his opinions, but he was very hostile to "direction of conscience." Waelti (*Morale kantienne,* 116) says that after 1879, Renouvier "would be considered an uncontested master in Protestant circles." But there was in fact a serious Protestant critique of Renouvier's philosophy. Méry (*Critique du christianisme,* I, 611, 616)

avoided involvement in the internal struggles of the Reformed church between orthodox and liberal theologies.[65] This indifference was in part philosophical. To friends who feared a backsliding from his philosophical positions he insisted that he had changed none of his beliefs and had not subscribed to any of the creeds and dogmas of the Reformed church.[66] This was the main thing that had attracted him to it: You could belong without adhering to any supernatural doctrines.

Because of this attitude, many have assumed, then and subsequently, that Renouvier should be classed among the liberal Protestants, many of whom had abandoned any literal belief in the Bible and had sometimes even put God in parentheses.[67] His sympathies were in fact as often with the orthodox. He was particularly critical of the liberal tendency to make social betterment and world peace the main aim of Christianity. Christ and his early followers clearly had not believed that this world could be reformed. The orthodox seemed to him closer to authentic religious feel-

---

believes that Renouvier's evolution toward monotheism was influenced by his Protestant friends, such as the pastor Armand Schloesing, who advocated adoption of neocriticism by pastors (Schloesing, "Le Criticisme de M. Renouvier," 274–78).

65. He declined an offer of the chair of philosophy at the Protestant Faculty of Theology of Montauban sometime in the 1880s (Méry, *Critique du christianisme*, I, 724). Schloesing ("Le Criticisme de M. Renouvier," 377–78) recognizes that Renouvier was neither liberal nor orthodox in terms of the current conflict. On Renouvier's influence on Protestant theology, see Méry, *Critique du christianisme*, II, 381.

66. Picard (*Idées sociales*, 298–99) expressed the fear that a change of religion is only movement from one heteronomy to another; Renouvier's criticist morals could stand alone. Renouvier did not share this confidence. In a letter to Dauriac, he insisted that there was no formal connection between his philosophy and any religion; Dauriac deduced that Renouvier felt free to draw on religious sources ("Moments de la philosophie," 42).

67. Renouvier (Renouvier to Secrétan, February 23, 1873, in *Correspondance de Renouvier et Secrétan*, 87) expressed more sympathy for liberal believers than for positivists, and *Critique philosophique* attracted more liberal than orthodox Protestant readers (Secrétan to Renouvier, December 12, 1872, in *Correspondance de Renouvier et Secrétan*, 84).

ing, even when he did not share their specific beliefs.[68] They displayed the kind of anthropomorphic conception of God that seemed to Renouvier the basic, natural religious outlook. The liberals, on the other hand, were often too close to the attitude of the metaphysical theologians of Catholicism, whose God he found excessively abstract.[69]

The extent of Renouvier's involvement in religious questions would remain determined by his philosophical concerns. In many respects his attitudes were more Catholic than Protestant, and in any case the reality of Protestantism was less important than the philosophical conception he had of it—the religion of Kant, the religion of the individual conscience, where no priest stood between man and God. Renouvier was clearly aware of how much his position differed from that of the great reformers,[70] however much he regretted that the Reformation had failed in France, that France had found an Henri IV and not a Henry VIII. Nothing in Christian theology can have been more repugnant to Renouvier than Luther's *De servo arbitrio* or Calvin's supralapsarianism.

The Catholic position on free will was much closer to Renouvier's,

---

68. "Christ had not been a doctrinaire advocate of social progress; He intended to open the road to salvation to individuals, to persons, not to states. . . . The confusion of Christianity with civilization, a common tendency of a large number of pastors, is a confusion in both directions and a pernicious error" (*Histoire*, II, 393, 394). See also *ibid.*, 401–402. Renouvier avoided the sentimentality of many liberal Protestants (Méry, *Critique du christianisme*, I, 523). See his comments on the Reformed Synod of 1872, reported by Méry, *Critique du christianisme*, I, 493. Renouvier considered J. S. Mill to have a similar view (*ibid.*, 399). He was suspicious of a religion without dogmas (*ibid.*, 401).

69. Renouvier attributed the liberal-orthodox split in French Calvinism to the intrusion of German pantheism (*Histoire*, IV, 468). He remained hostile to any theology of "raison raisonnante" but sought to ally his philosophy with a theology of "raison raisonnable" (Méry, *Critique du christianisme*, I, 407–408). He saw God in relation to this world, as a person, and thus did not void the idea of God of all content in the manner of the modernists (Méry, *Critique du christianisme*, II, 382).

70. He criticized them for not going far enough, for failing to avoid intolerance (Méry, *Critique du christianisme*, II, 245). They failed to rethink Christianity and to return to its sources (*ibid.*).

and he was more in agreement with Erasmus, or even Thomas Aquinas, than Luther or Calvin.[71] But the character of the churches was the reverse of what one might expect from this aspect of their doctrines, and this character was what mattered to Renouvier. He found the historical practice of the Catholic church totally destructive of the moral autonomy that was his highest value.[72]

What saved the Protestant churches from the consequences of their predestinarian doctrines was the inner logic of their commitment to the faith of the individual believer, directly in contact with his God. By its origins and essence, then, Protestantism was a religion of moral autonomy.[73] Individual believers and churches might forget this in their zeal, but they were always ultimately frustrated by the principle of individual choice. This has, of course, produced the "variations" of the Protestant

71. *Cf.* John Lukacs, *Confessions of an Original Sinner* (New York, 1990): What mattered even more in my mind was the fact that the Roman Catholic concept—doctrine as well as view—of human nature corresponded with what I was seeing and experiencing, especially during the last years of the war. . . . The teaching of free will—that men and women are responsible for what they do and say and even think, because they are free to do so—and original sin—that the moral range of a human being is infinitely greater and different from that of any other living being, since being naturally inclined to both evil and good, we are both beasts and angels—made a great deal of sense to me. (33)

72. *Histoire,* II, 483 (not one of his more convincing passages). Of course, contemporary Protestants were more likely to assert that God had given man freedom to choose (Arnal, *Hypothèse suprême,* 71). Renouvier noted that Michelet was wrong in thinking that belief in predestination favored despotism (*Histoire,* IV, 476–77). Benrubi (*Sources et courants,* I, 321) recognizes the moral and political reasons for Renouvier's preference for Protestantism.

73. See Méry, *Critique du christianisme,* II, 226–27; Schloesing ("Le Criticisme de M. Renouvier," 268) argues that Renouvier's view saves man's freedom without diminishing God, thus enabling Protestants to escape the troublesome problems of predestination. Whether liberal or orthodox, the believer chooses (Renouvier to Secrétan, April 13, 1869, in *Correspondance de Renouvier et Secrétan,* 21). Renouvier saw in Protestantism a return to the primitive character of the Pauline faith, which he believed respected human freedom (Méry, *Critique du christianisme,* II, 158).

churches, as Bossuet called them, but for Renouvier, this pluralism was a safeguard of freedom as well as its essence or source.[74] A Protestant could always rebel against his church without repudiating his personal beliefs. Protestant societies demonstrated, in Renouvier's opinion, the advantages of this moral position, for they were the societies that had also made the greatest advances in political liberty (with Prussia perhaps the exception). This combination of philosophical and political advantages surely formed the main part of his attraction to Protestantism.

For a Frenchman in the mid-nineteenth century to regret that his country had failed to turn Protestant in the sixteenth century can hardly have furnished the basis for an effective political action, even if his historical analysis of the consequences of this failure was correct. And Renouvier admitted that there was no chance that France would be converted to the *Réforme* in the future. As Secrétan wrote to him, "There are two traditions and too much blood, too many crimes."[75]

One suspects that Renouvier clung to a certain nebulous hope because he could not conceive any more likely way for the ideal of moral autonomy to take root in the French mind. Certainly the preachings of a philosopher were not going to have this effect, no matter how logical or how persuasive his arguments. Nor was some new religion founded by liberal men of goodwill likely to make a greater impression. The only religious attitude that seemed to be gaining ground in the nineteenth century was one that menaced rather than supported individuality and freedom—pantheism. Given this pessimistic analysis of the situation, what role was there left for the philosopher? Both the failure of the campaign for Protestant registration and the success of the effort to establish a program of laic moral education in the public schools left Renouvier with unsatisfied religious aspirations.

74. Pluralism was a natural consequence of freedom for Renouvier (*Histoire*, IV, 695).

75. Secrétan to Renouvier, January 26, 1870, in *Correspondance de Renouvier et Secrétan*, 47. Renouvier saw Maistre as right in predicting France would be the battleground over the future of Catholicism (*Histoire*, IV, 108). On why Protestantism was not possible in France, see *Histoire*, IV, 141. See also his reflections on Quinet's campaign for Protestantism (*Histoire*, IV, 479–81).

Renouvier had studied too deeply the lives of the great religious reformers to believe that he had a "reformer's calling."[76] He was greatly attracted by them, just as he was repelled by the evolution of the institutions inevitably founded on their visions. He could thus feel a great affection for Jesus of Nazareth without accepting the Christologies of any denomination. He was interested in recalling to Christians the character and virtues of primitive Christianity, and he clearly wished that their Church could embody more of those virtues, but his analysis of the history of religions showed why such a hope was futile. Renouvier did think he could effectively fight against the decline of Christianity by demonstrating the compatibility of primitive Christianity with the lessons of critical philosophy. This was obviously a message aimed at the intelligentsia, whose faith was being undermined by a misunderstood rationalism.

As far as Renouvier's sense of his religious mission is concerned, those who have seen in him a Pascal of the nineteenth century are perhaps closest to the mark. One German-Swiss observer called Renouvier a "Pascalian type," though "not much inclined to mysticism," and there was a sense in which Renouvier saw himself as having mutatis mutandis a position in his century similar to that of Pascal in his.[77] He explained the exceptional popularity of Pascal's *Pensées* in the nineteenth century as reflecting the concern of the educated classes in France generated by their religious indifference—and educated unbelievers were surely more numerous in Renouvier's day than in Pascal's. Renouvier was especially intrigued by the relevance of "Pascal's wager" for modern man.[78]

Pascal's version was vitiated by his insistence that man had to choose between Roman Catholicism and atheism, which was far from being true even in Pascal's time. But for Renouvier, there was a rational version, a genuine forced alternative, for man. Man had to believe or not believe in "the existence of a moral order in the world." This choice is forced in the sense that not to choose is also to choose; it is a choice that makes a

76. Méry, *Critique du christianisme*, II, 387.

77. Ascher, *Renouvier*, 55. And Rousseau in his? See Karl Barth, *Protestant Thought: From Rousseau to Ritschl* (New York, 1959), 85.

78. *Histoire*, IV, 688–69; *Esquisse*, II, 295–325.

difference.[79] Rationalists can thus act rationally in making this "moral wager," and their decision, however artificial it may seem at first, can lead to a genuine belief. Renouvier had long accepted Pascal's argument that if we act as if we believe something, we will through habit come to believe, for you can "bend the machine." [80] As for the benefits to society and the individual, what matters is not whether there is a moral order in the world but whether men believe there is one.

If Renouvier's message, like Pascal's, was thus addressed to the intelligentsia, it was not because he lacked "compassion for the multitude" but because he thought the religious needs of the multitude were largely catered to by existing churches.[81] It was the intelligentsia that needed help. Support for religion among the intelligentsia might also improve the character of popular religiosity: "If the philosophers make themselves devout," wrote Secrétan, "perhaps the common herd would let itself be persuaded to put a little more reason into its devotion." [82] Perhaps Renouvier would not have carried this argument as far as Secrétan, but he was concerned about the growing gap caused by the religious indifference of the educated.

Personalism

The centennial of the Revolution of 1789 marked the increasingly sure establishment of the republic and the termination of the *Critique philosophique*. Seeing himself as an old man racked by infirmities he diligently treated at one spa after another (but only once a year), Renouvier drove himself to an astonishing level of literary productivity in the last dozen or so years of his life. The greater part of this prodigious output was

79. Renouvier was much taken with William James's argument for the benefits of choosing to believe (*Esquisse*, II, 320–25); see Verneaux, *Idéalisme de Renouvier*, 311.

80. *Deuxième essai*, 309–12.

81. The charge was leveled by Moisant (*Psychologie de l'incroyant*, 316).

82. Secrétan to Renouvier, June 18, 1884, in *Correspondance de Renouvier et Secrétan*, 150.

devoted to religious questions, including a look back on the history of world religions and a theoretical development of a cosmological view that amazed and divided his admirers.[83] Drawing on the resources of his philosophical system building, Renouvier set out to explore more fully the logical consequences of his commitment to individual freedom and especially the significance of this commitment for his understanding of the preeminently religious question of evil. Out of that ultimate reflection emerged his *personnalisme*.[84]

83. *Philosophie analytique de l'histoire; les idées, les religions, les systèmes* (4 vols.; Paris, 1896–98) comprises 2600 pages. See especially, *La Nouvelle Monadologie* (with L. Prat) (Paris, 1899) and *Personnalisme*. On the reaction, see Louis Foucher, "Le Sens de la dernière philosophie de Renouvier," *Revue philosophique*, CXXXIV (1944), 317–21. Renouvier also published two other substantial, and more conventionally philosophical, works during this period: *Histoire et solution des problèmes métaphysiques* (Paris, 1901) and *Les Dilemmes de la métaphysique pure* (Paris, 1901). Dauriac argues that the metaphysical position of these last works is already to be found in the *Esquisse* and that his turning in the direction of a personalist metaphysics can be seen as early as the *Troisième essai* of 1864 ("Moments de la philosophie," 23–24, 26; *ibid.*, 33–34). Dauriac ("Le Testament philosophique de Renouvier," *Revue philosophique* [1904], 354–57) also argues that neocriticists need not accept any of this, even creation and the existence of God. Waelti (*Morale kantienne*, 61) agrees that the *Esquisse* marks an important turning point with Renouvier's acceptance of a personal God, creator of the world. Hamelin ("Philosophie analytique," 36) agrees. Pillon ("Ouvrage récent," 96–97) stresses the continuity between neocriticism and personalism. See also Méry, *Critique du christianisme*, I, 350–51, 642–43.

84. Mouy (*Idée de progrès*, 202) rightly rejects Séailles' idea that it was an effort by Renouvier to increase the appeal of his philosophy to Protestants. It was more likely to have the opposite effect with liberal Protestants, who rejected Original Sin. Dumas ("Renouvier," 2216) agrees that "it is unjust to see in personalism (1902) a 'cosmic adventure novel written by a polytechnician for Protestant pastors.'" Picard (*Idées sociales*, 307–308) suggests that his decline of hope for social reform led Renouvier to intensify his concern for individual salvation. Robert Le Savoureux (*L'Entreprise philosophique de Renouvier* [Paris, n.d.], 21) sees personalism as a new metaphysics toward which Renouvier had been consciously working all his life.

Personalism is a term that has had almost as many variants and has generated almost as many controversies as the word *humanism*. Thinkers flying this flag have been frequently at pains to distinguish themselves from one another. The most widely known personalist movement in France has been the Catholic one led by Emmanuel Mounier and centered around the review *Esprit*. Philosophically, it was closely associated with the Thomist revival, whose moving spirit was Jacques Maritain. From these points alone it is easy to see that Renouvier's personalism was something quite different, which the Thomists did not fail to point out.[85] Yet there were aspects of similarity on the political and social levels, for both were devoted to the defense of the individual against the oppressive forces of society and the state but also condemned the individualist egoism of laissez-faire capitalism.[86] The Catholics believed that the harmonization of the individual and society was possible only through a certain relationship with God, as conceived in Thomist theology, and with the community of Christian believers, both points on which they thought Renouvier fell short.[87] Both Renouvier and his Catholic critics were distinguished by their efforts to combine the maximum of respect for the individual human being with the building of a just society of such individuals.[88] Whatever nuances, or even antagonisms, may develop this is surely the basic element of any personalism.

85. Laberthonnière, *Critique du laïcisme*, 31; see also Lacroix, *Vocation personnelle*, 166.

86. "Before Mounier, this personalism [of Renouvier] was decidedly 'communitarian'" (Méry, *Critique du christianisme*, II, 447).

87. Renouvier saw "theological absolutism" as using individuals for God's purposes while he treats them as ends in themselves (*Personnalisme*, 79). In *Dilemmes*, 259, he charges that personalism is inconsistent with other elements of Catholic theology. Most Catholic critics were more understanding than Father Laberthonnière, who could find no difference between Renouvier and people like Gabriel Séailles and Ferdinand Buisson (Méry, *Critique du christianisme*, II, 480–81); see, for example, Moisant, *Psychologie*, 300–305, but he too felt that Renouvier lacked a sense of Christian community (*Psychologie*, 317–18).

88. Hamelin ("Philosophie analytique," 47) sees this as a distinction between Renouvier and Christian individualism, but he was writing before the appearance of Christian personalism. On William James as a religious personalist,

Thus it is true that while Renouvier began to call his philosophy *personnalisme* only at the end of his life, the basic elements of a personalist position were present throughout his mature thought.[89] His defense of individual freedom, never a license for the indulgence of egoism, was always connected to a sense of moral responsibility that was a counterpart of that freedom. He never assumed any "invisible hand" that would promote the collective good out of the sum of the actions of individual egos. His philosophy was never open to the anarchist temptation lurking in so many nineteenth-century versions of liberalism. However, it was not political and social issues that brought the personalist side of his thought to the forefront in the 1890s. This was rather the result of turning his attention to the largest issues of human destiny. Coming to terms with the sense of his impending death, he was not so much seeking consolation, which he knew was hard to derive from philosophy, as seeking to clarify his understanding, to fill in a philosophical framework that had been only sketched earlier.[90] And finally, though he found little satisfaction in the kind of immortality offered by eighteenth-century deists—the

---

see [François Pillon?], Review of William James, *L'Expérience religieuse, essai de psychologie descriptive* [*The Varieties of Religious Experience*], in *Année philosophique* (1905), 214–19.

89. See Dauriac, "Moments de la philosophie," 24; Verneaux, *Idéalisme de Renouvier*, 38–39. *Dilemmes*, 239, identifies personalism with the doctrine of *réalité*, which he always opposed to the Platonic *réalisme* of scholastic philosophy; see also *Dilemmes*, 262. As we have seen in the development of Renouvier's idea of free will, his conception of the person is less intellectualistic than Kant's; the person is a living being, a conscience where "phenomena of the intellectual order intersect with those of the sentimental and voluntary orders" (Parodi, *Philosophies d'hier*, 196). The person plays a crucial role in Renouvier's version of the categories, and his solution of an antinomies of the Western philosophical tradition hinges around his concept of the person (Waelti, *Morale kantienne*, 63). Renouvier also distinguishes between the empirical "individual" and the person: The person is more the goal, the end point of man's potential moral development. This distinction is also found in Mounier (Waelti, *Morale kantienne*, 63–64). Renouvier rejects Kant's identification of the person with the noumena (Waelti, *Morale kantienne*, 63–64).

90. Méry (*Critique du christianisme*, I, 62) sees Renouvier as a "*conscience malheureuse*" defending himself against "the anguish of death by recourse to

fame of one's surviving works—Renouvier may have wanted to mark the distinction between his thought and that of all the philosophers who had influenced him by giving his work a more distinctive name than neo-criticism.[91]

Though Renouvier's last work indulges in a more free-ranging speculation than his earlier *Essais,* one should not see in it the self-indulgent fantasies of an old man no longer capable of logical construction.[92] His wit remained acute to the end, and his speculation may have suffered more from an excess of logic than its absence: It was "too 'rationalist' to interest Christians, and too little 'rational' to interest philosophers."[93] His purpose, not always achieved to be sure, was to see what rational philosophy could tell us about human destiny, about those questions that were perhaps more usually taken to be the domain of religion.[94]

Unlike most nineteenth-century philosophers, he realized that the central question was the problem of evil.[95] The pantheist, evolutionist,

---

reason." *Cf.* Waelti, *Morale kantienne,* 61; Verneaux, *Idéalisme de Renouvier,* 2. Others, such as Foucher (*Jeunesse de Renouvier,* 3, "Sens de la dernière philosophie," 325), stress the connection of personalism with Renouvier's first philosophy; see Méry, *Critique du christianisme,* II, 438, 465–66.

91. Dauriac ("Moments de la philosophie," 25) is right in saying that personalism embodies a metaphysic and therefore goes outside the limits of criticism but that at the same time it remains *"rigoureusement néocriticiste."* Dauriac ("Testament philosophique," 346) says: "'Criticism' is the name of a method. 'Personalism' is the name of a doctrine." Méry (*Critique du christianisme,* II, 430) says it was a "definitive doctrine," which was not meant to break with neocriticism.

92. Roure (*Doctrines et problèmes,* 135–36), a Catholic critic of Renouvier, is wrong at both ends of his equation when he writes, "M. Renouvier only departs from positivism to enter into blind mysticism." See also Le Savoureux, *Entreprise philosophique,* 21.

93. Verneaux, *Idéalisme de Renouvier,* 4.

94. Méry (*Critique du christianisme,* II, 466–67, 496–97) thinks personalism breaks Renouvier's tendency to bring neocriticism and Christianity closer together.

95. Méry (*ibid.,* I, 542) argues that Renouvier began to confront the problem of evil in examining J. S. Mill's last works. Prat (*Charles Renouvier,* 8–10) exaggerates the degree of his original concern with the question.

or materialist views dominant in his age did not shed light on the origin and significance of evil, and many thinkers either ignored its existence or assumed that it was on the verge of being eliminated by the progress of science and enlightenment. This inconsequence was a source of weakness for a great deal of nineteenth-century thought and a danger when men tried to put that thought into action. Renouvier observed that Christianity had always drawn strength from its recognition of the reality of evil, but this virtue undermined its popularity in the face of the rise of modern optimism about man.[96]

While the twentieth century has renounced the naïve optimism of the nineteenth, we still have great trouble integrating evil into our thought and often repeat the errors of the last century without realizing it. This is perhaps because the idea of evil has seemed a relic of traditional Christianity in most minds. One of Renouvier's most pertinent legacies for our time is his insistence on bringing rational thought to bear on the subject of evil.[97] We are unlikely to accept much of his solution to the problem of evil, but we would do well to reflect on the example of his effort to come to grips with it.

The problem of evil is often divided into three categories (at least by the French): (1) *moral evil* (*le mal morale*), (2) *physical evil* (*le mal physique*), and (3) *metaphysical evil* (*le mal métaphysique*). The first two are of the greatest interest here. Once he had formulated his neocriticism, Renouvier had no trouble explaining the origins of moral evil. It was the inescapable product of man's free will, which could not make sense if man was free only to do good.[98] There are obvious analogies between Renouvier's version of the Fall of Man and the Judeo-Christian version

96. *Monadologie*, 369.

97. A.-D. Sertillanges (*L'Idée de creation et ses retentissements en philosophie* [Paris, 1945], 207) argues that the problem of evil is a major reason why pantheism and materialism have fought the Christian doctrine of the Creation. Dauriac ("Moments de la philosophie," 25, 40) says, "the last of the problems which, before Kant, no philosopher had seriously attempted to take away from the domain of theology." See also Dauriac, "Testament philosophique," 358.

98. According to Hamelin ("Philosophie analytique," 36) Renouvier's postulate of the Fall first appears in the second edition of his *Troisième essai* (1892). *Deuxième essai*, 602.

of Genesis.[99] But he always stressed their basic difference: "The person who violates the order of the world has not broken a promise or a commitment; he sins against himself and against society, which are two connected things; against nature as well."[100]

Renouvier thus rejected the idea of Original Sin in the common meaning of the theologians—guilt for something one did not do oneself—but accepted the concept as describing man's solidarity in evil. In his view, the legitimate meaning of original sin "is relative to the laws of heredity and of physical and moral solidarity, and to the law of habit, which, in human society, for the most part make our qualities and acts, vices as well as virtues, and, consequently, the destiny of our descendants, depend on those of our ancestors, and thus render all sorts of evil easier or even inevitable for these later generations as a result of the decisions of their ancestors . . . the successors will not fail to bear the *punishment* materially, but they are not morally responsible."[101]

He tried to connect his view of Original Sin to that of primitive Christianity by finding a similar idea in Saint Paul.[102] He thought it important for modern Christians to shed the traditional theological view because its immoral character was one of the things that most caused modern man to reject Christianity.[103] Whatever the origins of evil, Renouvier's concept of *solidarity in evil* (*solidarité dans le mal*) clearly made it easy for him to explain its propagation.[104] The question of where we should imagine evil to have first appeared, in or outside history, was not of pressing importance in the construction of Renouvier's social and political philosophy but acquired significance when he turned to the question of human destiny.

The origin of physical evil was more a difficult problem and had received a variety of solutions in Western thought that left him unsatis-

99. Arnal, *Hypothèse suprème*, 65–68.

100. *Personnalisme*, 82.

101. *Histoire*, II, 447–48.

102. *Ibid.*, 408, 447–49.

103. *Personnalisme*, 212.

104. *Quatrième essai*, 29–30. How did Renouvier's view differ from Rousseau's? On Rousseau's pelagianism, see Barth, *Protestant Thought*, 105–106.

fied. Was it inherent in matter? Was it a lack, a lack that marked the difference between the Creation and the Creator?[105] Was there any connection between the origins of moral and physical evil? Renouvier was, I suspect, always inclined toward this last possibility. The interrelations of physical and moral suffering are fairly obvious; the ability of each to contribute to the other is a commonplace of experience. Relating their origins raises more difficult questions, which Renouvier felt compelled to attack in his last years.[106] The solution at which he arrived was shaped more by his concern for the end of man than his origins, but the two could not be separated.

Renouvier's solution was to make the *mal moral* the source of the *mal physique*. Man's freedom was thus the source of his sufferings in this world as well as the instrument of his ultimate redemption.[107] Difficult as it was to connect the two evils, it seemed more difficult to separate them. If physical evil has a separate origin, then man may never be able

105. This is a common Christian theological view; see, for example, Sertillanges, *Idée de création*, 215–16.

106. In the *Essais*, Renouvier considered *mal physique* inexplicable (Mouy, *Idée de progrès*, 97). Renouvier wrote to Secrétan (March 23, 1872, in *Correspondance de Renouvier et Secrétan*, 66–67): "For a long time I have thought that the real problem of physical nature resides in the history of universal moral life. Only, you understand, I consider it just about impossible to strike the right note in our hypotheses about that history about which we know absolutely nothing before the appearance of the human race and even before a certain epoch of human existence." On the influence of Kant on Renouvier's views, see Méry, *Critique du christianisme*, II, 263–64.

107. This is also an element of theodicy (Mouy, *Idée de progrès*, 107). Sertillanges (*Idée de création*, 208–209) considers this view partially acceptable to Christians. Waelti (*Morale kantienne*, 73–74) argues that any other explanation destroys freedom and establishes determinism. See also Irène Cornwell, *Les Principes du droit dans la philosophie de Charles Renouvier: le droit international* (Paris, 1924), 86–87. See Mouy, *Idée de progrès,* 102–104, for a comparison of Renouvier's explanation with that of Joseph de Maistre. Renouvier says in the *Esquisse* (according to Miéville, *Philosophie de M. Renouvier,* 204–205) that this is what must have happened, but we cannot know how. Renouvier's agnosticism here is similar to his position on how the world was created (*Premier essai,* 359–60).

to master it. Physical evil as we experience it is built into the structure and functioning of the material world. Eliminating all the individual and social causes of human misery, even the elimination of hunger, disease, and accident, would still leave us face to face with separation and death.[108] One solution lies in the separation of the human essence from all materiality, but for Renouvier it made no sense to talk of man outside some corporeal embodiment, however modified from its present form. He praised Christianity for its adherence to a concept of bodily resurrection. Without this, there is no barrier against a sort of pantheist merger of the parts into the whole, with a resulting loss of individual personality.[109] Another alternative is that of the Indian religions, which place annihilation at the end of human destiny. But Renouvier could be satisfied only with a view in which man's corporeal defects are healed at the same time as his moral ones. The origins and the end of evil would have to be conceived as part of one project.[110]

This project immediately forced Renouvier to look beyond the present world in both directions. If the goal and destiny of man is the elimination of moral evil brought into the world by freedom, an elimination that can be carried out only by the further exercise of that freedom, it is futile to expect that goal to be reached in this world.[111] Moral progress

---

108. For Christians, physical evil is not always a moral evil for man; he may draw moral strength from it (Arnal, *Hypothèse suprême*, 72–80). Mouy (*Idée de progrès*, 117–19) sees Renouvier's view as related to that of his old friend Jean Reynaud, in *Terre et ciel*, Chap. I: "It will always be necessary to earn your bread by the sweat of your brow and to die in the end: no earthly progress will ever efface that."

109. On personalism as a weapon against pantheism, see Verneaux, *Idéalisme de Renouvier*, 317.

110. He also desired the elimination of the disharmony of the material world (*Personnalisme*, 217–18). There is an interesting parallel here between Renouvier's view and that of Charles Fourier. Parodi (*Du positivisme à l'idéalisme*, 170–71) notes that philosophy and science have come up with the same three conflicting doctrines about man's destiny that religions have arrived at: (1) progress, (2) decadence or fall, and (3) cycles.

111. For Renouvier's summary of his philosophy of the origins and destiny of man, see *Histoire*, IV, 742–82. He accuses those who seek or predict a paradise in this world of not aiming high enough (*Personnalisme*, 215).

is always possible, but so is moral regression, and Renouvier was always inclined to see the latter as easier and more likely. In any case, the power of *solidarity in evil* is too great for man to overcome in a world where he is also afflicted with a myriad of physical evils. This conviction was at the base of Renouvier's lifelong belief in immortality. There must, he was convinced, be a future world in which the moral potential of man's liberty can be worked out and his promise fulfilled.[112]

Renouvier's concern for the advancement of justice was evident in all aspects of his religious thought. He approached religion from the point of view of man, and it was man's fate that interested him. He was indifferent to the glory of God. God was the guarantee of justice, but justice as man conceives it. God, he insisted, cannot have a standard different from man's.[113] Renouvier's view of this "third world" in which human destiny will be fulfilled was to some extent a resurgence of his early Saint-Simonian belief in progress, with the important difference that its hopes were transferred to another world.[114] Despite Renouvier's

112. This is a belief he considered natural to man (*Premier essai*, 370). Mouy (*Idée de progrès*, 91–92) and Le Savoureux (*Entreprise philosophique*, 9–10) see a concern for death as early as the first *Manuel*. For Moisant (*Psychologie*, 328–29), Renouvier's view of immortality was that of a sage, a Socrates or a Plato, not that of a Christian. It was a view based on the philosophy of freedom rather than on a providential theology (Méry, *Critique du christianisme*, I, 200–201); see *Quatrième essai*, 772. *Deuxième essai*, 619–20.

113. *Histoire*, II, 602–603.

114. Foucher ("Sens de la dernière philosophie," 326–37) sees evidence of a revival of Renouvier's early Saint-Simonian belief in progress. Picard (*Idées sociales*, 301) stresses the role of Renouvier's idea of justice in generating a need for a "*métaphysique religieuse*" that promises satisfaction to his aspiration for man; Mouy, *Idée de progrès*, 94–95.

The hypothesis of the temporary character of evil, legitimately suggested by our desires and which can never be rejected except by another hypothesis, is nothing other than the *postulate of divinity*. In fact it consists of demanding that the world should be good in its origin and in its end, that is, such that it realizes the ends of beings, ends conceived and demanded by conscience, whatever the intermediate stages it may pass through. This is to demand, in accord with the most practical and best understood of all ideas of divinity, that the world should be the work of God. (*Esquisse*, II, 291)

continued devotion to progress through freedom, there was in his later work a strong sense of a destiny that man must someday reach, an outcome not entirely compatible with his idea of freedom.[115]

A future world in which the exercise of man's freedom would be irresistibly inclined toward the good would be a world very different from the present one, and Renouvier admitted that we cannot have a clear idea of what it would be like. He was caught in a dilemma similar to the one that led Catholic theologians to postulate the existence of Purgatory despite the absence of any biblical sanction for the idea. Like most Christians, Renouvier saw this world as a trial and preparation for the next, but he was acutely conscious that "the best of us leave this world in a state of preparation which is a long way from being sufficient for the realm of ends."[116] He therefore had to consider the possibility that further worlds of trial await us, but he was unwilling to enter into speculation that would risk leading away from his doctrine of finitism, which would certainly be the case if those future worlds resembled our own.[117]

Having pushed his philosophy into a realm usually reserved for theology, he also had to confront the question of punishment after death for those who have not merited a better world. He was revolted by the Christian idea of eternal damnation, which he insisted was not to be found in either Jesus' or Paul's teachings. Those who could not be redeemed would simply cease to exist, possibly after still further trials in other

---

115. On the importance of liberty for Renouvier's theodicy, see *Esquisse*, II, 291–92. Laberthonnière (*Critique du laïcisme*, 33) sees Renouvier's immortality as merely a displaced search for terrestrial happiness. Sertillanges (*Idée de création*, 106–107) argues that the idea of creation leads to a radical optimism about the ultimate ends of creation. Does not Renouvier share this opinion? See *Deuxième essai*, 626–27, and *Esquisse*, II, 292. The connection between belief in God and belief in the ultimate "realm of ends" (*règne des fins*) is supported by Miéville (*Philosophie de Renouvier*, 170) and Méry (*Critique du christianisme*, I, 658). Archambault (*Renouvier*, 31) sees immortality as an expression of the right to moral progress.

116. *Histoire*, IV, 771, 778; Méry, *Critique du christianisme*, II, 449.

117. *Histoire*, IV, 779. Man would have to pass through an infinite succession of future worlds to reach his end.

worlds.[118] Maintaining his philosophical approach, Renouvier rejected the idea of a last judgment and tried to conceive man's future as resulting from purely natural causes. Like Sartre, Renouvier thought that it was enough to understand that hell is the world in which we now live.[119] Clearly, Renouvier's philosophy was able to give us an idea of what the realm of ends would be like, but he had great difficulty telling us how we might hope to reach that realm with only the light of reason to guide us. In endowing his creatures with free will, God had given them both the thirst for justice and the means of achieving it. But his creatures are too weak to advance on that path without God's help, help in the face of the decisions that confront us every day.[120]

Because man is unable to achieve justice in this world, he needs to believe in the possibility of justice in a future life. Such a belief may be defended on rational grounds, as Renouvier tried to do, but it becomes easier to grasp, easier to accept, if we can conceive it as guaranteed by a divine personality whose very nature responds to man's longing for justice. Renouvier could not conceive that his feelings here were not natural to mankind. He personally felt the need for help, as he said to Louis Prat: "I have discovered, in examining my life, many reprehensible acts and, all told, I don't dare decide whether I've been less bad than the common run of men." [121] He hoped for another chance, for himself and all mankind.

118. *Ibid.*, II, 391–400, 470; *Esquisse*, II, 335–40. Thus, for Renouvier, in contrast with Hindu religion, the goal was not the annihilation of consciousness but its fullest possible development.

119. *Personnalisme*, 217–18; *Premier essai*, 369. He persisted in distinguishing this phenomenist immortality from that of the metaphysician's "immortal soul" (*Deuxième essai*, 596). Eternal rewards, yes; eternal punishments, no (*Histoire*, IV, 772, 776–77); see also Schloesing, "Criticisme de Renouvier," 211; *Histoire*, IV, 779.

120. Prat, *Renouvier*, 238–242. But the only kind of intervention of God in the world that Renouvier was ready to accept was action directly on the consciences of men (Miéville, *Philosophie de Renouvier*, 185–86). He considered physical miracles possible (*Histoire*, II, 366–67; *Deuxième essai*, 188–91) but insisted that they were not essential to religion (*Quatrième essai*, 193; *Histoire*, II, 368–69).

121. *Dernières entretiens*, 5, quoted by Moisant, *Psychologie*, 320.

If the solution to the problems of evil lies outside this world—and it certainly must if there is to be a solution—can the origins of evil nonetheless be found here? Renouvier seems initially to have made this assumption, but as he deepened his inquiry, he came to the conclusion that it was also necessary to postulate a "first world" before the present one.[122] The moral Fall of Man could be conceived as taking place in this world, but a physical context in which he would also have been free not to fall did not seem compatible with what we know of our physical world.[123] Determined never to reject the findings of natural science about this world, Renouvier had to postulate an earlier, perfect world, a world where physical evil was absent.[124] He could then imagine a process by which the free will of man, having chosen the wrong, should bring about the collapse of this perfect moral society in which men had been able to behave morally, and imagine that this moral collapse brought with it the disintegration of the perfect physical world, a disintegration into the chaos that Laplace's nebular hypothesis placed at the origin of the present world.[125]

The imagination that seeks to remain under the direction of reason has difficulty conceiving what these first and third worlds could be like, and Renouvier had the merit of admitting that we cannot go beyond

122. Arnal, *Hypothèse suprême*, 5. Renouvier (Renouvier to Secrétan, January 24, 1869, in *Correspondance de Renouvier et Secrétan*, 11) admitted that the idea of a first world did not much simplify the problem of creation, which he had always considered unknowable.

123. Hamelin ("Philosophie analytique," 44–45) says that before the second edition of the *Troisième essai*, Renouvier placed the fault in terrestrial man, which could explain the origin of moral evil but not of physical evil.

124. According to Arnal (*Hypothèse suprême*, 34–36), Renouvier's view of the first world shows pantheistic traits that he otherwise condemns. See Renouvier's summary description in *Personnalisme*, 81–82; see also *Personnalisme*, 89–91, 101; *Monadologie*, 470. Sertillanges (*Idée de création*, 216–17) sees the diversity of the physical world as one source of evil but also a necessary part of creation. Science cannot disprove the reality of a future life (*Premier essai*, 85, 364; *Deuxième essai*, 646–47). More generally, the beginning and the end of the universe surpass any possible knowledge (*Esquisse*, II, 387).

125. This world would probably have a similar end (*Deuxième essai*, 651).

certain generalities in constructing hypotheses about something necessarily outside any possible experience.[126] His effort to imagine a future world without physical evil reminds us of Fourier's cosmology, but Renouvier, by not trying to paint a detailed picture of such a world, largely avoided the ridicule Fourier brought on himself.[127] To examine the conditions for its existence was rash enough.

Renouvier's vision of man's origin and destiny was also to some extent a theodicy, though he preferred to call it a *cosmodicée,* a justification of the universe. There even creeps into his explanation of the origins some of the metaphysical concern for the nature of God that he regularly attacked as a vice of Catholic theology.[128] For he too wanted to conceive a world in which God could not be held responsible for the existence of evil, even though God created a world in which man could fall. Like many Christians, Renouvier saw the possibility of the Fall as balanced by the possibility of another world in which man could rise from his fallen state.[129] Renouvier did manage to avoid burdening his examination

126. He saw less risk of ridicule in hypothesizing about the ends of man than in speculating about his unknowable origins (*Troisième essai,* 187).

127. Insofar as he was inspired by Reynaud's *Terre et ciel,* Renouvier removed its elements of pantheist and infinitist inspiration (Mouy, *Idée de progrès,* 119). Roure (*Doctrines et problèmes,* 142–44) argues that rationalists who reject revelation (Renouvier, Reynaud, Flammarion) lack any solid ground for explaining the character of the future life and that Renouvier's phenomenology can make no sense of it at all. The Jesuit father has a loose grip on what phenomenism meant for Renouvier, but he does point to a difficulty. See Waelti, *Morale kantienne,* 65–66; Le Savoureux, *Entreprise philosophique,* 28–29. On Fourier and Renouvier, see Mouy, *Idée de progrès,* 120–22.

128. In his cosmological speculation, Renouvier arrived at a conception of God remote from both the theologians' Absolute and his earlier anthropomorphism, a God defined largely in terms of the schema of man's moral history. On its inadequacy from a religious viewpoint, see Miéville, *Philosophie de Renouvier,* 176–68, 212, 214–17, 223–24. See Méry, *Critique du christianisme,* II, 458–59. Prat (*Renouvier,* 207–208) says that neocriticism leads to a justification of a God of justice and goodness, the only kind of God conceivable by reason.

129. The promise of a future life was certainly one thing that made Renouvier feel close to the Christian faith (Renouvier to Hyacinthe Loyson, September 12, 1897, quoted in Méry, *Critique du christianisme,* II, 505–506).

with all the subsidiary questions that have arisen historically within the Christian framework, such as predestination and God's foreknowledge, but he also tended to avoid confronting issues inescapable for Christians, such as the role of Christ in man's redemption.[130] At the same time, he did push philosophical speculation rather uncomfortably into areas that had always been seen as the domain of theology.

Such cosmological speculation also had its impact on the inner balance of his philosophy. Renouvier's concept of the individual had always drawn something from the monadology of Leibniz, and his concern to move the human person through these three worlds brought this aspect to the forefront.[131]

Like Secrétan, I have some difficulty grasping this monadology and understanding how its apparently necessary corollary—the preestablished harmony of the monads—can be compatible with Renouvier's concept of liberty. It is even more difficult to see how he reconciles his monadology with his phenomenology, despite his assurances that the former follows from the latter, for the monads would seem to be a metaphysical concept and not phenomena.[132]

130. Protestant Jean Arnal (*Hypothèse suprème,* 61–62) draws attention to this.

131. Dauriac ("Testament philosophique," 346) states that personalism is a criticism with a Leibnizian metaphysics. Waelti (*Morale kantienne,* 42) sees an increasing influence of Leibniz as a result of an increasing concern with final causes; she also notes (*Morale kantienne,* 61n1) Renouvier's continued rejection of much of Leibniz's philosophy as linked to Leibniz's infinitism. Can Renouvier's movement from Kant toward Leibniz suggest a certain movement from Protestantism toward a crypto-Catholicism, in the sense of a more all-embracing system of values? (reflection suggested by Chap. LXII, "Dégradation des valeurs (8)," of Hermann Broch, *Huguenau oder die Sachlichkeit,* Vol. III of his *Die Schlafwandler* in the French edition [Paris, 1957]).

132. Verneaux (*Idéalisme de Renouvier,* 199) insists that phenomenology and monadology are in contradiction, but (*ibid.,* 164–65) he also believes that Renouvier's phenomenism required a *representation pour soi,* that is, a *personne* or a *monade.* A. Darlu raised this question in discussion of Dauriac's paper (Dauriac, "Moments de la philosophie," 42–43). Dauriac says Renouvier believed that the centrality of the idea of personality in his system of Categories provided

What matters, however, is that the monadology enabled Renouvier to conceive his *cosmodicée* in rational, philosophical terms rather than religious ones.[133] Unable to take some of the shortcuts a religious conception offers, he risks getting bogged down in the details of his explanation of how persons can have a real identity in their journey across the three worlds of existence.[134] His theory of the multiplicity of "germs" carrying each "person" through this world has been more than any commentator, however friendly, could swallow.[135] Excess of reason? Or at least of *raison raisonnante*?

None of this detracts much from Renouvier's stature as a philosopher. He knew what he was doing, and one of the things that make him an attractive figure is his willingness to take risks. This is not so common in a philosopher who still shared the system-building ambition of an earlier generation, for most of them were driven by an obsession to arrive at a complete and absolute certainty. Better than Kant, Renouvier took

---

an adequate bridge, but Dauriac is not sure that Renouvier was right; see his "Moments de la philosophie," 29*n*2.

133. Waelti (*Morale kantienne*, 22) accepts that Renouvier's "*rigoureusement phénoméniste*" criticism could, without inconsistency, include a theodicy. Discontinuity of the real world, necessary because of the law of contradiction, shows that the resumption of personal existence after long interruption cannot be ruled out (*Deuxième essai*, 649–50). "What I believe to be founded on science in spite of their extreme boldness, and what I believe to be Christian *in spirit*, though *materially* a thousand miles from the letter of the legends of the 2nd chapter of *Genesis*" (Renouvier to Hyacinthe Loyson, January 31, 1900, quoted in Méry, *Critique du christianisme*, II, 506–507). Renouvier insisted on the common rational foundation of his monadology and "*la philosophie chrétienne*" (*Monadologie*, 534).

134. See *Personnalisme*, 89–91. The possibility of such a journey was established as early as the *Deuxième essai*, 581–82. He compares it with the continuity of the individual through the many changes of his life (*Deuxième essai*, 644–45).

135. See *Personnalisme*, 114–17. Arnal (*Hypothèse suprême*, 45–46) notes a certain Brahminism in Renouvier's position. Mouy (*Idée de progrès*, 123–26) thinks Renouvier was unfaithful to his own concept of the person here and attributes this to a desire to arrange salvation for everyone.

the measure of these ambitions. None of his cosmological speculations are presented as certainties; they are meant to demonstrate what the mind can do when it tries to look beyond our existing world, not to prove the existence or nature of another world.[136] At the same time, they are not meant to be mere fantasies, and every effort is made to confine them to what he sees as the rules of thought. For Renouvier, both philosophical belief and religious belief had to be rational.[137]

There remains some debate whether Renouvier in his late works was simply pushing philosophy into the domain of theology.[138] Was he trying to make theology superfluous, repeating the syndrome of Saint-Simon and Comte, "crowning" his thought with a religion? Renouvier always insisted that he was not proposing a new religion, or even a religious philosophy, but a philosophy of religion: "We are far from attributing to the doctrine we are expounding the qualities of a religion, but we think that it can be presented as a philosophy of religion, a philosophy morally and logically superior, as far as the matters it deals with, to any religion whatsoever." [139]

136. Renouvier claimed only a verisimilitude (*Personnalisme*, 224–25). Immortality had always been only a moral certainty (*Deuxième essai*, 578). See Verneaux, *Idéalisme de Renouvier*, 301–302; Méry, *Critique du christianisme*, II, 388, 462. Höffding (*Philosophes contemporaines*, 87) recognizes that Renouvier proposes only a moral certainty. Renouvier was more sober than Camille Flammarion, who combined serious astronomy with vast cosmological speculation.

137. Renouvier was hostile to fantasy in religion (Méry, *Critique du christianisme*, I, 421). He insisted that religion does not need the support of miracles and old superstitions (*Quatrième essai* 776–77). Mouy (*Idée de progrès*, 195) agrees with Hamelin that Renouvier's *cosmodicée* is reasonable in principle and with Prat that its excesses can be treated as deliberate myths. Renouvier certainly viewed a future life as natural, not as miraculous (Miéville, *Philosophie de Renouvier*, 169). Verneaux, *Idéalisme de Renouvier*, 305–307.

138. Yes, according to Miéville (*Philosophie de Renouvier*, 192); yes, and it was a mistake, according to Verneaux (*Idéalisme de Renouvier*, 324–25); see Renouvier's reflections in *Esquisse*, II, 405.

139. *Monadologie*, 522. Méry (*Critique du christianisme*, I, 87) places Renouvier's personalism somewhere "between" the religions of Saint-Simon and Comte. For the parallel between Comte and Renouvier, see *Critique du christianisme*, II, 300. I cannot agree with Méry (*Critique du christianisme*, I, 178) that

With these last works Renouvier was admitting to himself that he would never find a home in the positive religions of Western tradition—still less in the Eastern—and he wanted to see what light his philosophy could shed on the perennial questions of man's destiny. The imminence of his death and his increasing pessimism "about the situation in France and the world" perhaps made him more willing to force the limits of philosophical speculation: "Everyone still seems to believe in progress. I no longer do. At our age, one must rather try to believe in another world better than this one." [140] He did not, however, alter his fundamental approach. His method was always that of rational argument.[141]

He could not, as a philosopher, turn away from the questions of God, Creation, and immortality, and it is far from certain that contemporary philosophy has done itself a service by severing these subjects from its domain.[142] He clearly demonstrated the negation of man that

---

Renouvier ever reached a "religious faith" (*foi religieuse*). Archambault (*Renouvier*, 53, 56) sees Renouvier as moving from immanence to transcendence, but I would prefer to describe it as an emergence of transcendence within immanence.

140. Renouvier to his nephew Georges d'Albénas, December 31, 1898, quoted in Méry, *Critique du christianisme*, II, 15. "The world appears to me to be in one of these great eras whose spirit and outcome can only be measured by looking ahead a thousand years and not merely a hundred years. A confused synthesis is developing which will embrace all climates, races, and religions; what appears most clearly in the ways and means is the evil which men are seeking with all their strength to do to one another—for their good! More than ever it is necessary to lift our views and our hopes above this unfortunate earthy globe to Heaven" (Renouvier to Hyacinthe Loyson, January 31, 1900, quoted *ibid.*, II, 506).

141. Pillon, "Ouvrage récent," 96. Verneaux (*Idéalisme de Renouvier*, 279–80) argues that Renouvier's philosophy only brings him to the threshold of metaphysics, but draws back from examining the "mystery of being." Dauriac, "Testament philosophique," 337.

142. Méry (*Critique du christianisme*, II, 455) finds that both Renouvier's metaphysics and his sociology lead him to a concern with an afterlife, and (*ibid.*, II, 475) argues that his last philosophy had Judeo-Christian roots. Renouvier (*Histoire*, IV, 75) insisted that immortality was a philosophical question.

accompanies the negation of God in the materialist or pantheist philosophies of the nineteenth century.[143]

Renouvier's error was in presenting these speculations in the usual format of his philosophical inquiry. What was needed to give them their true weight and intention was a great cosmological poem. Renouvier knew he had to work within the limits of his literary talents, but he lamented that he could not be the Victor Hugo of *personnalisme,* just as he regretted that Hugo's capacity of expression was wasted in the defense of an untenable metaphysics.[144] The irony is that Renouvier's contribution to the spread of critical philosophy contributed to the disappearance of the audience for such metaphysical poetry.

The Religious Crisis of the Nineteenth Century

It should be clear by now that any understanding of Renouvier the philosopher or Renouvier the man must take into account the nature and strength of his concern for religious questions. However, just what light does this study shed on the religious crisis of the nineteenth century? Renouvier was deeply involved in that crisis, and in many ways he is a representative figure, but he also exhibits some distinctively personal reactions that need to be stressed.

From the point of view of this study, it is most useful to look upon

143. The deterministic view of the universe
is called by some *atheism,* by others *pantheism,* and it cannot be denied that the former use of words is most in accord with the common idea of God held in all ages. But the two terms can be brought together under another, more general one, which would be *impersonalism.* The negation of the human person, really, of Man, is allied with the negation of God, or the person of God; for Man, his principle and his end, is effaced if the individual human does not exist in perpetuity, if his existence is not equivalent to that of his species and his world, if the world and Man do not explain one another with reference to God. (*Dilemmes,* 233)

144. See Waelti, *Morale kantienne,* 62, and Renouvier's *Victor Hugo, le philosophe* (Paris, 1900).

the religious crisis as one aspect of the emergence of modernity, one of the factors that make the modern Western world distinct from its predecessors: "The present state of religion is nothing less than a visible, complete, and universal decadence, which, moreover, every church recognizes, except for Muslim fanaticism. But Islam is plunged into barbarity. The religious existence of the old races of Asia is no more than the memory of their past, all that remains living are superstitions." [145] From Renouvier's point of view, the religious crisis was particularly important in both the sphere of ideas and the sphere of politics and there was a mutual interaction between the two. We will look at both.

In the intellectual sphere, I want to draw attention to three areas in which religious questions are deeply embedded in the crisis of modernity: (1) the conflict of reason and authority, (2) the conflict of the individual and the community, and (3) the struggle for a whole view of man. All of these issues were evident to contemporaries, though few saw as clearly into them as Renouvier.

There was never any doubt that the rise of the authority of reason, usually defined as the application of scientific methods, and the corresponding decline of the authority of tradition, whether expressed in secular or religious institutions, was a major feature of the new age. It was a process that had begun well before the nineteenth century and indeed had reached crisis proportions in both religion and politics during the eighteenth century. As a youth, Renouvier was immersed in an atmosphere where the supremacy of reason was taken for granted.[146] That supremacy would never be a question for him. In religious matters, he could never accept anything without submitting it to the verdict of his reason. That verdict was very severe regarding the mythological and theological traditions of Christianity.[147]

But this rationalist enthusiasm had its self-generated limits. While

145. *Histoire,* IV, 648.

146. For Renouvier's version of the distinction between philosophy and religion and the origins of their conflict, see *Esquisse,* I, 101–104.

147. "But how can reason recognize itself in the mythical and legendary parts of the Christology?" (Renouvier to Secrétan, April 13, 1869, in *Correspondance de Renouvier et Secrétan,* 21).

Renouvier was far from the first French philosopher to study Kant, he may well have been the first to take seriously Kant's message about the limits of reason. He would apply this insight to develop a critique of "scientism" that I have considered elsewhere, and he also saw that it implied the permanent existence of a sphere of action for religion. Unlike others who recognized a religious sphere, he would not treat it as a residue, a shrinking portion destined to disappear with the march of knowledge.

Thus in religion as in other questions, Renouvier combined an uncompromising rationalism with a vigorous critique of the abuse of the name of reason, an abuse that was one of the most widespread and damaging habits of the intellectual world of the nineteenth century. Moreover, he would show that this sense of the limits of reason need not lead us into philosophical skepticism, and this too was not easy in the nineteenth century, for skepticism makes its appearance whenever old authorities have been undermined and the rationalist claims of the new authorities are obviously too pretentious.

Renouvier saw that in religion agnosticism has its place where we do not yet have enough information and where we can never have enough information, the first a personal situation, the latter more general. By temperament, he hated to have to say "I do not know" but was easily reconciled where he could say "I cannot know." He made a great effort, which others would have done well to imitate, to measure the degree of certainty with which he could rationally adhere to each of his beliefs in religious matters. Because of the atmosphere of religious struggle, this attitude was not common in his century, and Renouvier had not reached it from indifference. It was an expression of his concern.

The conflict between the individual and the community is an eternal one in the history of Western Christianity, inherent in its religious nature. In his "analytic" history of Christianity, Renouvier insisted that the message of Jesus was one of individual, not collective, salvation.[148] But he recognized that when expectations for an early end to this world were disappointed, the ongoing institution of the Church naturally brought to

148. *Histoire,* IV, 347; see also, Méry, *Critique du christianisme,* I, 344, II, 125.

the fore the communal aspects of the faith. In this it would be aided by the sociopolitical developments of the Middle Ages, though Renouvier is not far from attributing these to the influence of the Church. In matters of doctrine the Church had a natural penchant for the creation of an orthodoxy beyond individual challenge, but the leeway allowed varied considerably from age to age. The rise of an intellectual theology seemed disastrous to Renouvier because it contributed to the impulse for uniformity and belief in the certainty of dogma. The value of individual thought and religious conscience would be effectively reasserted only by the Renaissance and Reformation, as a result, he thought, of their reference to the values of classical antiquity and the early Church.

From the fifteenth century on, individualism became increasingly the dominant characteristic of the modern mentality, in religion as in every other sphere. By the beginning of the nineteenth century, it was also recognized as not an unmixed blessing, and the values of community were being reasserted from both a religious and a rationalist viewpoint.

Renouvier's individualism took shape in the conflict with the social views of his early Saint-Simonian friends even more than from his earlier clash with religious authority as embodied in the schools. The residue of Saint-Simonian community remained stronger in him than the sense of belonging to a Christian community, a sense that had never been more than weak. As a result, his effort to promote social and political policies that would take into account both the value of the individual and the importance of the community would be more important than his effort at a similar balance in religious matters. The modern Catholic community seemed to him so determined on the suppression of individual conscience that he remained blind to the human values of its community. Contemporary Protestantism was clearly committed to the individual conscience and thus attracted Renouvier, though he would never really enter into its spiritual community.

He recognized intellectually the strength that people may draw from belonging to a religious communion, but he could not feel it himself, a trait he certainly shares with many nineteenth- and twentieth-century intellectuals. Still, he recognized as ideal a situation in which the individual through the exercise of his moral free will chose to belong to a religious community and respected the right of others to choose differently.

Renouvier's arguments in favor of individualism were philosophical rather than historical and thus another aspect of the way he set himself against certain basic trends of his century. But his position was not one taken in ignorance of the historical development of Western individualism, though it was in opposition to an historicist explanation of that development. Religion could remain important in Renouvier's overall scheme of thought in no small part because he could see a thread of individualism running through Christianity from its beginnings. He could thus see the possibility of a faith compatible with the ideal of moral autonomy that his reason had chosen as a supreme value.

To what extent did Renouvier's religious opinions contribute to the effort to balance the individual and the community that marked his thought as a whole? It is difficult to disentangle cause and effect here. To what extent did he see religion as having a useful role in promoting this balance in everyday life? He does seem to have seen some potentiality in Protestantism but to have underestimated the civilizing role of Catholicism.[149] But clearly he saw this role as important for the future as long as men lived in a state of war, that is, for the remainder of the existence of the human race on this planet.

Did he see any hope for ending the religious crisis of his century? His excesses of optimism in this direction were rare, but he set himself to thinking about the grounds for an escape from that crisis even though he was basically pessimistic about the chances of achieving very much, at least in Catholic France. Yet he avoided the excesses of hope and despair that have been the more common reaction of Western intellectuals over the past two centuries.

The struggle for a whole view of man is perhaps a less well-defined concept, and in any case I will have to deal with it more briefly. One of the most obvious consequences of the developments of the nineteenth century was to fragment the study of man: Physiology and psychology, philosophy and sociology, would increasingly go their own ways, each claiming at least implicitly to embody the most important insights. Even where the conclusions of different specialties tended to converge, such convergence would seem only fortuitous.

149. He did recognize it as having helped protect the West from orientalism in religion (Méry, *Critique du christianisme*, II, 188).

There were, to be sure, heroic attempts at integration, as in Auguste Comte's vision of "sociology" or Herbert Spencer's evolutionism. But in both this integration of the study of man was bought, in Renouvier's opinion, at the price of the loss of human individuality. The religious orientations of these two thinkers were not important in this outcome. When Comte became convinced of the inadequacy of his (yet undeveloped) sociology, he formulated on top of it, at the newly raised summit of his scientific pyramid, the Religion of Humanity. In this a certain wholeness was achieved only by reduction of the individual to a worshiper of the community. Spencer's evolutionism, paired with an agnosticism in which religion dealt with the unknowable, seemed to Renouvier just another modern pantheism that like its predecessors solved the problem of the individual by abolishing him. The price in both cases was not simply intellectual confusion but the promotion of despotism and the abolition of freedom. Was this what modernity would inevitably mean?

As in the intellectual, I want to draw attention to three areas in the political sphere in which religious questions are deeply embedded in the crisis of modernity: (1) democracy and the separation of society from the state, (2) the loss of sacred authority by the state, and (3) the role, a necessary one, of anticlericalism in the founding of the Third Republic. To some extent, these developments were less evident to contemporaries than the ones addressed above, perhaps because they were to become clearer only with a certain experience of the later nineteenth or even the twentieth century.

The distinction of society and the state became fully conscious to French political thinkers only with the Revolution when Rousseau was recognized as the founder of modern French thinking on this subject.[150] Rousseau pointed out the difficulties that arise from this separation when it comes to legitimizing any actual state. But it was Saint-Simon who first gave full expression to the feeling that the state, as it had existed for centuries, was superfluous in the modern world.

Society in its economic and intellectual functions becomes all that matters. Western religious tradition had tended to blur the society-state

150. For a recent analysis of how Rousseau has been interpreted and misinterpreted, see Julliard, *Faute à Rousseau*.

distinction in theory and in practice. Catholics persisted in seeing the state, in the person of the ruler, as established by God and under the general oversight of his ministers, so that the only "society" they recognized, that of the community of believers, could not effectively be opposed to it. The state could fail in its duties to the society only in the sense of failing to conform to the laws of God as interpreted by his voice on earth. The attitude of the Protestant reformers was not fundamentally different, though political realities forced them to an accommodation expressed in the motto *cuius regio eius religio*. Like Renouvier, one may see in the attitude of the Saint-Simonians and others a kind of laic transcription of the Catholic attitude.

When one looks at nineteenth-century political doctrines, it is sometimes difficult to say whether they should be classified as absorbing the state in society or society in the state, so much do the practical consequences of such views resemble each other. Renouvier, I think, tended to view the Catholic ideal as an effort to monopolize the power of the state in the interests of one part of society (which claimed, to be sure, to speak for the whole). This is also the view he had of socialism and communism. In the circumstances of nineteenth-century France, he recognized these as the main dangers to individual freedom. At the same time, he recognized the danger of another kind of absorption of the state by society, that embodied in the extremes of laissez-faire liberalism, a view in which the state becomes—almost—as superfluous as it was to Saint-Simon. Laissez-faire was an idea that could make sense only in the state of peace. In this world, something more than the night-watchman state would always be necessary.

Renouvier's position is one essential to the viability of democracy. Society and the state are both distinct and necessary. The state is (or should be) the political expression of the common interests of society's members. Society is not a "thing in itself," for its reality is found in the individuals who compose it, but *solidarity in evil and in good* means that it is not just an aggregate of atoms. Political life is an area of struggle over issues that cannot be definitively resolved.

His religious views have a definite if subordinate part in the formation of these conclusions. The state is always a necessary counterweight to those social forces that seek to compel conformity to a nonrational doctrine. Without it, a free society cannot exist. Religion in society, on the other hand, may function as a safeguard against the monopolistic inclinations of any state, provided that the religion itself respects the dictates of individual conscience. The religious crisis of the nineteenth century produced a restricted group with a nostalgia for the days when the state recognized itself, at least verbally, as subordinate to the church but also a more numerous group that sought to make a religion of the state and a God of humanity. Renouvier showed that it was possible to be modern without accepting the inevitability of either radical solution.

Another way of looking at the change in the relations between society and the state is to say that with the Revolution the French state (and others to follow) suffered a permanent loss of their sacred authority. While this is most obviously a political development of the greatest importance, it also entails a change in the traditional relations between church and state that radically alters the place of the church in society. When the authority of the state is believed to derive from man, as organized in society, the state has no further need for a divine sanction. Indeed, such a sanction would be a source of conflict unless that particular church and society happened to coincide, which was far from the case, even in Catholic France.

The state may respect the Catholic church as "the religion of the vast majority of Frenchmen" (as one French constitution put it) but must consider itself independent from and superior to the Church in those areas of legitimate state action. The secular arm can no longer be invoked to execute the will of the Church. The Catholic church—like the other churches, whether recognized by the state or not—becomes a part of society on a par with other social organizations regarding its relations with the state.[151] There can be no doubt that the logic of the modern state entails the separation of church and state.

Logic and experience, however, are two different things. Renouvier and other French liberals recognized the logic of the separation of church and state but were also aware that it could not be achieved overnight. For one thing, the Church could hardly be expected to surrender readily

---

151. His idea was for all churches to have the common status of private associations, none to have a privileged relation with the state.

the privileged position of centuries. The doggedness with which it fought back from the dark days of the Convention showed that it was still a church militant.

Despite the efforts of a few liberals, most Church leaders understood that the kind of church-state relations they were accustomed to could flourish only under a monarchical form of government. Experience led them to prefer the traditional monarchy, of course, but they found it was also possible to adapt to a more modern form of authoritarian government. Bonaparte would do, no matter how nostalgic one might be for Bourbon. This is why the movement to establish a democratic republic in France in the nineteenth century had to be anticlerical.

It was also why the republicans could not be content with a simple separation of church and state. The functioning of a modern democratic state requires its citizens to have an attitude about the relations of society and the state different from the attitude inculcated by the French Church in the nineteenth century. The undoubted support to authoritarian government given by that teaching may not be absolutely inherent in Catholicism, as Renouvier and others thought—at least the twentieth century has offered some hope on this score—but the history of France to that time offered no reasons to believe in the possible reconciliation of Rome and a French republic. Their historical analysis of the failures of the First and Second republics led French liberals to the conclusion that a people must be educated to believe in the value of a free society and a responsible government. To the extent that the Catholic church was in fact and not just in the liberals' imagination an obstacle to that education, the anticlerical campaigns of the early Third Republic were fully justified.

None of this justifies the revolutionary history of violence against the Church, the clergy, and the faithful, a violence that disgraced and threatened to discredit almost every uprising. Nor does it justify the hatred of religion common on the extreme Left, even when not manifested in violence. But to interpret the republican anticlerical campaign as an ideological mask for the advance of bourgeois economic interests is to put oneself on the side of an ideology as hostile to democracy and freedom as the French Catholic church itself in the nineteenth century.

Renouvier's part in the anticlerical struggle (discussed earlier) was distinguished by the vigor with which he pursued the necessities for the creation of a modern democratic society and his ability to avoid all antireligious excesses in the process. His religious thought and his sympathy for the differing religious faiths of others ensured an alertness to the rights of others. His polemic was always aimed at ideas, institutions, and practices rather than individuals. Catholics who set out to argue with him by correspondence were astounded to discover the mildness and modesty of this vigorous debater.[152]

Renouvier frequently expressed his regret that differences of opinion could rarely be kept from becoming conflicts of persons. He could not be hypocritical and mask his opinions, but the charm of his apologies for having to differ revised the opinion more than one Catholic held of this resolute enemy. In his last years, Renouvier would be in friendly correspondence with both Protestant pastors and Catholics priests; he felt more at home with them than he did in the free-thinking circles of anticlericalism.[153]

One of the reasons Renouvier was able to maintain contact, however attenuated, with Christianity was his rejection of two of the more popular responses to the religious crisis of the century: positivism and pantheism.[154] This was a part of his resistance to all forms of determinism and antihumanism. Christianity, though in his opinion much corrupted, had the merit of preserving the distinctiveness and centrality of man and the potentiality of reinforcing man's aspiration for freedom. This was one of the reasons he quarreled with liberal Protestant pastors over their efforts to assimilate evolutionism, in which he saw a mechanistic, dehumanizing view of the universe. Interested though he was in a future life, the central focus of Renouvier's religious thought was on this world and the consequences of religious beliefs in contemporary society. He saw clearly that a world from which religious faith was absent would not be a better world and would not, contrary to the views of many

152. See, for example, Moisant, *Psychologie*, 270–71, 280.
153. Méry, *Critique du christianisme*, II, 498–99; most notably, the dissident priest Hyacinthe Loyson, married and foe of papal infallibility (*ibid.*, I, 482–84). Méry publishes several of Renouvier's letters to Father Loyson.
154. He saw any possible religious revival as tending to Gnosticism or a modern Alexandrianism (*Esquisse*, II, 330). He likened the present to a new Hellenistic age (*Histoire*, IV, 742–45).

rationalists, be a freer one or even a more rational one.[155] "The depths where the religious conscience is seated in man show us in the decadence of formal beliefs and organized practices the gravest of alarming symptoms for the future of European society." [156]

Still, Renouvier's approach was an intellectual one. Despite a knowledge of religious history and Church doctrine that would have done credit to a theology professor, he did not have the inner experience of a believer.[157] It is an exaggeration to portray him as a pagan, pre-Christian philosopher, even when this is meant to be sympathetic, though his enthusiasm for classical thought was strong.[158] He was very much a modern man, even a child of his century (so fertile in nostalgias), and his efforts to grapple with the religious question of that century are those of a post-Descartes rationalist philosopher. Though presenting his philosophy as compatible with the "essentials" of Christianity, Renouvier would to the end believe that his philosophy was morally and logically superior to any religion.[159]

What marks Renouvier as belonging to his century rather than ours is his faith in the capacity of philosophy to provide both true and useful answers to those questions that man persists in posing to himself: "My

155. He felt a need for the alliance of religion and philosophy against their common enemies (*Esquisse*, II, 353–54). Méry (*Critique du christianisme*, II, 270) says that for Renouvier, "Irreligion goes hand in hand with irrationalism"; see also *Critique du christianisme*, II, 280–81.

156. *Histoire*, IV, 740.

157. Moisant (*Psychologie*, 297–98) was impressed. Renouvier was up to date on biblical exegesis, especially Protestant (Méry, *Critique du christianisme*, II, 105*n*2).

158. If Prat is to be believed, Renouvier's last search for consolation took him from the Bible to Lucretius and Epictetus (Méry, *Critique du christianisme*, II, 469–70). Prat was a Hellenist hostile to Protestantism.

159. *Personnalisme*, 223–24. Renouvier's rationalism here is far from the arrogance of gnosticism or even the assurance of the theologians. He never lost sight of the limits of reason; see Méry, *Critique du christianisme*, I, 172. Méry (*Critique du christianisme*, II, 497) insists that Renouvier's philosophic method prevented him from following out his religious sentiments. The very strength of his philosophic faith isolated him from religion.

ambition, for which I was no doubt destined by the form of the talents heaven gave me, has been for nearly 50 years to labor in the traces and at my rank in that lineage of thinkers who have set out to discover the high truths through reason—and later to assure themselves of the limits within which this is possible, and the means, if there are any, of satisfying both mind and heart independently of any recourse to those affirmations of belief which rely on history and traditions." [160]

At the same time, he had to admit that philosophy could not save the world, in the sense of bringing about a world ruled by reason. Religion was more capable of motivating the majority of mankind. [161] What makes him of continuing relevance for our century is his demonstration that one can avoid the pitfalls of scientism that have left so much of modern thought helpless in the face of totalitarianism. There would be no point in seeking to revive Renouvier's philosophical faith in all its complexities, but his philosophical approach to the problems of this world has not exhausted its beneficial potential.

Any movement that aspires to introduce more justice into society, Renouvier insisted, will destroy itself if it tries to rely on a purely "scientific" or "natural" view of man, for such views are hostile to the idea of individual rights and to human solidarity. "Materialist and atheistic socialism is unaware that, outside of the sects, many thinkers who have a feeling for the moral needs of the human soul have for a long time— since the theological doctrine of the Middle Ages ceased to rule men's spirits—felt that the world is suffering from the lack of faith in a transcendent truth." [162]

160. Renouvier to Hyacinthe Loyson, February 13, 1889, quoted in Méry, *Critique du christianisme*, II, 504–505. Renouvier considered the lack of philosophy to be a mark of inferiority in a society (*Quatrième essai*, 723).

161. *Histoire*, IV, 776. Cf. Roure, *Doctrines et problèmes*, 151–52. Renouvier wrote to Loyson (February 2, 1903): "Philosophers are isolated men" ("*Les philosophes sont des isolés*") (quoted by Méry, *Critique du christianisme*, II, 509).

162. *Histoire*, IV, 741; cited by Méry, *Critique du christianisme*, II, 348, as on p. 742. The last part of this paragraph was used by Julien Benda as an exordium to *Trahison des clercs*.

IV

Individualism and Community

The great modern liberal movement which
began during the Renaissance and Reformation, has reached its apogee in our century and, at least in economic matters, is
ending at this very moment, in a reaction
proportionate to the action, and which is
the most extensive, the most serious, the
least accidental manifestation of the socialist spirit that can be cited in the history of
Europe. The liberal reaction will perhaps
appear in its turn.

—Renouvier, *Histoire*

One of the key questions facing Western society in
the nineteenth century, as in the twentieth, was the
proper relations between the individual and society. Nowhere was this
problem more acutely felt than in France, the Revolution having made
evident the practical character of the question. The impact of the Revolution on French thinking about the relations of the individual and society was to aggravate both the individualist and communitarian strains.
People saw individualism as either one of the great gains of the Revolution or one of its most pernicious outcomes.

The former were concerned to defend it against a recrudescence of
the Old Regime in politics or in religion; they were the heirs of the liberal
strain of the Enlightenment. The latter, more varied and inventive,
mostly conceded the impossibility of restoring society on its old bases
and were therefore compelled to seek a new order. This applied to the
so-called theocrats or traditionalists as well as the utopian socialists.
Most pregnant for the future was the Saint-Simonian interpretation,

which put the need for restructuring society into the framework of a philosophy of history. In various ways the search for a new "organic" age would dominate much of nineteenth-century thought. There were also a few thinkers, of whom Renouvier was the most profound, who tried to transcend this distinction and to incorporate the supreme value of the individual into a viable concept of social order.

There was general agreement that the dominant attitude of post-Revolutionary France was one of individualism. While some might deplore this development, even see it as an offense against God, and others might feel that it had not gone far enough, that it characterized only the elite of the nation, all agreed that it was both dominant and growing. So inescapable did this fact seem that French sociology—Durkheim's science of social facts—took as one of its initial tasks the sociological explanation of individualism.[1] However much sociology might be rooted in a belief in the importance of community, indeed in the historical priority of society over the individual, it had to come to terms with the social fact of individualism. Most nineteenth-century thinkers did not need the sociologists to remind them that man cannot be fully human, perhaps not human at all, except in the context of some society. But what sort of society was appropriate for the new individualist?

One of the aspects of this question most variously answered in the nineteenth century was scale: What size community best suits modern man? There were thinkers, like Auguste Comte, who responded in terms of mankind as a whole, abstracting all differences of civilization, race, or level of development, whether out of genuine universalism or having failed to notice the existence of non-European peoples. There were others who, on the contrary, focused on the minimum size of a viable, autonomous human community, though usually loosely federated into some larger grouping. These small communities might be conceived to give the freest range to individualism, as with Charles Fourier's phalansterian communities, or to root out all such individualism through the techniques of social conditioning, as with Robert Owen (the B. F. Skinner of the nineteenth century).[2]

---

1. See the chapter on Durkheim in my *From Philosophy to Sociology*.
2. For Renouvier on Robert Owen, see *Histoire*, IV, 176–87.

The French and American revolutions had not brought a definitive answer to the long debate in Western political thought whether freedom could coexist with large-scale states. Renouvier would have a nostalgia for the Greek polis like that of Rousseau for the Genevan republic, but he did not imagine that it was worthwhile to propose a restructuring of society on the basis of mere considerations of size.[3] Catholic thinkers, sometimes forgetting the direct relation of the individual to God that, as Renouvier pointed out, is at the origins and center of Christianity, sought to counter individualism by stressing man's place in the community of believers, organized in widening circles from the parish to the nation to the universal Church.

Surprisingly enough, serious reflection paid less attention to the most successful idea of community in the nineteenth century: nationalism. It was perhaps inevitable in the age of evolutionism and the rise of modern biology that the most popular conception of nationality would be racial. Renouvier was one of the century's most vigorous critics of the idea of "natural nationality," which he attacked as false to the reality of human history and an idea with harmful consequences. Without denying the diversity of human communities, without falling into the humbug of twentieth-century anthropology that finds them all of equal value, he insisted that these differences resulted not from primitive, natural characteristics but from what peoples had done with their human potential and especially their moral liberty. The true races were not ethnic (*éthnique*) but ethical (*éthique*).[4] The same physical qualities could produce highly different results, which tended to have cumulative effects as a result of solidarity. But even those races which had sunk so low as to be incapable of moral progress should be recognized as part of the same humanity.[5]

Renouvier argued that our common humanity did not depend on a common origin. He felt that the linguistic differences between, for example, Aryans and Semites were evidence of separate origins, but this radical incompatibility of language was no detraction from their com-

3. *Personnalisme*, 152–55.
4. *Quatrième essai*, 212, 552; see Cornwell, *Principes du droit*, 139–41.
5. *Quatrième essai*, 85, 87, 724.

mon humanity. Semites and Aryans had displayed different characters in their history, though they were not clearly distinguishable physiologically.[6] Both were essential parts of the heritage of Western man. Renouvier would bitterly denounce the rise of anti-Semitism at the time of the Dreyfus affair. What mattered for a human community was not similarities of origin but the existence of common concepts of justice and law. The idea of natural nationality was thus destructive of historically evolved communities and a powerful source of international conflict.[7]

Though nationalism was becoming the attitude of most thinkers, it was seldom subjected to much analysis as a mode for bridging the gap between the individual and the community, except when it became a political instrument in moments of crisis or war.[8] And yet the nation was increasingly the one community for which Europeans were willing to sacrifice the individual, and not just others but themselves. However conceived, nationality was a potent source of conflict both within and between existing states in the nineteenth century. Renouvier was sensitive to the problems of minority nationalities and defended the right of oppressed peoples to revolt and to seek their liberty. He irritated French nationalists by insisting that Alsace did not naturally belong to France any more than to Germany and that Alsatians alone had the right to decide their future.[9]

At the same time, he had no romanticized concept of the moral superiority of small national groups and was well aware of their propensity to quarrel and fight. Even the Greek polis had been far from admirable

6. *Ibid.,* 558–64, 553–54.

7. Archambault, *Renouvier,* 49–50; Picard, *Idées sociales,* 167–79.

8. The German annexation of Alsace-Lorraine in 1871 brought forth an outpouring of argument over the nature of nationality, with German scholars like David Friedrich Strauss and Theodore Mommsen asserting the rights of natural nationality, while Fustel de Coulanges and Ernest Renan defended the concept of elective nationality. See the interesting discussion in Alain Finkielkraut, *Le Défaite de la pensée* (Paris, 1987), 39–46.

9. Renouvier actually welcomed the defeat of 1870 (Renouvier to Secrétan, August 7, 1871, in *Correspondance de Renouvier et Secrétan,* 64–65). For him, no people was good as a people but only by the measure of its deeds. If he rated the French above the Prussians, it was not meant as high praise.

in this respect. He was even prepared to concede that for all its faults, the Habsburg Empire was a factor for peace in Europe and thus to hope for its reform rather than its disappearance.[10] What mattered was that people should have moral reasons for attachment to their communities, moral reasons applicable not to utopian dreams but to the actual state of war (see Chapter I). A certain sense of national community was thus necessary if France was to defend itself against the newly risen German nation.[11] The defense of the nation by intellectuals is usually seen, even by themselves, as a temporary deviation from their more serious thought about the individual and society, as if this could be abstracted from the realities of modern human organization.

At the practical level, one of the most pressing issues for Renouvier was what Leonard Krieger has called "the ultimate question of all politics—the limits of civil obedience."[12] Renouvier's combination of individualism and solidarity leads to a balanced solution to this question, but not one that offers easy answers, for his solution requires the integration of moral ideals as defined by philosophic reflection with an appreciation of the realities of a particular situation.

He remained constant to the orientation he had shown in the *Manuel republican* of 1848: "I am not dreaming of the ideal community nor of total devotion, but I am reconciling liberty with equality, the independence of persons with the power of the Republic, and property with public welfare."[13] Evaluation of situations is by nature more difficult to achieve than the formation of right principles, and Renouvier always advises us to take our ignorance into account. At the theoretical level, his doctrine gives full support to the supremacy of the individual over the state or any other social institution. The main function of such institutions is to "defend, with the common force, the rights or liberties of each

10. *Histoire*, IV, 727–28. Since 1919, an increasing number of liberals have come to share this view.

11. *Ibid.*, 572. The necessity for national defense created a kind of vicious circle; there could be no duty to sacrifice one's nation by disarmament (*ibid.*, 705). On Renouvier as advocate of a purely defensive army, see Benda, "Idées d'un républicain," 224–25.

12. Leonard Krieger, *The German Idea of Freedom* (Boston, 1957), 251.

13. *Manuel républicain* (1904), 298–99.

individual against the unjust activities of others."[14] But, as Renouvier says, a little reflection on this phrase shows us that in reality rights and liberties always have limits and that force and constraint are essential in any social order.[15]

The perfect social order, in which constraint would be unnecessary, is a utopian fantasy, hence outside the realm of practical morality. But its opposite, a social order in which the individual yields all his natural rights to the community, is immoral.[16] Though the individual accepts the limitation of his rights in order to defend them better through collective action, he must still retain the right of defense against the unjust action of the very organ of that collective defense—the state. Not the least of those rights is that of property, including the right to make a profit from its exploitation.[17]

Renouvier devoted an extensive section of his *Science de la morale* to the examination of civil disobedience. While the right is clearly established in pure morals, its applicability in practice is considerably circumscribed by the fact of solidarity.[18] No individual is sufficiently innocent of responsibility for the evils of society to be justified in claiming the benefit of an absolute application of his rights.[19] Moreover, the state of war obliges us to take into consideration the effect of exercising our right of defense on other members of society. Renouvier was thus most favorable to those methods of civil disobedience that have the least impact on others, such as emigration and passive resistance. While acknowledging the virtues of struggling for a more just society rather than withdrawing from the effort, he insisted that no one can be obliged to make the self-sacrifice such a struggle may entail.

Renouvier considered that the degrees of resistance permissible in practice depended both on the character and degree of oppression and on the possibility of successfully replacing the existing order with some-

---

14. *Histoire,* IV, 629.
15. *Ibid.,* 629–30.
16. See Picard, *Idées sociales,* 202; *Deuxième essai,* 555.
17. *Histoire,* IV, 630–31.
18. Cavallari, *Charles Renouvier,* 102–105.
19. See Picard, *Idées sociales,* 179.

thing better. Purely individual revolt risked doing more harm than good. Joining with others was potentially more efficacious, but also more risky. Group action had the merit of a greater possibility of being justified because many had to agree on the existence of the evil to be remedied. But those prepared to take action against an unjust government were almost always a minority, and it was not easy for an active minority to avoid offending the rights of the majority. Even if the position of the revolutionaries was morally superior, if it was also too far ahead of the general population, the revolutionaries would be likely to resort to violence and coercion not merely against the unjust government but against the recalcitrant majority and would thus provoke a reaction likely to return the society to a condition worse than before.[20]

With the experience of the French Revolution before him, Renouvier did not conceive the possibility of an enduring Jacobin success like that of the Bolsheviks. On the other hand, the Bolshevik revolution, like others of the twentieth century, seems to have amply justified his pessimism. Revolution, in his view, was likely to be successful and morally justified only when the rottenness of the existing order was so evident and generally acknowledged that little effort was needed to topple it. History afforded but few examples: 1688, 1776, 1830, 1848.[21] The balance that Renouvier achieved between the rights of the individual and the demands of solidarity was thus very much in the tradition of John Locke.

Laissez-Faire and Socialism

Whether limited in vision to the existing political states or national communities, most nineteenth-century French thought about the relations of individual and community took one or the other of two sharply conflicting approaches: laissez-faire liberalism or socialism and communism.

The common usage of the French language has made it difficult to talk about liberalism because of its tendency to equate the term *libéralisme* with laissez-faire economic theory. I have argued elsewhere for the

20. See *ibid.*, 180–81.
21. *Ibid.*, 181–84.

importance of a larger sense of the term for understanding the history of French political thought, and I will try here to use the term *laissez-faire* to designate a view of the proper relations of the individual and the community derived from the economic theory of Adam Smith, given its classic French development by Jean-Baptiste Say and Frédéric Bastiat.[22]

It is important to recognize that laissez-faire has its origins in economic theory, more specifically in an effort to discover the conditions that would maximize the production of wealth for society as a whole. Individualism thus appears in it as a means rather than an end. The free pursuit of individual advantage is justified as serving the interests of society. In the process, it also benefits given individuals, but only *à titre provisoire*, for what the society of free competition raises up it also brings down. No one acquires any right to an established position; hereditary advantages are easily lost. Indeed, the greater the individual insecurity, the more freely the mechanisms of the market can function and the greater the benefit, at least in aggregate wealth, to the society as a whole.

One of the drawbacks of the laissez-faire approach is its unidimensional view of man, its confinement to "economic man" as if he were all of man. The German historical school of economics in the nineteenth century would try to overcome this limitation, and twentieth-century economists would generally recognize its artificiality.[23] This awareness, however, is counterbalanced by the sense that all sciences proceed by abstraction and that no "*science humaine*" would have any chance of success if it was required from the beginning to take account of the whole man.

Unfortunately, when they proceeded from the abstract world of economic laws to the advocacy of public policy, nineteenth-century advocates of laissez-faire tended to forget that it is necessary to restore many of the considerations that were excluded in the process of developing those "laws."[24] It is not simply that the conditions for the functioning of a laissez-faire economy as dreamed of by the economists have never ex-

22. Logue, *From Philosophy to Sociology,* Chap. I.
23. See Richard, *Question sociale,* 345.
24. Renouvier considered economics a pseudoscience (*Histoire,* IV, 560).

isted and appear unlikely ever to be realized. There are more fundamental difficulties with laissez-faire as an approach to the question of the individual and society, some of them recognized in the nineteenth century, others clearer in the light of later experience.

Laissez-faire did not make its appearance in a vacuum of intellectual abstraction, and Adam Smith was certainly aware of having to work within a political as well as an economic context.[25] In France, laissez-faire was clearly a liberating movement in the face of the Old Regime's economic order. It was a significant part of the individualist movement that has made modern society distinctively different from that of the Old Regime. It was thus a good illustration of why Saint-Simon would baptize the eighteenth century a "critical period," and it gives us some idea why Marx would develop the idea of "bourgeois ideology."

But these reactions against laissez-faire would present their own difficulties and dangers, sometimes surprisingly linked to those of their rival. The laissez-faire economists would see their position as a limit beyond which thought could not progress, except in detail, and their critics would see it as a transition, a historically necessary phase but one that would necessarily disappear in the development to follow, that is, in the near future. Experience would disappoint both groups, which is another way of saying that they all developed only partial truths, the common experience of man in the face of life's most difficult questions.

Conservative critics of laissez-faire saw in it first an affront to their moral ideas. It appeared not merely to advocate the right of the strongest but to show a cruel indifference to the fate of the weak, the victims of progress, the poor in general. Laissez-faire was an affront to Christianity, especially in its Catholic version, for Protestantism had open before it more possibilities for adapting Christian charity and love to the conditions of an individualistic society.[26] Advocates of laissez-faire were sel-

25. Renouvier credited the German *Kathedersozialisten* with a greater sense of the factors other than pure material interests that affect men's conduct with respect to their interests (*Histoire*, IV, 612). But he also noted that the experience of Germany was more favorable to the action of the state as an agent of progress than was the case in Great Britain (*ibid.*, 613).

26. Renouvier welcomed Christian concern for the poor, but he believed that religion offered no insights into how the problem of poverty might be solved (*ibid.*, 617).

dom so detached from Christian morality as to consider charity an out-moded idea, at least until biological evolutionism produced its impact on the thought of Herbert Spencer later in the century. As we shall see, the dangers of amoralism in laissez-faire turn out to have a great deal in common with the same dangers in socialism. Both derive from the way they consider the relations of the individual to society.

Both socialist and conservative critics of laissez-faire—and socialists sometimes acknowledged their borrowings from the conservatives in this matter—saw in laissez-faire a potential anarchism, a destruction not merely of government but of any viable social order.[27] The minimum of government advocated by the economists as necessary to make the laissez-faire system work was a concession to the real world, out of harmony with the foundations of their system.

Laissez-faire in its essence leads to the total absorption of the state by society and continually challenges the existence of the state as an evil, however necessary. Starting as an argument for the primacy of economics over politics, an argument perhaps necessary to liberate economic activity from the dead hand of the Old Regime state, laissez-faire recognizes as legitimate only a politics in the service of economic interests. Economic interests themselves are presented as an adequate foundation for the community in the absence of any autonomous political life. Even if it were certainly true that such a society would maximize the wealth of the society, it could not provide an adequate basis for human community. And it could not serve as an adequate foundation for the liberty of the individual.

What laissez-faire gives to the individual's freedom in one sense it takes away in another, for the free competition of individuals for economic survival (or wealth) is, after all, justified by an argument that is a kind of historical determinism.[28] Not only do the laws of the market produce their beneficial results for the community regardless of the intentions of those who are trying to benefit only themselves, but those laws also ensure that when men act for other than selfish reasons, the results tend to diminish the wealth of the community. Adam Smith's "in-

27. On the Saint-Simonians and Maistre, see *ibid.*, 189.
28. I got this idea from the discussion of Friedrich Hayek in Ferry and Renaut, *Des droits de l'homme*, 149–51.

visible hand," by shaping the consequences of men's actions, deprives them of any meaningful liberty. It is not that liberty requires that our choices should always produce what we intend; human experience is too marked with the contrary. But if there is no possible correlation between our chosen ends and the outcomes of our actions, we are no better than puppets of forces acting on or through us.

The "invisible hand" is thus a close relative—more narrowly conceived and based on a different philosophical tradition—of Hegel's "cunning of reason," which so cleverly uses the human race to produce the results only it has consciously aimed at.[29] Nevertheless, it must be acknowledged that to the extent that the determinism inherent in laissez-faire is not always acknowledged by or even conscious in most of its defenders, the antiliberty consequences of it do not appear as readily in real life as do the similar consequences of socialism.

In the real world, a modified laissez-faire has to be preserved as a barrier against the more virulent forms of suppression of the individual by society or the state threatened by modern socialism. Renouvier defended a large measure of economic freedom as essential to other freedoms, but he repeatedly and vigorously condemned laissez-faire doctrine. The intellectual error of laissez-faire, as he saw it, was to confuse—just like the utopian socialists—the real world, the "state of war," with the ideal but nonexistent "state of peace."[30]

The moral ideal of an economic transaction, a view he shared with many laissez-faire economists, was one of perfect reciprocity freely entered into by both parties. But such transactions do not exist in this world any more than moral actions in conformity with the categorical imperative. Except in the rarest cases, it would be as disastrous to the individual to attempt the one as the other. In economics as in morals it

29. As Richard (*Question sociale*, 6–9) argues, "The doctrine of the harmony of interests is immoralist and it prepares the way for the acceptance of overtly immoralist doctrines like social darwinism."

30. Picard, *Idées sociales*, 124, 195–96, 218. The laissez-faire thinkers offended Renouvier by treating the state of war (which they failed to recognize as such) as legitimate and recognizing no higher justice than the rules of prudent conduct.

is necessary to recognize the state of war. An economic liberalism that recognizes this, that sets as its objective the kind of liberty attainable in this world, that does not repudiate the pursuit of justice—a liberty organized, in other words, around the "right of defense"—would have his support.[31]

Renouvier's critique of laissez-faire theory is to some extent linked to his moral critique of contemporary society. At the level of theory, it is joined to his critique of utilitarian moral philosophy. Utilitarians are unsuccessful in their effort to derive the general interest from individual interests: "The greatest interest of each individual, in effect, would consist in being excused from having to observe the rules of justice that everyone else observed."[32] Renouvier's reaction reflects his early support of Saint-Simonian socialism, and though he repudiated his Saint-Simonianism and became a strong opponent of socialism, he retained substantial elements of the socialist critique of modern society.

It was the socialist remedies that he believed would be worse than the disease. The main intellectual danger came from the socialists' historical determinism—and here Marx was repeating the errors of Saint-Simon—and the political dangers came from their statism, their reliance on the state to create economic justice.[33] Renouvier thus sought to remain at a distance from both those who made too much of the role of the state and those who made too little. The failure of the 1848 revolution he attributed to those socialists like Louis Blanc who naïvely believed the state could play a role that went against the habits, expectations, interests, and desires of most of the population and to those antisocialists who refused to recognize that the state had a responsibility

31. Renouvier, like Fourier, had great reservations about the morality of commerce (*Histoire*, IV, 599), but he admitted that "merchants are the most energetic defenders of economic liberty and of the civil and political liberties that are connected with it" (Richard, *Question sociale*, 310; see Picard, *Idées sociales*, 243–45). Nonetheless, Renouvier preferred commercial to military civilizations (*Quatrième essai*, 568).

32. *Esquisse*, I, 359; see also 435.

33. Use of the state to maintain equality among citizens would destroy everybody's liberty (Cavallari, *Charles Renouvier*, 163).

in the face of the social problem.[34] Neither state nor society could remain indifferent.

The continuing failure of the French state in the nineteenth century to deal adequately with the socioeconomic problems of the working class was a major source, in Renouvier's opinion, of the growing success of the socialist movement.[35] "The progress of socialism in the public mind, its entry into militant politics, have been inevitable in spite of everything, because the function of manual labor has undergone a painful crisis after the abolition of the guarantees of the Old Regime in favor of pure liberty. The promises of the optimistic economists, the benefits of *laisser-faire* have not been realized."[36] The workers could not be faulted for seeking to ameliorate their miserable conditions or following a false route if nothing better was offered them. Renouvier's analysis of why it was a false route that had come to dominate the thinking of the socialist movement was always balanced by a search for those elements in the socialist tradition that took some account of the potential of human liberty. He would always prefer Fourier to Saint-Simon, Proudhon to Marx.[37]

34. *Histoire,* IV, 204; see Agulhon, Preface to *Manuel républicain,* 22.

35. *Histoire,* IV, 3–4.

36. *Personnalisme,* 199–200.

37. In the socialist aspects of his thought, Renouvier was nobody's disciple (Picard, *Idées sociales,* 322). Fourier was one of the few—perhaps the only— socialist to recognize the *solidarité du mal* (*Histoire,* IV, 171). Renouvier applauded his reliance on individual freedom as the means to reform but deplored his neglect of duty and reason (*Quatrième essai,* 180). Renouvier felt that Fourier came the closest to offering a practical economic organization because of his recognition of the interrelated roles of capital, labor, and talent (*Histoire,* IV, 202). Unlike Fourier, Proudhon was a strict moralist (Mouy, *Idée de progrès,* 61–62), and Renouvier saw in him a defender of the individual (Cavallari, *Charles Renouvier,* 164–66). He felt that Proudhon's socialism was in the same line with his own "garantism" (*Histoire,* IV, 559) and insisted that the main economic theses of *Das Kapital* were to be found in Proudhon. Mouy (*Idée de progrès,* 60) is wrong in thinking Renouvier adopted Proudhon's economic doctrine with little reservation. Renouvier chided Proudhon for believing in the social efficacy of political revolutions (*Histoire,* IV, 222) and for confusing the state of war with the state of peace (*Histoire,* IV, 219–20). See also Tint, "Search for a Laic Morality," 13.

The statism that Renouvier condemned in French socialism had its roots in Saint-Simon and the development of his doctrine by the Saint-Simonians. Convinced that society had to be led by an elite, they had no interest in raising the capacity of the vast mass of society to independence or self-government.[38] The state would be run by a self-selected oligarchy of experts, a new "spiritual power," whose qualifications would include those necessary to direct the economic activity of the society. Saint-Simon and the other constructors of a new authority taught that "liberty can never achieve anything except destruction, and it ought to be banished from any true *social organization*." They intended to put a benevolent elite in charge, and Renouvier did not doubt the benevolence of their intentions.[39]

But he was also convinced that it was utter fancy to imagine that the Saint-Simonian elite could be trusted to follow their ideal of using their power to improve the moral and material conditions of the poorest and most numerous classes. In any case, the mass of men, or indeed an individual, cannot be made better by the actions of an outside force. This outside force would have to consist of men who were already of a moral superiority not attainable in existing society. The nineteenth century was not short of reformers who imagined themselves endowed with the necessary qualities, and they were often superior men in many respects, but their thought ran in this familiar vicious circle.[40]

38. Renouvier placed the intellectual roots of the different varieties of socialism in three thinkers: Saint-Simon, Fourier, and Robert Owen (*Histoire*, IV, 483–84). Renouvier attributed to the Saint-Simonians something very much akin to the *Führerprinzip* (*ibid.*, 194–95).

39. *Ibid.*, 151, 147, 160. He notes that they are not motivated by any concept of justice (*ibid.*, 155–56).

40. For a socialist economy,

One must suppose these magistrates to be invested with the same power and endowed with all the virtues as well as provided with all the necessary knowledge. This is transporting the Saint-Simonian utopia from the aristocratic and clerical mode to the democratic mode. The utopian character remains the same. It does not principally consist, as one might believe at first view, in the material difficulties of the double office of distribution of work and of consumption, enormous though this would

Renouvier saw the socialist movement as both inspired by and reacting against the French Revolution, in particular reacting against "the
spirit of civil equality and of pure liberty" that had made the Revolution
effective in destruction.[41] They could not accept the uncertainty that went
with leaving the reconstruction of post-Revolutionary society up to the
free initiative of individuals. Not wishing a return to the old order, they
proceeded to the a priori construction of a new *order,* manifesting, Renouvier insisted, the continuation under different labels of the "Catholic
spirit."[42] Experience, however, demonstrated that it is never possible to
translate a priori theories into social reality.[43]

While the Saint-Simonian movement was fractured by the rival views
and rival ambitions of its leaders, becoming bogged down in religious
mysticism, its legacy of statism was to be found in other branches of pre-
1848 French socialism. Even a socialism that sought to rebuild economic

---

be. The vices of the reigning social system founded on liberty, laisser
faire and chance, are such that we do not have the right to demand that
the system of authority, community and universal regulation should be
exempt from errors and difficulties. The utopia is especially political
and consists in the optimistic double hypothesis that the persons who
would exercise, under whatever titles, the functions of direction, sur-
veillance, and distribution would be and would remain at the moral
level of their mission, and, an even more difficult thing, that the persons
directed, supervised, who would be given their tasks for labor and their
shares of the product, would remain satisfied with their condition and
their fate whatever it might be. In sum, conscience and constant, emi-
nent good will are expected from both sides.

The improbability of this is perhaps less in the religious system
than in the others. . . . The democratic communists are under the self-
made illusion, which the Saint-Simonians avoided, that they can preserve liberty and equality while at the same time establishing a power
of constraining each citizen at his task of production and of limiting
him to his ration as consumer. (*Ibid.,* 196)

See also *Monadologie,* 274–75, 528–59. More recent technocrats continue to
display the same inconsequence (Spragens, *Irony of Liberal Reason,* 91–127).

41. *Histoire,* IV, 145.
42. *Ibid.,* 145–46.
43. *Personnalisme,* 162.

life from the bottom, like that of Louis Blanc, called upon the state to play a guiding and directing role. Renouvier did not do justice to Blanc's desire to make this a temporary role, necessary to make the transition from contemporary society, but he appreciated better than Blanc the likelihood that such a state role would become permanent and increasingly dictatorial.[44]

After 1848, the antistatist wing of French socialism was the one that followed Proudhon (more or less, for it was not always easy to tell where Proudhon was headed), and even he had a moment of weakness for the attractions of a benevolent despot.[45] When socialism passes from the realm of intellectual speculation to that of everyday politics, those socialists who conceive a positive or even a central role for the state have an advantage. However much they claim to reject the existing order of society and the state, they offer the possibility of acting within the existing framework, if only for the purpose of overthrowing it.

The extreme of believing that control of the state is the key that will permit any desired social transformation was embodied in Louis-Auguste Blanqui, whose life was one long effort at a coup d'état.[46] The seizure of power was so central to his thought that he would probably have had no idea what to do next if he had found himself in the Tuileries or the Hotel de Ville instead of Vincennes or Sainte-Pélagie. But Blanqui became one of the symbolic heroes of French socialism and its preoccupation with the state. All these statists agreed with Proudhon that the working classes were enslaved, and none imagined that a socialist state could become an even greater slave master.

If all these socialists, the statists as well as the others, believed that they were aiming at the liberation of mankind, why would Renouvier by

44. On Louis Blanc, see the fine biography by Leo Loubère, *Louis Blanc: His Life and His Contribution to the Rise of French Jacobin-Socialism* (Evanston, 1961). Blanc, Renouvier believed, explicitly identified the state and society, thus destroying individual liberty (*Histoire*, IV, 208).

45. Mouy, *Idée de progrès*, 64. For a further look at Proudhon, see Robert L. Hoffman, *Revolutionary Justice: The Social and Political Theory of P. J. Proudhon* (Carbondale, Ill., 1972).

46. For Renouvier's view of Blanqui, see *Histoire*, IV, 576–78. For a modern view, see Alan B. Spitzer, *The Revolutionary Theories of Louis Auguste Blanqui* (New York, 1957).

the end of the nineteenth century believe that "collectivism," as it was then calling itself, was the principal menace to liberty in modern society? It is easy to be convinced of this truth a hundred years later—many former socialists know the experience—but what was there in Renouvier's analysis that made him see clearly that this was the destiny of socialism?

The few socialist writers who have dealt with Renouvier have failed to come to grips with his critique and have largely been content with an "ideological unmasking" based on his social origins. Attempts to dismiss his position as an ideological defense of the old Orléanist bourgeoisie, or more commonly the ascending middle classes who made the Third Republic in their image, have failed to come to grips with the positions he actually took.[47] Renouvier's contempt for the ruling bourgeoisie of nineteenth-century France was exceeded only by his hatred of the kings and aristocrats who preceded them. He was far from satisfied with contemporary society, although he did think it was possible to do much worse.[48] The twentieth century would prove him only too right.

Renouvier continued to accept much of the pre-1848 socialist critique of the liberal economy. He turned against socialism only when it completely adopted the amoral scientism and naturalism that he denounced in laissez-faire theory. Renouvier's philosophy of liberty, not an attachment to conservative social interests, enabled him to penetrate the illusions of nineteenth-century socialism.[49] With the exception of Fourier and Proudhon, the socialists—whether utopians before 1848 or "real-

47. This is true even of John A. Scott in *Republican Ideas and the Liberal Tradition in France, 1870–1914* (New York, 1966).

48. Renouvier to Secrétan, August 13, 1875, in *Correspondance de Renouvier et Secrétan*, 118. Renouvier thought that the French lack of respect for authorities developed because of the latter's unworthiness (Benda, "Idées d'un républicain," 27). See Renouvier's remarks to Louis Prat (Prat, *Charles Renouvier*, 97–98), in which he expresses more hope for the people than for the bourgeoisie. On his continued attack on the bourgeoisie, see Picard, *Idées sociales*, 130–31. Renouvier did not hesitate to call himself a "*socialiste libéral*" or "*garantiste*" (see Picard, *Idées sociales*, 331; Jules Thomas, Preface to *Manuel républicain* [1904]).

49. See Richard, *Question sociale*, 18, for an interesting analysis of the split between philosophy and socialism in France after 1848; for a good summary, see Thomas, Preface to *Manuel républicain* (1904), 34–35.

ists" after—excluded liberty as means and end from their conceptions of social reform. The disastrous consequences in practice reflected their theoretical rejection of man, his dissolution in the realm of matter and universal determinism.[50]

The basic intellectual flaw of socialism was not its materialist metaphysics (though that did mislead many socialists into believing that they were being scientific when they were actually adhering to a metaphysical conception dating from ancient Greece) or its tendency to hypostasize "society," that is, to treat it as if it were a real person capable of having responsibilities. More fundamental was socialists' historical determinism, or to be more specific, their optimistic historical determinism.[51] The particularly dangerous socialist manifestation of this optimism was their belief in the possible—no, necessary—emergence on this earth of perfect community.[52] Even if they conceived perfect community in terms identical to Renouvier's concept of a state of peace, and some perhaps did, he saw the dangers in their conviction that it could be attained in this world,

50. Renouvier wrote, in *Histoire*, IV, 741:

In the most *advanced* parties, atheism is the undisguised profession of faith of those who take science for their banner. Pure naturalism, however, seems ill-chosen as a doctrine to furnish arguments—at least arguments drawn from the sentiment of justice—for the party of social demands. Isn't the condition of proletarians, like that of capitalists, or vice versa, the result of natural forces and of the sequence of causes? But God being part of the old social order must, like the other powers, be banished from the new order! It remains to be seen whether a moral society can do without a sovereign principle which connects man to the world, explains and guides his existence, and at least gives the idea of duty, on which every society of free men is based, a claim to our respect which the variable opinions and tastes of individuals do not have. What will this social principle be?

51. *Ibid.*, 633. Richard (*Question sociale*, 315, 339) points out the similarities (and differences) of Renouvier's critique on this point with those of the German neo-Kantians. Renouvier considered Marx and Lassalle debased Hegelians (*Histoire*, IV, 552–53). On historical optimism, see also *Monadologie*, 529–30.

52. *Histoire*, IV, 587–88, 626–27.

53. And, Renouvier points out, the effort to reach utopian goals usually provokes a reaction that leaves us with less liberty than before (*Histoire*, IV, 623–34).

especially by political action.[53] The dangers of this belief were aggravated by the expectation that the goal was near, attainable in the lifetime of those then living.

Renouvier's philosophical understanding of the conditions for true community made it clear that those conditions did not and could not ever exist in this world. As Karl Popper says, "It is indeed a principle of rationalist politics that we cannot make heaven on earth." [54] The philosophical equivalent of what Christians would call man's fallen nature was an unbridgeable obstacle to any earthly paradise. Regardless of how this came about (and Renouvier did think of a "fall"), when man has once departed from observation of the categorical imperative, no recovery of that perfect community is possible.

The very solidarity of human relations binds us more easily, Renouvier thought, to the perpetuation of evil, *solidarité du mal,* than any propagation of good. Man's liberty makes it possible for him to contract, or expand, the realm of evil in this world, at least a little bit, more in some times and places than others. But any sustained movement in the direction of perfect community is made still further impossible by the human freedom that permits any movement. What philosophy shows to be true is emphatically confirmed by any reflection on human history that is not distorted by optimistic determinism.

But even if the goal is impossible to achieve, why is it dangerous to pursue it? Does not man need ideals? Of course he does, but much depends on how he interprets them. As the French Revolution had demonstrated, secular ideals may be used to justify sending men to the scaffold as readily as religious ideals in an earlier age. Ideals must be combined with a realistic understanding of what can morally be done to advance them in the state of war in which we live.

An impossible goal, more readily than any other kind, generates fanaticism in its pursuit. The more desirable the objective, the more the true believer feels hatred for anything or anyone that appears to stand in the way, the easier it is to feel justified in whatever crime is "needed" to clear the way, to make men better, to "force them to be free": "At bottom . . . it is difficult for a collectivist like Marx, given the opinions he proclaims, to have imagined a system of community that would not be

54. Popper, *High Tide of Prophecy,* 245.

tyrannical. . . . What other outcome than absolute power does logic leave him to conceive a means of restraining individual instincts? To what sort of moral authority would he have recourse?"[55] Rulers have always made free use of *raison d'état* to justify the pursuit of their particular interests or the preservation of their power. How much more readily would governments that believed sincerely in their mission to give man perfect community trample every human right underfoot.

The real values of actual people are inevitably lost in the struggle for the unattainable—as Pascal said, "He who wants to create an angel creates a beast" ("Qui veut faire l'ange fait la bête")—and the victims are not abstractions like liberty and justice but real people.[56] Increasingly dominated by Marxism, post-1848 socialism in France adopted a determinist view of history that designated certain elements of existing society as the enemy, a powerful enemy to be respected and feared but also hated. The earthly paradise could not be attained until the bourgeoisie was eliminated "as a class." It was easy to forget that while the aristocrats had been eliminated "as a class" with the abolition of their privileges in 1789, this would not save thousands of the *ci-devants* from the guillotine a few months or years later. But their elimination did not make the Revolution "safe."

Unable to deliver its promises, the Revolution had to find new enemies continually, even within its own ranks. It was no accident, as Marxist writers like to say, that the vast majority of the victims of the Terror were ordinary working people. The socialist revolution, because it was committed to radically unrealizable goals, was bound to be even more frustrated if it kept its ideals, but almost equally driven to justify its exercise of power if it lost them. It could never run out of enemies, and it would be no accident that Russian bolshevism would massacre far more peasants and proletarians than aristocrats and bourgeois.

I doubt that even Renouvier's pessimism could have foreseen the magnitude of this human disaster (and certainly not that it would take place in Russia, the least advanced of the great powers of his day), but he would not have been greatly surprised by it or by the character of the

55. *Histoire*, IV, 567–68; see also 624.

56. Méry, *Critique du christianisme*, I, 72. Pensée No. 346, in *Les Pensées de Pascal*, ed. Francis Kaplan, (Paris, 1982), 227.

Soviet and Eastern European governments of the mid-twentieth century. He was aware of the dangers of trying to be a prophet in political matters and tried to confine his analysis to indicating large-scale trends, the conclusions to which certain positions were likely to lead. I do not, however, think it exaggerated to say that he saw the totalitarian potential in the socialist movement of the later nineteenth century. No determinist, he did not think that those potentials had to be realized, but he greatly feared that they would.

Socialism threatened to be the political realization of many of the intellectual errors of the nineteenth century: determinism, which denied man any freedom and therefore justified treating him as a thing; historical optimism, which justified any present crime in the name of an ideal future; even pantheism, which absorbed the individual in the whole, distinct from or even against the aims of individuals.

On the political level, socialism was calling for a concentration of power in the state so great that society would be not merely under its domination but utterly crushed. The absorption of society by the state had been only hinted at in the Terror. With the growth of modern industry, the levers of centralized power were longer than ever. The destruction of a society independent from, yet closely associated with, the state would be catastrophic for the individual, who would lose any refuge from state power.

The socialists complained that in any case the workers had no security in present society. Renouvier agreed, and agreed that the aim of social reform must be to provide a basic minimum of security to all members of society. But socialism was on a path that would destroy all possibility of security for the worker and enslave him to a power more remote and alien than that of the capitalists, with the added irony that this power would claim to represent the working class.[57] Socialism, he recognized, was a recipe for the most complete despotism, a dictatorship with a good conscience.

Renouvier and Liberal Democracy

The deepening pessimism of Renouvier's later years did not destroy the

57. *Histoire*, IV, 565.

social-reforming spirit with which he approached the questions of the relations of the individual and society. His philosophy of liberty rejected any fatalism of the pessimistic variety, the most common before the eighteenth century, as well as the optimistic. He knew that the influence of philosophers on the course of human events has always been minimal and indirect, but he also thought that they had a responsibility to seek truth and propagate their ideas. One never knew where or when a seed might bear fruit. Renouvier might regret that the dominant ideas of the time were not closer to his own—and even miss the more egoistic pleasure of being recognized, which came to him very late—but he understood that philosophers need not worry about being on the bandwagon of history or in tune with the evolution of the universe, without being any less concerned about the world around him. He would try to find and show to others a way to avoid the self-delusions of doctrinaire laissez-faire and deterministic socialism.[58]

Always a realist, Renouvier sought to work within the realities of contemporary society, however distasteful, and to base his reform programs on the nature of man and the human condition as his philosophy understood them.[59] Starting from the basic concept of the individual with free will, he would, not surprisingly, make political liberty the central feature of his vision of the best attainable structure of the relations of the individual and society. The aspiration to self-government is the means to the best of possible societies: "The moral and political system of the world which tends to define itself as a *government of beings by themselves*, . . . under the general laws both of the conscience and of nature, . . . necessarily engenders religions of liberty, doctrines of action, moral dignity, and exaltation of the human personality."[60]

A community of perfect freedom being impossible, one can still seek to improve existing relations. The great advantage of the liberal democratic regime is that it is the modern regime most open to reform and the

58. "Renouvier rejects all authoritarian theories as immoral and all purely liberal theories as utopian" (Lacroix, *Vocation personnelle*, 132–33).

59. Picard, *Idées sociales*, 185. Picard (*ibid.*, 319) saw Renouvier's sociopolitical thought as derived from his philosophy; see also Lacroix, *Vocation personnelle*, 140.

60. *Deuxième essai*, 688.

most capable of resisting the extremes of reaction and revolution. The exact form of the regime depends upon national circumstances. The parliamentary monarchy suited Great Britain, but in France a liberal regime would have to be a republic, at least after 1792.[61]

At heart, Renouvier's preference for the republic was philosophical, derived from its theoretical harmony with human freedom, but he also knew how far actual republics differ from the ideal.[62] Given that mankind always lives in a state of war, freedom can exist only under a political order that does not pretend to be able to give a permanent solution to all social conflicts. Regimes that are ideologically committed to such a solution, whether from a religious or a secular point of view, are necessarily oppressive in spirit, though there can be wide variations in practice. Liberty can thrive only in the framework of a government that furnishes an arena for, but puts limitations on, social conflicts.[63] Only under such a government can the idea of the rights of man find its true expression, which comes from men's recognition of the freedom inherent in each human being. The main responsibility for the defense of his rights

61. See Cornwell, *Principes du droit*, 149. Picard (*Idées sociales*, 189) says, "He concluded, however, that the republic is the form of state which best permits man to carry out his duty of [promoting] social justice." Renouvier (*Deuxième essai*, 687) equates democracy with "the free and full development of men's faculties in society" and monarchy with *repos* and stagnation. On Renouvier's great admiration for Britain, see Cornwell, *Principes du droit*, 132.

62. "Applied neo-criticism becomes the philosophy of respect for law or, as Renouvier himself put it, the philosophy of the republican idea" (Cornwell, *Principes du droit*, 138). See Picard, *Idées sociales*, 96, 121, 127. Mouy (*Idée de progrès*, 169) argues that for Renouvier, democracy integrates means and ends: "*pour la liberté par la liberté*" ("for liberty by means of liberty"). Cavallari (*Charles Renouvier*, 102) stresses the importance for the development of Renouvier's ideas of his "direct observation of the social and institutional dynamics of his time."

63. See Renouvier to Secrétan, August 13, 1875, in *Correspondance de Renouvier et Secrétan*, 120. Renouvier favored the leadership of "*radical-conservatives* who fight within their country by legal means. They are radicals with respect to their goals, but always conservatives in the choice of means to attain them" (Cornwell, *Principes du droit*, 171).

still rests, Renouvier thought, on the individual, but to prevent rights from being simply the privilege of the strongest, government must also have a role.[64]

This is why the republic has to be not only liberal but democratic. Given the egalitarian character of Renouvier's concept of justice, both theoretical and applied, he had to be a democrat. The republic was the means of reconciling liberty and equality.[65] Without a system of universal suffrage, there would be too much concentration of power in society. "Also, I am a strong democrat, though I believe as you do that the collective is by nature inferior to the individual."[66] Even if the elements of social and economic power have an influence disproportionate to their numbers under democracy, they are compelled from time to time to take account of the interests and will of the weaker but more numerous.[67]

The masses, it is true, are often ignorant, impulsive, easily swayed to the support of bad causes, like that of Louis-Napoléon, and "many democrats nourish thoughts of community or of hierarchy which would be oppressive."[68] But in Renouvier's opinion, the upper classes were not that different, and superior education was often counterbalanced by greater pride, egoism, and the sheer weight of material interests. Democratic politics will not produce perfect harmony among all these conflicting

64. *Monadologie*, 387. See Picard, *Idées sociales*, 187. Renouvier also recognized the need in practice for intermediate bodies in society (*Histoire*, IV, 536–37). For an argument in favor of the multiplication of social groups as a practical defense of freedom, see Lacroix, *Vocation personnelle*, 184–85.

65. See Cavallari, *Charles Renouvier*, 86–88.

66. Renouvier to William James, May 14, 1878 quoted in Méry, *Critique du christianisme*, I, 467.

67. Lacroix (*Vocation personnelle*, 128–29) sees a latent personalism in Renouvier's view of democracy. Majority rule is a form of organization inspired by the state of war (*Deuxième essai*, 554–55; Picard, *Idées sociales*, 144). Renouvier came to favor indirect election of deputies as a means of combining the voters' knowledge of the people they were voting for (and he preferred voting for men, not for ideas) with efficacy at the national level; see Picard's critique (*Idées sociales*, 140–43).

68. *Quatrième essai*, 130.

wills, but it does keep the verdict from ever being closed in favor of one group or another.[69]

Renouvier recognized the need for "a political and cultural growth of everybody, which allows a transformation of society 'from the bottom,' the sole guarantee against every form of despotism."[70] We easily forget how rare the defense of democracy was among political philosophers during the century of the rise of democracy.[71] The growing political strength of democracy worried most intellectuals, who saw only its drawbacks, especially those that would follow from the political incapacity of the undereducated masses.

The socialist critique of the democratic republic in France was that it did not bring genuine, let alone equal, freedom to the working class. Though Renouvier considered the socialists mistaken on the question of freedom, he did recognize an element of truth in their critique. The socialist conception of freedom as effective power, enunciated clearly by Louis Blanc, misplaced the locus of human freedom and led to a politics that effectively denied freedom to individuals.

> It was a snare, he [Louis Blanc] said, to make liberty as a *right* shine in men's eyes without giving them the assured *power* to exercise and develop the faculties for which the recognition of this right opens the way. This sophistry tended to reverse the clearest and most categorical meaning of the word *liberty* in political language, but it was very well chosen to deceive unenlightened minds. The logical vice of the idea led to the greatest possible error in social philosophy. The promise of *true li-*

69. Renouvier recognized that power corrupts (Lacroix, *Vocation personnelle*, 128). "A democrat in power is always an aristocrat, if he isn't already one before coming to power" (*Monadologie*, 376). On the weakness of the Third Republic, see *Histoire*, IV, 730. Cornwell (*Principes du droit*, 183, referring to *Critique philosophique*, 1872-I, 226, and 1873-I, 373) says that under majority rule, "an empirical law possesses only a *provisionally obligatory* value." Democracy keeps open the possibility of reform (Cornwell, *Principes du droit*, 180–81).

70. Cavallari, *Charles Renouvier*, x.

71. See Picard, *Idées sociales*, 334, on Renouvier's originality here.

berty, as communism calls that which includes certain material powers to exercise it, can only be maintained for this or that person at the price of harming the rights of others to exercise similar powers, since one is aware that they conflict with one another by the nature of things, and one doesn't know in advance to what degree they can be allowed or restrained for each person. This true liberty brings with it the renunciation of *simple liberty.*[72]

The socialist position, however, did have the merit of drawing attention to the practical problem of establishing liberty in society. To deal with liberty as a practical problem, it is necessary to focus on the question of the right of defense. This perspective shows that the workers in early industrial society, though they might have been materially better off, were lacking in mechanisms of social defense, more lacking even than many in more traditional societies.[73] A rigorous laissez-faire would prevent the development of new modes of defense, as the Le Chapelier law (1791) had shown.[74] Socialism, in pursuit of an ideal where defense would be unnecessary, would in fact simply make it impossible. Any comparison of the role of trade unions in the "capitalist" and "socialist" worlds of the twentieth century would amply confirm Renouvier's views here. What was needed was the development of new forms of defense suitable to the modern competitive industrial economy.[75]

While the liberal democratic republic did not guarantee the devel-

72. *Histoire,* IV, 203–204.

73. Socialist internationalism also draws attention to the supranational character of the problem, but the program of the Second International, while promising a "miracle en sociologie," offers in reality the ruin of freedom (*ibid.,* 573–74). He stresses (*ibid.,* 603) the "lack of fixed connections between the contracting parties and of stability in their relations." This lack of security leads modern workers to fear liberty (*ibid.,* 622).

74. Renouvier found it unacceptable that societies could leave the weak without defense (*ibid.,* 389).

75. Renouvier saw the spread of machinery and large-scale factories and commerce as having both bad and good effects (*ibid.,* 599–600).

opment of these forms, it was open to their possibility. Renouvier was concerned that not enough progress in that direction had been made in France in his lifetime.

> The dominant character of the nineteenth century has remained to its very end the same as that which applied to the end of the preceding century, to the Revolution, to the spirit from which it developed, carried to its culminating point: to sum it up in a few words, it is the inability to attain the ideal which charmed people, the infirmity of the masses in the face of what was demanded of them by way of intelligence and devotion, the egoism of the very persons who had offered themselves as guides when they had in their hands the instrument they had asked for to fulfill the promises they had made, finally, the check or the abortion of serious reforms in the incessant clash of abstract principle, passions and interests.[76]

What did he think was needed? One line of research was suggested by his reflections on the importance of property. He was less interested in questions about the origin or justification of private property and probably doubted that a single theory, such as the labor theory in all its variants, was of much practical use, given the weight of historical prescription. Experience, however, suggested that the possession of property had served in all ages as one of the most effective instruments for exercising the right of defense. It offered an element of security for the individual against the powers of government and against the infringements of other members of society.[77] Was it not the possession of property that

76. *Ibid.*, 3–4; see also 729.
77. Property is thus legitimate even in societies where it is very unequally distributed (*ibid.*, 215). But Renouvier also agreed with Marx that the basic social problem was the workers' lack of capital (*ibid.*, 564). On the value of property in defending the individual against the royal and priestly powers in antiquity, see *Personnalisme*, 146–47; see also Lacroix, *Vocation personnelle*, 155. "Society would make him [the individual] pay too high a price for the means of defense it furnishes him if it confiscated, in the claimed interest of all, his right to

currently most distinguished the bourgeoisie from the working classes? What was needed in modern society was a generalization of property.[78] The lack of property in the vast majority of workers was a major origin of the society's ills.[79]

In Renouvier's opinion, the socialists' emphasis on the ownership of the instruments of production somewhat confused the issue, not because this form of property was unimportant but because of the conclusions they drew from their too exclusive focus on it. Since the instruments of production were becoming increasingly social rather than individual in character under the influence of both modern technology and modern

---

possess [property] and to freely enter into contracts, which is half of his personality" (*Histoire*, IV, 632).

78. Cavallari, *Charles Renouvier*, 112 (speaking of his 1851 work).

79. Modern society finds itself

in such economic conditions that the class of workers, opposed to that of owners, cannot derive from contracts freely entered into that share of the fruits of labor necessary to support it in an acceptable manner. The free worker will not even obtain guarantees of that share, whatever it may be. This is in fact what has happened. The liberty conquered by the worker has freed the employers from the obligation [to provide that guarantee]. From liberty has come competition, and from the increase in population, the invention of machines, the lack of capital or loans to the worker, has come poverty on the one hand and the accumulation of wealth, and luxury on the other. Society is thus divided from the economic point of view into two classes without any regular links between them, either of law or of custom, and their relations are based on chance circumstances, on temporary contracts between isolated persons whose sentiments have become, on the whole, ones of mutual hostility. (*Monadologie*, 386)

Not so far from the picture painted by the *Communist Manifesto*, is it? Like Marx, Renouvier admitted that the accumulation of capital also had benefits for society (*Histoire*, IV, 632). Renouvier agreed that the existing great inequality of property was a major problem for any government of laws (*Monadologie*, 373). But equality of property is a goal hostile to freedom, though he was prepared to admit a limitation on the degree of inequality through progressive taxation (Picard, *Idées sociales*, 231–35); see also *Histoire*, IV, 564.

business organization, they concluded that collective ownership was necessary.[80] Lack of participation in the ownership of these instruments was undoubtedly harmful to the workers in many ways, material and psychological, but the socialist solution would make the situation worse. Collective ownership of the instruments of production would diminish the security of the workers. Faced with only one possible employer (in the most extreme case, perhaps never fully realized), they would lack any leverage against that employer. The socialist argument that they would not need any such leverage because the employer would be devoted to their interests, would "be them," was sheer utopianism, subject to the same arguments as the similar position of the Saint-Simonians at the beginning of the century.

How can society hope to produce a management that despite being "other" than the workers is totally devoted to their interests rather than its own? The socialists' materialistic sociology should suggest that this is impossible, and in practice they always fall back on the moral appeal of "socialism," as if this could be somehow exempt from the weaknesses they denounce in all other moral appeals. Once again, as Renouvier pointed out, we are caught in the vicious circle of postulating for the construction of a virtuous society the existence of men who could emerge only from an already perfect society.[81]

Does this mean that nothing can be done and that we must be content with present society in all its injustice? Renouvier did not think so, but he recognized that getting the changes he thought necessary would be difficult. Rather than advocating a universal (and therefore chimerical) solution, he proposed several lines of advance that did not demand the overthrow of the present economic system to be implemented.[82] Workers can acquire an element of ownership in the instruments of production in more than one way. Renouvier's most general solution was the

80. In the sense that individual ownership by workers of modern instruments of production is not possible, collective forms are necessary (*Histoire*, IV, 635).

81. See Picard, *Idées sociales*, 154, 197–98.

82. Picard (*ibid.*, 249–50, 257) fears that Renouvier's methods would overthrow the free economy. Renouvier says that reforms cannot wait for a more radical restructuring of the economy (*Histoire*, IV, 596–97).

recognition by society of the "right to work." He considered this right a necessary deduction from the fact of solidarity, and thus his commitment to it survived the debacle of the 1848 revolution.[83] It was supported by his mature moral philosophy, and he considered it antithetical to any collectivist socialism.

For Renouvier, the right to work was a form of property, a "moral equivalent of property," as Picard remarks.[84] Renouvier certainly saw it as a moral exigency:

> The *right to work,* a principle of justice, a *guarantist* principle, to borrow the excellent language of Fourier, excludes, rather than presupposing, the communist principle for it implies by its very terms, . . . an opposition between the existing society, on the one hand, in which the instruments of labor—land and capital—are entirely appropriated, and the individual, on the other hand, who demands the use of those instruments as a necessary condition of his existence. This demand is just, in principle, though means must be considered, for it cannot be rejected without placing the individual under the rule of a social contract which, while stripping him of his natural liberties, gives him *nothing* in exchange. Without the possibility of living there is nothing else. When the Constituent Assembly of 1848 refused to recognize the right to work it committed a grave injustice as well as an evident philosophic error—unless one advocates the most brutal materialism in human relations.[85]

The right to work in nineteenth-century French terms was not the anti-union measure that goes by that name in the United States today. It meant the right of every human being to earn his daily bread by his own

83. See Picard, *Idées sociales,* 266–67, Méry, *Critique du christianisme,* II, 336, on the idea of *"dette sociale"; Monadologie,* 394.

84. Picard, *Idées sociales,* 241; Lacroix, *Vocation personnelle,* 156–57; see also Richard, *Question sociale,* 305–307, 315.

85. *Histoire,* IV, 205.

labor and thus the obligation of society to guarantee the practical application of this right.

Since 1848, Renouvier had also been a consistent advocate of production cooperatives, while admitting that only an elite of the working class possessed the qualities needed to make them work. The numbers of that elite could grow over time as a result of the experiences of the cooperatives themselves.[86] With the growth of industries requiring large-scale organization, other forms of worker participation were also needed, but the corresponding development of the joint-stock form of capital ownership showed that new possibilities existed. Renouvier was particularly interested in the potential of profit-sharing schemes.[87]

This latter approach showed that he did not think everything had to take the form of direct individual ownership. There are other forms of participation that can provide a measure of security and independence as long as the worker has established rights in them that cannot be arbitrarily withdrawn by employers or the state. These may take the form of insurance programs, for example, or pension funds. Renouvier preferred programs that evoked the individual initiative of the worker or depended on his freely given consent.[88] On the other hand, he was sure

86. Lacroix, *Vocation personnelle*, 159. Renouvier praised Fourier repeatedly for the practical character of his idea of cooperation (for example, *Histoire*, IV, 175). Secrétan (Secrétan to Renouvier, March 25, 1871, in *Correspondance de Renouvier et Secrétan*, 56) saw Renouvier as close to the Swiss economist Léon Walras; see Richard, *Question sociale*, 313–15. Picard (*Idées sociales*, 264–65) noted the hostility to freedom of association among French democrats following Rousseau. Renouvier, on the other hand, consistently supported that freedom, but not to the point where the existence of the state was threatened. Renouvier noted the nature of the socialists' opposition to cooperatives (*Histoire*, IV, 596). His views were similar to those of Charles Gide (Méry, *Critique du christianisme*, II, 331). On the persistence of Fourier's influence, see Richard, *Question sociale*, 276–79. According to Picard (*Idées sociales*, 110), after 1870 Renouvier returned to his earlier support of a role for the state in promoting cooperatives. *Monadologie*, 390–91.

87. *Histoire*, IV, 603, notes J. S. Mill's support.

88. *Histoire*, IV, 633–34. Renouvier noted the backwardness of French social legislation (*ibid.*, 733); see Richard, *Question sociale*, 307–309, Picard, *Idées*

that substantial governmental action would be needed and that the workers were not in a position to do everything for themselves.[89] Democratic suffrage did not by itself guarantee the advancement of workers' interests.

Renouvier frankly admitted that the workers were right in thinking that their rulers did not care much about their misery.[90] Indeed, the existence of a socialist political movement might be necessary to overcome the inertia of the existing system, but he advocated a "liberal" socialism that guaranteed individual property within limits. He considered the existing socialist parties as much an obstacle to moral reform of the economy as the oligarchs of wealth, and he urged French socialists to form a parliamentary movement like the German Social-Democracy and to give up their belief in revolutionary miracles.[91]

For significant reforms to become possible, the political leaders of the country, guided by right principles, must demonstrate the will to reform, and he saw little evidence of this in France.[92] Republican politicians seemed "secretly paralyzed by the opinion that in *these matters nothing can be done.*"[93] Leadership does not automatically emerge to fill a need, whatever the deterministic philosophies of history may say. The democratic republic, despite its weaknesses, remains the best possible

---

sociales, 255–56. Social insurance was seen as a major instrument of solidarity. There was also the moral problem of assistance to the needy. For Renouvier, it was a social duty, because it was first an individual duty but one best carried out through common action (Picard, *Idées sociales,* 227). Cavallari, (*Charles Renouvier,* 161) sees Renouvier's social individualism as having affinities with the contemporary syndicalism of Pelloutier and the socialism of Jaurès.

89. Renouvier saw the economists coming to recognize the need for state intervention if the economy is to become more just (*Histoire,* IV, 601); on the need for state action, see *ibid.,* 636–37. Picard (*Idées sociales,* 257) fears Renouvier would confer too much power on the state.

90. *Histoire,* IV, 624.

91. *Personnalisme,* 200–201; *Monadologie,* 392–93; *Histoire,* IV, 638–40. In fact, the French socialists at the turn of the century were increasingly mating their revolutionary rhetoric to a parliamentary reformist practice.

92. *Histoire,* IV, 625.

93. *Ibid.,* 733.

context for reform, he insisted, because it virtually guarantees that nothing will be enacted before it has become acceptable to the *moeurs* of society. As a result, gains may be smaller and slower, but great disappointments and frustrations will be fewer.[94]

The lesson of the revolutions of the nineteenth century, in Renouvier's opinion, was the impotence of revolution to create great social transformations. Liberal democracy was the form of government most in harmony with human freedom and most likely to promote enduring social reform.

Individualism and Society

Because he started from the individualist premise essential to moral philosophy and denied any existence to the species or society apart from the individuals that compose them, Renouvier had to face a certain difficulty in explaining the existence of society and the reality of social solidarity without using the organicist concepts so popular in the nineteenth century. The only "natural" society he would concede was the family, the basis for a potential social development. In the abstract, man "is both social and antisocial, as he is both good and bad."[95] Kant's "unsociable sociability" expresses well the antinomy of man's condition, and Renouvier admitted that the passage from the individual to society is an insoluble question. Social solidarity is nonetheless a reality of man's historical experience, which permits us also to describe man as a social being.[96]

Renouvier initially formed his idea of solidarity while still under the

---

94. On the impotence of reason and laws to reform society, see *Monadologie,* 399. But, he admitted, liberty was more established in the constitution of the Third Republic than in the *moeurs* of the population (*Esquisse,* II, 331); see Cornwell, *Principes du droit,* 185. *Histoire,* IV, 224. On the tendency of revolutions to escape the control of their authors, see *Personnalisme,* 157, and to delay progress by trampling on liberty, *Quatrième essai,* 107–11.

95. *Quatrième essai,* 92–93.

96. *Personnalisme,* 131; *Quatrième essai,* 92–93.

influence of the Saint-Simonians.[97] Tracing its philosophical origins to Bacon and Descartes, he attributed its current popularity to the fact that "it gives a very beautiful and very precise form to the principle of necessity in the social relations of men" and that "love of self and love of others, individual perfection and collective perfection, all find a common foundation in this idea."[98] Though he would soon repudiate Saint-Simonian historicism and reject its easy solution of the conflict between individual and society as leading to the extinction of the individual, he retained the sense of solidarity as expressing the aspect of necessity in human relations.[99] Renouvier's repudiation of universal necessity was not a rejection of all determinisms governing human action, certainly not all social determination.

Renouvier was able to reconcile his moral individualism with social solidarity because the former did not prevent him from accepting the latter as a reality of historical experience. What was vital was to prevent the reality of solidarity from subverting the value of individuality. In his mature thought, Renouvier came to see this issue in the perspective of a centuries-old struggle between religion and rationalist philosophy. The medieval Church's conception of Original Sin was an effort to give solidarity a moral character and to impute guilt to individuals for acts not their own, a position Renouvier vigorously rejected: "Theologians, by imputing evil to the species, have suppressed the moral individual."[100] Only the Pelagians were headed in the right direction. Philosophy, on the other hand, tended to view the individual in isolation. Renouvier's moral philosophy would try to remedy both these errors and "conciliate individual responsibility with human solidarity."[101]

Renouvier's moral philosophy was thus able to solve the problem that frustrated eighteenth-century individualism because he was seeking

97. Mouy, *Idée de progrès,* 89.·
98. *Manuel de philosophie moderne* (Paris, 1842), 440.
99. On this outcome of organicism, see Renouvier to Secrétan, May 21, 1870 (annex, in *Correspondance de Renouvier et Secrétan,* 51).
100. *Histoire,* II, 679.
101. *Ibid.* See also Picard, *Idées sociales,* 27, Richard, *Question sociale,* 294–98, 317.

to promote not "utility" or "happiness" but justice.[102] He demonstrated clearly that neither utility nor happiness can bridge the gap between the individual and society; neither offers a principle on which to adjudicate the inevitable conflicts between the utility or happiness of different individuals. Only justice can carry that burden. Justice must be rational in its basis, not empirical or emotional. Its foundation is the reason of the free individual, who imposes on himself moral duties that can readily be deduced, as Kant showed, from our nature as beings possessing reason and free will. Justice thus transcends our individual interests or sentiments but at the same time comes from within us. It was, for Renouvier, simultaneously social and individual.

Freedom and Society

The dominant trends of nineteenth-century French social and political thought were not able to find a path toward the reconciliation of the individual and society without leading to the sacrifice of liberty. This conclusion has become evident enough in our century. That the nineteenth century was not entirely without resources in this matter, however, is the message of my analysis of Renouvier's approach to the problem.[103] It seems unnecessary to demonstrate that the nature of the problem is essentially similar in our time. Democratic societies, despite their weaknesses, have shown that it is possible to make some progress along lines Renouvier would have approved. Even the slowness with which that progress has been made would have seemed a good thing to him.

For Renouvier, the problems of the relations of the individual and

102. Picard, *Idées sociales*, 328–29.

103. On Renouvier's view of the nineteenth-century obstacles to the resolution of the social question, see Méry, *Critique du christianisme*, II, 282. There was a strong tendency in the nineteenth century to see society as the ultimate reality and therefore the supreme value, thus subordinating the individual (see Lacroix, *Vocation personnelle*, 121). On Renouvier's insistence on social reform through liberty, see Cavallari, *Charles Renouvier*, 149–50.

the community are basically moral problems, that is, problems for which only a moral approach can show us the direction of their solution and its practical limits.[104] Moral solutions, as we have seen, are those that tend within the limits of the possible toward the promotion of the moral autonomy of the individual.[105] The limits of the possible in any given time or place are the historical results of the social ramifications of man's exercise of his free will—that is, of what Renouvier called *solidarity in evil* (*solidarité dans le mal*). The existence of this solidarity makes this essentially moral issue also a political one.[106] Governments may seek to promote *solidarity in good* (*solidarité dans le bien*), but a more fundamental justification for their existence is the solidarity of evil. In Renouvier's philosophy, government cannot escape having a moral mission.[107] Political life itself will decide how, and how far, that mission is carried out: "The debate between authority and liberty . . . can only result in a conciliation of a practical nature." [108] Only philosophy can show what principles should guide that practical effort.

104. "The question of the social order is not one of the distribution of material goods, but one of duty, right, and constraint" (*Monadologie*, 382). On the relations of moral philosophy to social questions in the nineteenth century, see Richard, *Question sociale*. Mouy (*Idée de progrès*, 194) sees Renouvier's commitment to individualistic solutions as having reached a peak with the *Science de la morale* and then declining, but this seems to me a misunderstanding.

105. See Picard, *Idées sociales*, 332.

106. Renouvier adapted to his philosophy the expression of Schopenhauer: "The victim and the executioner are the same man" (*Personnalisme*, 221). Only Secrétan stressed the connection of the social question and the problem of evil as much as Renouvier (Richard, *Question sociale*, 284). Renouvier thought that "the road to the emancipation of the people ought in reality to be rather longer than that imagined by Marx and also more tied to 'political' and 'superstructural' facts" (Cavallari, *Charles Renouvier*, 97). Renouvier paralleled the modern situation with that of the ancient democracies (*Monadologie*, 387).

107. But does he go as far as Fichte in recognizing a state "endowed with the fundamental authority to coerce individuals toward their moral freedom but in the name of moral freedom itself" (Krieger, *German Idea*, 188)? Necessary government, he admitted, necessarily has a moral authority (*Histoire*, IV, 392).

108. *Histoire*, IV, 389.

Renouvier's philosophy shows that there are two concepts that form the axis on which the existence and development of liberty in the real world hinges: the idea of moral responsibility founded on free will and solidarity in evil, the main characteristic of our "state of war." The sociopolitical philosophies of the nineteenth century that failed to incorporate these concepts, whether from optimism or determinism, would not merely fail to promote liberty and "progress" but would contribute to the growth of the modern mentality that made twentieth-century totalitarianism possible.

The state of peace of which they dreamed is so impossible for man that "if ever the pretentions and appearance of such a regime could appear by government action, it would be in contradiction to the goal being pursued; it would announce the most complete tyranny that can be conceived over persons and their relations, so complete that the least experience of human nature as it really is would not permit us even to believe that the undertaking was possible, until it reached the point where the trend toward it was noticeable and menacing." [109] I know of no better demonstration of the potential value of philosophical reflection on public issues than the long effort Renouvier gave to his countrymen in the last four decades of the nineteenth century.

109. *Ibid.*, 631.

V

The Philosopher and His Age: Mirror or Critic?

> I hope I'm wrong, but it seems to me that
> we are watching the beginning of an intel-
> lectual and moral decadence which will
> lead us rapidly to a new night of the mind
> and the heart.
> —Renouvier to Louis Prat, in Prat,
> *Charles Renouvier*

A thinker may come to seem interesting or even important for the manner in which he reflects the
dominant characteristics of the movement of thought in his age. Even a
relatively unoriginal mind may acquire a lasting reputation if he is taken
as a "representative man" of his time. On the other hand, a thinker who
sets himself up as a critic of much that his contemporaries hold sacred
may also acquire a posthumous fame when the dominant ideas of his
time seem discredited to a later generation. Renouvier has not enjoyed
the benefits of any of these positions, yet his relationship to the main
currents of his age is one of the things that make him interesting; even
more, it is what makes it so instructive to reexamine his thought today.
It is not just that Renouvier doggedly battled against several of those
main currents but that he did so within the larger framework of modern
philosophy, a framework he shared with those he criticized. It is easy to
show that he owes a great deal to some of the currents he most bitterly
criticized, but far from discrediting his criticism, this position, simulta-

neously within and without, makes it all the more valuable and penetrating.

A sense of having shared the common errors of his day before discovering that they were errors, a reluctance to gain polemical advantage
by exaggerating the differences that separated him from other thinkers,
gives Renouvier's critique a subtlety that detracts nothing from its vigor.
He was fully aware that, critic or mimic, a thinker is part of his age.
Indeed, the relativism that is one of the foundation stones of Renouvier's
mature philosophy stresses the implantation of the thinker in his time.[1]
But he arrived at this position in a manner very different from that of the
historical determinists.

A common weakness of philosophers, a source of their arrogance
and dogmatism, is their tendency to imagine that they are working in the
realm of pure spirit, guided only by logic and/or intuition.[2] Renouvier's
reflections on the apparently irreconcilable differences among philosophers over the ages, combined with his doctrine of free will, convinced
him that philosophical doctrines, however soundly argued, should be
understood as *beliefs*.[3] As beliefs, they are shaped by an enormous va-

1. Verneaux (*Idéalisme de Renouvier*, 329–30) sees Renouvier's neocriticism as expressing the spirit of the age, namely relativism. There is another common critique, especially popular on the Catholic Right, that sees as one of the
main (disastrous) characteristics of nineteenth-century philosophy a tendency to
subjectivism, which makes it an ally of Protestantism; see Ollé-Laprune, *Certitude morale*, 326–27, 334–35, who also says (329) that Renouvier "sums up
and translates after a fashion the spirit of the present age." Cited by Roure,
Doctrines et problèmes, 126.

2. Spragens (*Irony of Liberal Reason*) is particularly good on this characteristic of those he calls the "technocrats."

3. It would be interesting to know how Richard Rorty would situate Renouvier in the history of philosophy he develops in *Philosophy and the Mirror
of Nature*. "On the periphery of the history of modern philosophy, one finds
figures who, without forming a 'tradition,' resemble each other in their distrust
of the notion that man's essence is to be a knower of essences. Goethe, Kierke-
gaard, Santayana, William James, Dewey, the later Wittgenstein, the later Heidegger, are figures of this sort. They are often accused of relativism or cynicism.
They are often dubious about progress" (*ibid.*, 367). Renouvier fit these qualifications, but he was also engaged in "solving the traditional problems of philosophy."

riety of forces, ranging from the psychological quirks of the individual to the impact of current events to the weight of a particular philosophical tradition.

Free will does not deny that the individual is implanted in history and especially in that of his own time.

> There cannot be any independence more complete than that which excludes in theory the influences on a thinker and his participation in the dominant ideas of his time. But, in fact, the higher his ideal of the autonomy of reflective thought the more he should confess his weakness, and *a fortiori* he ought to assign little value to the coefficient of action which can derive from his own labor, his personal effort, within the general movement of ideas whose nature and direction he is criticizing; for he is forced to recognize the vast role of common determinism outside him as well as the elements of dependency of his own moral constitution.[4]

Renouvier was clearly aware that he did not stand above the limitations common to thinking men. As we have seen in the chapter on free will, he always insisted that on major questions man can never reach apodictic certainty. This awareness shielded him from the "totalitarian temptation" inherent in the social philosophy of many of his contemporaries.

Deterministic philosophies of history, on the other hand, lead to the conclusion that a thinker's work has meaning, and indeed truth, only in the context of his own time. Outside that context it has meaning only as part of a process leading to the development of some future—higher— stage of philosophical understanding. Given sharp form by Hegel, but more loosely and diffusely penetrating the assumptions of a large proportion of nineteenth-century thinkers, this outlook has continued to exercise a strong influence.[5] Even those who see this process of development

4. *Histoire*, IV, 750–51 (note how Renouvier's phrasing here reflects his mathematical training).

5. Hegel at least tried to see within each stage the relation of views to the thinker who held them, without falling into a reductionist psychology (Kaufmann, *Goethe, Kant, and Hegel*, 263). In his youth, Renouvier was quite

as leading not to the triumph that Hegel imagined his own work to be but to the liquidation of philosophy in our time are forced to reshape the history of thought to force it into their schemata.[6] They have to ignore or dismiss any thinker or thought that does not fit into their view of the significance of a period, or if the person is too well known to be dismissed, they have to reinterpret his ideas to fit the ordained line of development.

Renouvier's view of the history of philosophy, regardless of whether he "correctly" interpreted the ideas of this or that thinker, brings us closer to the history of Western thought than any developmental scheme can, but it also shatters any hope of grasping the overall "meaning" of that history. Renouvier's resistance to his century's passion for finding that meaning is one of his most important legacies. It shows us that the Western philosophic tradition is not necessarily dead, that it has survived many deviations, dead ends, and repetitions in the past. However much it is shaped by the circumstances of an age, philosophy also responds to man's perpetual search for answers to questions that continue to matter, even though he is unable to give them definitive answers. It is this quality that most binds the fate of philosophy to that of religion. As long as men remain unable to delude themselves into believing that they possess, or can possess, definitive answers to the questions of man's origin and fate and how he should act in this world, both philosophy and religion will find a place in our world.

Renouvier's great interest in the history of philosophy is one of the things that mark him as a philosopher of the nineteenth century. In France, at least, an extensive familiarity with the history of philosophy or the great thinkers of the past was de rigueur if you wanted to be considered a philosopher. Outsiders to the educational establishment, like Renouvier and later Alfred Fouillée, bought their ticket of admission to respectability with works of historical erudition. Highly original minds uncontaminated by historical knowledge, like that of Charles

---

strongly, if indirectly, influenced by Hegel as well as the Saint-Simonians (Cavallari, *Charles Renouvier*, xi).

6. There is a sense in which the triumph of philosophy and its liquidation are the same thing; for example, in Marx's concept of *praxis*.

Fourier, were not even considered philosophers.[7] Joseph Ferrari, in his well-known diatribe against the Cousinian Eclectics, *Les philosophes salariés,* even accused Victor Cousin of steering young philosophers into historical work to inhibit the development of original thought because original thought might upset the political security of the "University" professors.

For all his criticism of the Eclectics—and he often expressed the conviction that they did not merit the title of philosopher—Renouvier considered Cousin's promotion of historical study a good thing on balance, having really expanded and deepened and made more accurate our knowledge of the work of earlier philosophers. The depth of his historical knowledge was one of the things that saved Renouvier from the pitfalls of historical determinism. It also served him well when he wanted to show that ideas passing as the products of modern science were often unconscious paraphrases of ancient metaphysical doctrines. This mode of argument he shared with the despised Eclectics, but he did not use it, as they did, as a means to reduce conflict or minimize differences.

For Renouvier, the positivists were a more serious enemy than the Eclectics, but there are also elements of positivist influence on his philosophy that mark him as a man of his century. His respect for science was scarcely less than theirs, though he understood science more broadly than Comte permitted. Renouvier and Comte shared, after all, the same early intellectual formation, and the younger man actually studied mathematics under Comte at the Ecole polytechnique. Renouvier was inclined to think, like Plato and Aristotle for that matter, that the study of mathematics was a prerequisite for the study of philosophy. One of the weaknesses of the English empiricists since Locke had been, in his opinion, their lack of familiarity with mathematics.[8] Mathematics was also central to his concept of science: Studies acquired the character of science when they reached the stage at which the data they worked on could be quantified.

7. Renouvier, on the other hand, argued that Fourier ought to be considered a major philosopher (*Histoire,* IV, 161–62).

8. Many of today's French philosophers congratulate themselves on their lack of scientific training, which they think would interfere with their imagination (Bouveresse, *Philosophe autophages,* 48–49).

It is true that Renouvier also used the term *science* more broadly. While considering a science of morals possible, he ridiculed Bentham's efforts to quantify pleasure and pain, but he did consider that a higher degree of certainty is possible where quantification is legitimately used. Renouvier also praised positivism for encouraging the phenomenological approach to scientific inquiry, dismissing concern for "causes" and other relics of the metaphysical interpretation of nature. The search for laws of the behavior of phenomena constituted science for Renouvier as much as for the positivists. He was much less sanguine about the possibility of applying any narrow conception of science to the study of man and society.

What marks Renouvier most clearly as a nineteenth-century philosopher is the magnitude of his ambition. Having staked out the extent of the intellectual domain of philosophy, he did not then specialize in this or that aspect of it but set out to develop his own views on every philosophical question in the belief that they could all be organized around a few central ideas. It was not just his genius but also the particular character of his situation that made it not only possible to conceive but to execute such an ambitious program, and it is fair to say "execute" despite the fact that when he died at age eighty-eight, he had plans for three more books.[9]

Secure in an inherited income, he was free from the necessity to give lectures, to read students' papers, to attend committee meetings, free from the hundreds of everyday cares that keep the twentieth-century intellectual from sustained mental effort. Renouvier was inclined to think that almost any form of employment, like Spinoza's lens grinding, was better for a philosopher than teaching philosophy, but independence was the best of situations.

While the development of his thought benefited by his independence, Renouvier's reputation may have suffered. It was too easy for those who did not bother to read him to dismiss him as a representative of a vanishing class. The sheer volume of his published work, estimated at over 25,000 pages by Méry, has been an obstacle to the scholarly examination of his work, since no one today wants to expose himself to the charge of not having been thorough enough. It has also disadvantaged him in the

9. Prat, *Renouvier*, 296.

French secondary-school philosophy program that prefers authors who can be adequately presented in brief extracts or wrote very little. While sharing the great ambition of many of his contemporaries, Renouvier lacked the dogmatism that makes it easy to boil most of them down to a more digestible size. His apparently irreducible bulk makes him seem too much a man of his day.

Man of his day? Yes, but Renouvier certainly thought of himself as an outsider, engaged in an unending struggle with the dominant intellectual trends of that day. One can always make a case for any individual being more reflective of his time than he would admit, but this would substantially misunderstand Renouvier's importance. It is true that the sense of being an outsider to the dominant society was a common experience of nineteenth-century intellectuals, so common that for some it was no doubt a pose. For many, this sentiment was a reaction against the rising industrial society, which seemed to devalue traditional learning and to be philistine toward the arts. Renouvier was not so much against industrial development as the overoptimistic interpretation of its value.[10] He was especially critical of those who praised its virtues while ignoring the damage it caused, and his criticism of the evils of large-scale industry was in full accord with the socialists'. It is true that like most socialists he failed to notice that the products of large-scale industry were not luxuries for the rich. But he condemned laissez-faire economists and socialists alike for believing that the happiness of mankind was to be found in more material wealth rather than justice and peace.[11]

Given our incapacity to handle the moral problems created by modern industry, Renouvier confided to Louis Prat at the end of his life, it would have been better if science had remained theoretical.[12] One frequently hears, among intellectuals, the nostalgic wish to live in the eighteenth century—with modern medicine, of course, false teeth and eyeglasses, central heating, and . . . the list rapidly grows when we start to think about it. But in judging nineteenth-century nostalgia for preindustrial civilization we should remember that many of what we consider the benefits of modern industrial society had not made their appearance by

10. See, for example, *Quatrième essai*, 307.
11. *Monadologie*, 421–22, 431–32.
12. *Derniers entretiens*, 84–85.

the end of the nineteenth century and that many of the drawbacks were only too evident.

The reaction against the industrial present could take different forms and lead in different directions. Among intellectuals there would always be some who were outsiders in the name of a lost and better past—if not the society of the Old Regime, then that of ancient Greece or Rome. Renouvier thought that classical Greece had been one of the high points of Western civilization, and there were times when he may have thought it the highest of all, but he was never as completely absorbed in it as his friend Louis Ménard, a Hellenist. The glory that was Greece stood for Renouvier mainly as an argument against all optimistic philosophies of history.

More common than those who yearned romantically for a lost past were those who considered themselves outsiders in the name of a glorious, inevitable, and near future. The evils of the present were for them not the decaying relics of some forgotten glory but the necessary birth pangs of a shining future. Those nineteenth-century "futurists" who relished the prospect of a scientific-industrial civilization also failed to foresee what it would be like. Their alienation from the present was worn as a sort of badge of merit, a proof of one's superiority to the satisfied common herd. This sort of outersiderism, whether manifested in revolutionary socialism or evolutionary philosophy, was indeed so common in the nineteenth century as to constitute one of the main intellectual trends, which makes its quality of being outside somewhat ambiguous. Rather, these outsiders were part of the dominant ideas that made Renouvier an outsider.

For Renouvier was an outsider for philosophical rather than historical reasons. He was not outside in the name of either an idealized past or an ideal future. He was outside in the name of a perennial ideal, unattainable in any period of human experience, though some periods had come closer than others. His outsiderness did not derive so much from reaction against the injustices and immoralities of his age, for on that score all societies present more negative than positive features. What made Renouvier feel an outsider was his differences with the main intellectual trends of his time, whether or not their proponents were defenders or critics of the existing social order.

It has been argued that the outsiderness (*alienation* is the more fashionable term) of the modern intellectual is essential to his productive capacity, the source of his insights, the generator of his energy. As a sociological generalization, this is perhaps too much based on the experiences of a particular time and place. It has also served as a rationale for irresponsibility, individual and collective. Renouvier's sense of being an outsider was a motive that drove him to remind his society of the risks involved in the neglect of certain universal values.[13] After all, someone who was really "outside" his age could hardly function as a critic of it because he would lack sufficient contact to say anything relevant to its problems.

What Renouvier saw was that the dominant intellectual trends, though responding to social, political, and philosophical developments, were likely to harm the perennial values he held dear. This gave him a sense of the outsider's mission to combat those trends. He did not have a naïvely optimistic belief in the capacity of philosophy to change the world, in this being closer to Hegel than to Marx, but he did believe that ideas were one of the things that mattered, slow and subterranean though their influence often was. It was thus his responsibility as a philosopher to address not just the questions that philosophers have found professionally interesting over the centuries (though he had a lively interest in technical questions, especially in mathematics) but the questions that matter to everybody in his society.

Being outside was thus for Renouvier the opportunity to achieve a critical distance from both the social and intellectual milieus, a distance that enabled him to see not only the flaws in the existing society but the dangers in the ideas of those who proposed to change it. The thought of the defenders of the existing order was too easily influenced by nonphilosophical considerations, as demonstrated by the Eclectics in their efforts to conciliate the political power of the Church while distancing themselves from its doctrine.[14] The thought of the revolutionary opponents of the existing order was more influenced by intellectual concep-

13. The modesty his relativism imposed on Renouvier did not detract from his duty to be critical of his age (*Histoire*, IV, 751).

14. Ferrari (*Philosophes salariés*, 162–63) called the Eclectics the nineteenth-century equivalent of the Jesuits, *i.e.*, the representatives of the clerical monarchy to the rich.

tions, to be sure, but conceptions that had not been subjected to sufficiently rigorous analysis and hence were little better than Francis Bacon's "idols of the tribe." The ideas of the defenders scarcely presented an intellectual challenge, and Renouvier was usually content to ridicule their superficiality. The ideas of the critics presented a greater challenge, especially as their influence grew later in the century.

Renouvier considered the position of a voice crying in the wilderness an honorable one, perhaps the only possible one in some ages. He greatly admired those Hebrew prophets who stood against the powers of their day. But he preferred to have some influence, provided that he could do so without sacrificing his independence and his ideals. After 1851, he realized that his only path to influence would be through the pen, that he was not cut out for the rough-and-tumble of public life.

Not only did he feel the need to rethink his philosophical position; he would from the beginning seek to communicate his new ideas first to other philosophers, then to a wider public. He was disappointed, but not surprised, that the philosophical establishment took little notice of his first *Essai de critique générale* (1854). Even had his views not been so strongly in conflict with those of the Eclectic school, he was in a narrower sense an outsider to their establishment, not a product of the Ecole normale supérieure or a candidate for the *agrégation de philosophie*, necessary to become a university professor. His struggle for recognition would always be a battle against the University, where the influence of the Eclectic pupils of Victor Cousin would persist into the twentieth century.[15] Philosophy was not yet a monopoly of university professors in the nineteenth century, but the complete centralization of philosophical education in France, in contrast to Germany or Great Britain, made it difficult for those outside the system to gain attention, even negative.

In his later years, Renouvier was not far from believing that there had been a deliberate effort by the last generation of Eclectics, led by the mild-mannered Paul Janet, to keep his ideas from being considered in academic circles. He knew at least one young man whose effort to do a neocriticist thesis had met with such resistance that Renouvier felt obliged to advise him not to risk his career by persisting. Despite these

15. On their domination, see *ibid.*, Chap. X, "L'Eclectisme au pouvoir," 100–123.

difficulties, he was to enjoy the satisfaction of seeing his ideas adopted in the work of some young academics and seeing one of the brightest of a younger generation, Octave Hamelin, adopt an avowedly neocriticist position and recognize Renouvier's influence. Renouvier would have missed this pleasure had he not lived to a ripe old age. The belated character of his "official" recognition probably also shortened its duration. A new star was emerging whose thought would seem, rightly or wrongly, more in tune with the sensibilities of the twentieth century, especially after 1914—Henri Bergson. Bergson would also demonstrate the continuing power in French philosophical education of the spoken work and a certain rhetorical eloquence that Renouvier did not possess.

Renouvier was aware of his handicap in this area. His first youthful competition essay had received an honorable mention despite some rather pointed remarks by one judge about the gaucheness of his language.[16] He would remain motivated to make his arguments as clear as possible. Unlike Kant and most of his followers, who were willing to sacrifice clarity in the vain search for absolute truth and as a result introduced the confusion between profundity and obscurity that has been the bane of so much modern philosophy, Renouvier would never cease to rewrite his ideas, to present them from different angles, in the hope of making them better understood.[17] Despite a certain weakness for digressions, his mature style is not really prolix or obscure. It does not suffer from the rhetorical inflation common among his contemporaries; indeed, it was too prosaic for their taste. His language reflects his self-awareness and modesty; it is direct and even vigorous, full of striking and forceful expressions of his views (as I hope this work demonstrates). Renouvier is one of the few voluminous philosophical writers of the nineteenth century who can be read today, and read with pleasure, not just out of duty.[18]

16. Hamelin, *Système de Renouvier*, 8; see Foucher, *Jeunesse de Renouvier*, 37–41, for more on the judge's comments.

17. Regarding Kant, see the analysis of Walter Kaufmann, *Goethe, Kant, and Hegel*.

18. Given the pretentious, jargon-ridden, willfully obscure writing that has been so common in French philosophy since 1945, perhaps it would be well if reading Renouvier were made a duty today. It would be a salutary shock even to

The Eclectics have had their revenge. The penetration of Renouvier's ideas into the university that began in the 1890s petered out in the 1920s to become a total neglect that can be qualified only as a scandal. One can understand that the new eclectics would ignore a position that constituted as direct a challenge to their assumptions as to the original Eclectics. It remains a scandal that the French philosophical establishment in 1986 could propose as one of the themes for reflection for the academic year the idea of liberty but (as far as my limited search discovered) did not include any mention of Renouvier in any of the required manuals or any extract of his works in the required anthologies. Fortunately, this neglect (can it really be ignorance?) does not prevent him from remaining the most powerful advocate of the idea of liberty in modern French philosophy, a thinker worthy of being placed in the lineage of Benjamin Constant and Alexis de Tocqueville.[19]

After 1871, Renouvier would add little to his basic arguments in favor of liberty and would concentrate on developing its applications.[20] In addition to a monumental effort to explore its meaning for the history of philosophy, he would be much concerned with philosophy's relevance for contemporary politics and would seek to have a political influence. I doubt that he was much more satisfied with the results than he had been in 1848, though he was now much more realistic in his expectations.[21] Again, it was entirely through his writings that he hoped to have an influence. The *Critique philosophique* aimed not at influencing political leaders directly but at reaching some of the opinion makers who were in contact with the politicians, as Renouvier was not.

---

the critics of this postwar pandemonium whose own prose is not so liberated from it as their ideas.

19. Secrétan to Renouvier, September 13, 1874, in *Correspondance de Renouvier et Secrétan*, 105–106.

20. "It could be said that his book [*Science de la moral*, 1869] is a kind of higher Manual for the liberal publicist, if you don't give the word *liberal* too narrow a definition" (Hamelin, *Système de Renouvier*, 401).

21. Renouvier certainly lacked the utopian confidence in the power of true ideas expressed by Proudhon in his polemic with Renouvier (Proudhon, *Justice dans la Révolution*, 455).

The political founders of the Third Republic preferred to associate themselves publicly with what they saw as the dominant idea of the day; they did not want to be thought less than progressive. As Péguy said later, "It will never be known what acts of cowardice have been motivated by the fear of not looking sufficiently progressive." [22] But the need of the new regime to establish itself as promoter of public morality eventually led to a recognition that Renouvier's work helped establish the moral credentials of the republic. [23] He did not seek any of the honors the republic liked to give in such cases but did accept a subsidy for the publication of his *Philosophie analytique de l'histoire* (1896 to 1898). He would not be seen in the republican salons of Paris. He would find the republicans too contented with the little that they had accomplished. He would no doubt have shared Péguy's complaint that *"mystique* ends up as *politique."*

It was surely to Renouvier's advantage, and one of the things that gives him a continuing value, that he was vitally interested in the political struggles of the republic yet sufficiently detached from them not to be compromised in the failures (or the successes) of the political leaders or parties. He would never have to trim his thought to protect the interests of any group. His republicanism, his attachment to social reform, and his anticlericalism detached him from socially conservative causes. His commitment to liberty and his pessimism separated him from any movement promising *"des lendemains qui chantent."* [24] Renouvier's social status as a *rentier* demonstrated the validity of his argument in favor of property as promoting independence. Of course, the conditions of independence draw their value from the use made of them. If he were only one of the many intellectual godfathers of the Third Republic, Renouvier would have little more value than the others. The effort to apply his thought to the specific political issues of the early republic is nonetheless one of the sources of his continuing relevance, for he furnishes a model

22. Quoted by John Lukacs, *Confessions,* 318.

23. As Thomas (Introduction to *Manuel républicain* [1904], 3–4) remarks, Renouvier certainly was a better model for democrats than Comte, Taine, or Renan.

24. Literally, "singing tomorrows," perhaps translatable as "a shining future"; this was a phrase popularized by Maurice Thorez, longtime Stalinist secretary-general of the French Communist party.

of the application of universal ideas to concrete circumstances devoid of the fanaticism that has so often accompanied such efforts in modern times.

As a critic of the social and political problems of his time, Renouvier acknowledged his indebtedness, even to thinkers with whom he had major disagreements. He claimed no greater capacity to foresee the flow of day-to-day events than any other contemporary. He agreed with Herbert Spencer on the inability of men and governments to anticipate the consequences of their actions but did not share Spencer's politically quietist conclusions.[25] He was mainly concerned to show how men's ideas influence, but do not determine, the positions they take and the actions they attempt. He was far from claiming any exclusive influence and even remarked how often men act in ways contrary to their explicitly acknowledged ideas. This was, he thought, not an evil since men's acts are often better than a strict deduction from their ideas would lead one to expect. His was a philosophy that attempted to take into account a realistic picture of man's behavior in the real world.

One of the advantages of a philosophy of liberty is that it does not generate unrealistic expectations or exaggerate our capacity to understand the world.[26] These "limitations" make it a more valuable tool for the interpretation of our experience than any of the deterministic philosophies that have claimed the transparency of history under their analytic vision.

Renouvier believed that ideas do matter and that the philosophical positions of the active part of society (whether majority or minority, more commonly the latter) do have an influence on the course of events. It is therefore important to be aware of contemporary currents of ideas,

25. *Histoire*, IV, 359–60. Cornwell (*Principes du droit*, 111) notes the activist character of neocriticism.

26. Most philosophers are driven toward doctrines of necessity out of fear of adopting positions whose validity is uncertain. Kaufmann (*Goethe, Kant, and Hegel*, 239) cites the examples of Hegel and Kant. In his *Without Guilt or Justice: From Decidophobia to Autonomy* (New York, 1973), Kaufmann develops a provocative analysis of this fear of making intellectual and moral choices which he calls *decidophobia*. Renouvier's philosophy made him remarkably immune to this common complaint.

the ends they tend to promote, whether they really lead where their promoters think they will. A philosophical critique of contemporary ideas
may not have much direct impact on the course of events, nor may it
cause many men to admit the errors of their ideas, for the forces of convention and habit, the desire to be "progressive," make most immune to
argument. At least Renouvier's critique does not furnish, as the deterministic philosophies of history have, reasons for justifying the murder of
those whose ideas differ from ours.[27] This is a negative virtue, but not a
small one. The more positive value of his critique is that it helps us to
understand the intellectual origins and practical inclinations of those
ideas that have proved so murderous in the twentieth century.[28]

I do not want to claim more for Renouvier's philosophy than he
would. Its greatest value for us is in a sense retrospective: It provides a
vantage point from which to understand better the intellectual currents
of the nineteenth century. The responses provoked by his work also add
to our understanding: "Reexamining the literature on Renouvier, it is
possible to distinguish some problems which emerge in French thought
from the middle of the 19th century to our own day: the critique of the
infinite, the search for an individualist philosophy founded on contingency, the impact of rationalism on the debate within Christian thought,
the antagonism between the individual and the state, in which the anti-
Hegelian component present in the tradition of French political thought
appears."[29]

Historians of Western thought can benefit not merely from studying
Renouvier's analysis of his century but from applying his approach to the
development of their own analyses. We have become well aware of the
totalitarian and antihuman potential of many progressive doctrines of
the nineteenth century. We can understand them better if we also try to

27. For a sense of how murder can lurk behind even what is ostensibly
literary criticism, see Jean Marie Goulemot, "Candide militant: la littérature
française et la philosophie des lumières dans quelques revues communistes de
1944 à la mort de Joseph Staline," *Libre*, VII (1980), 199–245.

28. Twentieth-century writers who have performed a similar role—*e.g.*, Jacob Talmon, Karl Popper, Thomas Spragens, and Alain Besançon—have generally failed to note that any nineteenth-century writers had similar insights.

29. Cavallari, *Charles Renouvier*, vii.

examine why Renouvier was able to diagnose the dangers to which these ideas were exposing Western society well before those consequences worked themselves out in the twentieth century.

It was not just that Renouvier was pessimistic about man's capacity for improvement or that he feared the "lights were going out all over Europe" well before Sir Edward Grey marked the hour of their extinction in 1914. There were many other pessimists in the nineteenth century, and Renouvier saw a pessimistic mood spreading at the end of the century. It is easy to be a Cassandra, and prophecies of doom are often enough satisfied in human history, even if the worst does not always happen. Renouvier was no Schopenhauer. Man's capacity for evil certainly outweighed his inclination to good, but he did have a capacity for good. Renouvier would not hope for man's extinction. Renouvier's analysis remains valuable because it helps us to understand why things went wrong insofar as wrong ideas were a factor in what went wrong.

What distinguishes Renouvier from other critics of the nineteenth century is not just the accuracy of his forebodings, well above average though that was, but his demonstration of the continuing value of philosophical reflection for the understanding of historical experience and contemporary issues. In this too he was fighting against one of the trends of his century, which was to consider philosophy, like theology, as part of a dead or dying past. Had not Comte proclaimed the end of the metaphysical age and the advent of the positive age?

Even those who did not directly follow Comte increasingly looked to the physical or the social sciences to furnish, in the not too distant future, answers to all the questions that "science" permitted us to ask (assumed to be everything worth knowing). The unrealistic expectations that almost invariably accompanied this orientation were a product not just of an optimistic temperament, common though that was, but of a failure to conduct any philosophical analysis of the premises on which the "scientific" construct was based. No criteria were established that would permit a judgment about the legitimacy of the social programs deduced from "scientific" bases, hence the propensity of most nineteenth-century thinkers to swallow anything with the outward trappings of science.

This weakness of nineteenth-century thought made its first influential appearance in the positivism of Comte, who dogmatically asserted, rejecting any further examination as unnecessary, that any reflection on the nature and conditions of scientific thought was of no importance. Comte was apparently aware that such reflection cannot form part of science itself and that to admit its legitimacy would be to admit the legitimacy of an inquiry outside positive science. This he could not consistently do, and he was thus led to assume as absolute truths certain philosophic positions whose very existence he had to deny.

For many scientists, the positivist view was a convenient one, since it enabled them to pursue their investigations without engaging in a type of reflection foreign to their inclinations. And Renouvier recognized that no harm usually came from this as far as scientific research was concerned. He was well aware of the element of routine and convention in scientific work, and he was not far from Thomas Kuhn's view of the role of dominant paradigms in the life of science. Still, he was comforted by the emergence of a few scientist-philosophers who stressed the role of hypotheses in scientific research, like Claude Bernard, or who acknowledged the role of undemonstrable hypotheses in the foundations of science, like Henri Poincaré.

Gödel's theorem—"all consistent axiomatic formulations of number theory include undecidable propositions"[30]—which has so impressed twentieth-century scientists, would have seemed to Renouvier a confirmation of the position he had held all along. Positivist dogmatism and Comte's hierarchical view of the historical emergence of the positive sciences could have a harmful impact on the future development of science. This dogmatism imposed far greater restrictions on legitimate inquiry than Renouvier's critical analysis, which had more faith in the creative possibilities of science even as it attempted to define science's legitimate domain. Comte's dogmatism left him vulnerable to certain pseudoscientific appeals. Having declared a scientific psychology impossible, he was unable to judge critically any purportedly physiological explanation of mental phenomena and accepted Gall's phrenology, just as Herbert Spen-

---

30. Douglas R. Hofstadter, *Gödel, Escher, Bach: An Eternal Golden Braid* (New York, 1979), 17. The significance of Gödel's theorem is explored throughout Hofstadter's work.

cer readily accepted a direct correlation between size of the brain and human mental ability.

However, Renouvier was less concerned about the impact of positivism on the physical sciences, which were mature enough to take care of themselves, than the comfort given by an unreflective view of science to the proliferation of pseudosciences purporting to explain man and society. The legitimate prestige of modern science made its misappropriation to justify this or that social doctrine all the more dangerous. It was bad enough that the mass audience for such doctrines always lacks the critical perspective, but the greater danger was the elimination of a philosophical reflection that, however few its practitioners, was always needed to prevent the triumph of unreason.[31]

We have seen the thrust of his critique of social doctrines based on historical determinism or optimistic evolutionism. Renouvier was not indifferent to efforts to create a more genuinely scientific sociology. He was sympathetic to some of the efforts of Gabriel Tarde, another provincial thinker, to formulate the laws of imitation, though he also found that Tarde failed to take adequate account of the role of freedom and the capacity of the individual to change the world.[32] It is not clear to what extent Renouvier was aware of the emergence of Durkheim's sociology, though there are hints that he did know of it and doubted that it had yet sufficiently defined itself as a science. On the other hand, it would not be too fanciful to suggest that Durkheim's awareness of Renouvier was one of the things that pushed him to a greater reflection on the nature and conditions of a social science than had characterized earlier nineteenth-century social theorists.

Renouvier remained convinced that neither science nor social science was capable of making a contribution to man's moral progress. He greatly feared that Western man was living on his moral capital and had found no way to replace it: "The truth is that society up to the present

---

31. "The conflict between rationalism and irrationalism has become the most important intellectual, and perhaps even moral, issue of our time" (Popper, *High Tide of Prophecy*, 212). Some who have misunderstood Renouvier's relativism have placed him on the side of the irrationalists. The error of this view is forcefully exposed by Pasquali (*Fundamentos gnoseològicos*, 130–35).

32. See, for example, *Histoire*, IV, 706.

has lived morally on a very mixed set of sentiments and ideas which have their roots in Hellenic civilization, Roman law, Roman administration, Judaic tradition, Christian revelation, scholasticism, and the works of the great learned philosophers and artists of the grand European nations since the 16th century. This moral life rules mainly by custom and is transmitted by education."[33] Despite the very real benefits of modern science, its accomplishments "are not those . . . which support moral life, nor those which can prepare minds for the coming of a better moral regime than the present one."[34]

What Renouvier's work shows us is the need for a philosophical reflection on the foundations of all other areas of intellectual activity, which are not capable of justifying their operations from within. This is a high conception of the mission of philosophy but not a return to the medieval pretension of "metaphysics, queen of the sciences."[35] Such reflection has great potential value for all other disciplines of thought, whether physics or history, biology or sociology. The failure of twentieth-century philosophers to accept this mission is surely one of the sources of the discredit into which philosophy has fallen. Too many philosophers seemed to accept the legitimacy of the death sentence passed on philosophy by positivism and have devoted their philosophical effort to demonstrating, directly or indirectly, the uselessness of philosophy. All the surviving philosophical traditions seem to have been afflicted. Anglo-American empiricism either turned toward a reduction of philosophy to symbolic logic, obscuring its distinction from pure mathematics, or, eschewing such rigor, toward a trivialization of philosophy into the linguistic game playing of amusing Oxbridge dons.[36]

33. *Ibid.*, 718–19.
34. *Ibid.*
35. Boutroux ("Philosophie en France," 714) could still claim that philosophers are distinct from scientists because they are concerned with a total, living experience and because philosophy is devoted to the ideal and not merely to the knowledge of what is. Thus, while Rorty is justified in attacking the excesses of the claim that philosophy should judge everything, he fails to see the pragmatic value of the philosophical approach taken by a Renouvier.
36. Jacques Bouveresse, whose critique of recent French thought I have largely followed, would insist that this is unfair to Wittgenstein. I am sure he is

The debasement of philosophy in France after 1930 would go even further. The importation of German existentialism took root with such little conviction that Sartre seems not to have hesitated to sacrifice his philosophical convictions on man's absolute freedom to the political convenience of the crudest Marxist-Leninist determinism. Postexistentialist French philosophy has seemed devoted to proving the impossibility of philosophy and freeing the philosopher from any responsible search for truth. Art having long become anything done by a person calling himself an artist, philosophy has now become anything asserted by someone calling himself a philosopher. The legitimacy of the former may be debated; the latter is a contradiction in terms.

Renouvier recognized the nineteenth century as an era of great development in historical scholarship. He conceded that some valuable gains had been made, especially in our knowledge of classical antiquity and pre-Greek civilizations. But he found that most modern historical writing was antimoral in effect, and he suspected that this was a tendency inherent in historical study. Historians seemed inclined by the very nature of their study to see whatever has happened as having had to happen. The most diverse explanations may well be equally deterministic; they have in common the tendency to believe that things could not have happened differently.

This retrospective determinism is a cut-rate sort of determinism: It cannot tell what is going to happen but offers only to explain why what happened had to happen. It is easy enough to find reasons for everything that has happened; our common embarrassment is rather that there are too many reasons and it is not easy to choose among them. Renouvier was perfectly willing to admit a certain retrospective determinism: This, after all, did happen rather than that. But he insisted that such a determinism had to be coupled with a recognition that before the fact different outcomes were possible and that human choices—which may include acts of freedom, even if not always or often—are among the factors in

---

right, but it nonetheless seems to me that linguistic philosophy and its deconstructionist offshoots are dead ends. See his discussion of Popper's critique of the linguistic philosophers in Bouveresse, *Philosophe autophages*, Chap. V, "La philosophie a-t-elle oublié ses problèmes?"

determining those outcomes. Historians who understand the significance of freedom will write a somewhat different sort of history than those who do not. For one thing, it will be a history open to a recognition of the significant role played by individuals and therefore a history that does not banish all moral judgment.[37]

Deterministic history, like deterministic philosophies of history, appalled Renouvier by its apology for the crimes of the past. This was one of the less appealing features of the nationalistic history that dominated so much nineteenth-century scholarship. The present nation-state was regarded as such an absolute good that anything that could be interpreted as helping to bring it about was promoted if not always to the status of a good in itself, at least to the status of a necessary evil out of which good had come. God's mysterious ways were replaced by the no less mysterious workings of the "cunning of reason" or, for less philosophically inclined historians, by the working of "History."

Renouvier particularly castigated French historians for their apology for the sins of the monarchy, a tendency even republican historians were not immune to. He would not have been surprised to find Soviet Marxist historians glorifying Ivan the Terrible or Peter the Great. French historians in the nineteenth century had to deal with the problem of their Revolution, and they found it difficult to do anything other than to accept or condemn it *en bloc*.[38] For Renouvier, the benefits of the Revolution were too important simply to condemn it for its errors. Even though he was skeptical of revolutions in general as vehicles for social improvement, he could not write off the effort to promote liberty and equality. But neither could he share the outlook of those historians who with similar values felt called on to excuse the Terror or find benefits in Napoléon's dictatorship. French revolutionary scholarship is still grappling with these problems. A franker recognition of the legitimacy of moral judgments would do much to clarify the issues.

Renouvier's personal contribution to historical scholarship was

37. A history that excludes moral judgment is left with no standard but happiness (*Esquisse*, II, 246).

38. See Jean-Marie Mayeur, "La Révolution française est un bloc . . . ," *Commentaire*, XII (1989), 145–52.

"confined" to the history of thought. The main thing that prevents him from being considered one of the great historians of Western thought is his rejection of historicism, his refusal to impose any developmental scheme on that history. On the contrary, he emphasized its dialectical character, its perpetually renewed conflicts, its dependence on both external circumstances and the deepest continuities of the human person. It was not a static conception, however, but one that incorporated the reality of time and saw humanity as having a real history, moving from its unimaginable beginning to its unknowable end.[39] In contrast with much twentieth-century writing, Renouvier's intellectual history was a history without heroes—only men—and this is one of the reasons, as Giovanna Cavallari has noted, that it has a "liberating, anti-authoritarian value."[40]

Moral considerations were initially banished from historical scholarship in the pursuit of objectivity. The mistake of the nineteenth century was to conceive historical objectivity on the model of the natural sciences.[41] It thus became easy to introduce not the indifference but the positive immoralism of determinist philosophy into the mainstream of historical explanation. Marxist historiography, like Marxist economics, was thus rooted in certain aspects of mainstream thought in the nineteenth century. If it has lost ground in recent years, that has been largely a by-product of the perception of the larger failure of Marxist socialism. Historical study will liberate itself from the bonds of a naïve determinism, Marxist or other, only when it learns how to deal with the reality of human freedom. There are doubtless other means to achieve this liberation than reflection on Renouvier's philosophy, but for the historian of the nineteenth century, I can think of no other reflection that takes us so directly to the heart of the issues.

I have argued elsewhere for the relevance of nineteenth-century authors for the examination of twentieth-century intellectual (and social)

39. See Mouy, *Idée de progrès*, 128.
40. Cavallari, *Charles Renouvier*, 183.
41. There are a number of interesting reflections on this topic scattered throughout John Clive, *Not by Fact Alone: Essays on the Writing and Reading of History* (New York, 1989).

issues. I would go even further, to suggest their superiority over most twentieth-century thinkers. Therefore, I would not call this chapter an appeal to "go back" to Renouvier, or to the nineteenth century more generally. Given our present intellectual disarray, I am more inclined to describe it as an appeal to go forward.

It would be a mistake to see Renouvier simply as a representative of the bourgeois individualism of the nineteenth century, as both Christians and Marxists have been inclined to do.[42] His individualism was profoundly social, as his decision to call his philosophy personalism shows. While this choice came late, the integration of the person into the community was established very early with the development of Renouvier's understanding of solidarity. That concept combined the pessimism of experience and the optimism of reason in a flexible balance capable of adapting to all the vicissitudes of man's future. Reason and liberty were inseparable concepts, and Renouvier very early had a profound sense of the grandeur and misery that liberty establishes as the human condition.[43]

The most important contribution of Renouvier's confrontation with the intellectual currents of his century is his consistent devotion to the distinctiveness of man.[44] The twentieth century has recognized that many nineteenth-century strains of thought end in an explicit antihumanism, and humanism has been the subject of repeated attacks in our day. The feebleness of the pretension to science of all antihumanisms was shown clearly enough by Renouvier, but it remains difficult for the twentieth century to accept his insistence that the only point of view compatible with moral thought is to "take man as the center of the universe, as did Aristotle and the Bible."[45] This is perhaps the most important legacy of a dying Christianity to the modern world.

Renouvier's vision of man was complex and nuanced. He did not forget that man is also an animal and insisted that freedom and reason

---

42. Lacroix, *Vocation personnelle*, 166; see, for example, Scott, *Republican Ideas,* 55, 59, 67.

43. *Deuxième essai,* 456–57.

44. See, for example, Méry, *Critique du christianisme,* I, 382.

45. Höffding, *Philosophes contemporaines,* 87.

are not enough to ensure his survival. Instinct will always remain necessary.[46] There is nonetheless a radical distinction between man and all other animals that the most antihumanist ambitions of a few scientists will never be able to erase. Morality is one of the key elements of that distinction: "Man seeks *the better,* where animals only pursue *their good.*"[47] The moral uniqueness of man is an essential basis from which to resist all the efforts to absorb the individual into a society that becomes the whole of reality. Renouvier's concept of man puts us on guard against the utopian illusion of a perfect community and thus opens the way to thinking about man *in* society that will free us from the consequences of man's fear of abandoning a commitment to the perfect integration of man into his moral world.

Man is not capable of perfect justice any more than perfect knowledge, but he is capable of the pursuit of truth and justice. Philosophical reflection is an integral part of that pursuit.[48] It is necessary to guard us against the overestimation of man that has made modern Gnosticism one of the foundations of totalitarianism.[49] Renouvier calls on us not to despair of man but to understand him: "To want to make himself a god, I mean a god of justice, is, I fear, for a man to singularly overestimate his intellectual power and, even more, his moral worth."[50] For all his weakness, man is not impotent against the evils of the world. He has his conscience, and "conscience is above the world; even when it surrenders to the world, it dominates it, since in order to submit itself it has first to judge it."[51]

Renouvier believed that man should transfer his hopes for perfect justice and community to another world and seek in this world only to satisfy his conscience, because that is within his capacity.[52] It was not common for Renouvier to refer to Voltaire, but he was convinced of the

46. *Deuxième essai,* 576–77.

47. *Ibid.,* 196; see also Méry, *Critique du christianisme,* I, 609.

48. See Boutroux, "Philosophie en France," 716.

49. See the profound interpretation in Alain Besançon, *Les Origines intellectuelles du léninisme* (Paris, 1977).

50. Quoted in Prat, *Renouvier,* 299.

51. *Deuxième essai,* 546.

52. *Histoire,* IV, 781–82.

wisdom of Candide's dictum: "The very profound saying of a philosopher, that unique recipe against the sufferings of life and against pessimist theories: 'We must cultivate our garden,' is no less true of the highest speculations than of moral philosophy. We cannot approach any reality, neither God nor the world, except by the side that faces us, and nowhere can we go beyond the coastline of the country where we are landing. It is there that we ought to establish our culture." [53]

A final word on the philosopher and his time. By precept and example, Renouvier insisted that the philosopher be attentive to his time as well as knowledgeable about the past. He often had occasion to lament that his fellow thinkers were blinded by their doctrines to the realities of the world around them. In the last decade of his life, Renouvier gave up trying to keep up with what was new in contemporary intellectual life and concentrated on his personal message,[54] but from his retreat at Prades in the Pyrenees he formed a solid view of the way the world was heading, a view that often escaped the professors living in the capital. What he saw most clearly was the imminence of a great war: "The spectacle our times offers to the philosopher is one of the greatest efforts ever seen, perhaps, to arm the peoples and to train the rival nations for the struggle for existence. The world in the last half-century has been taking great steps toward a return to barbarism, and thinkers do not seem to be paying any attention. A strange contrast reigns between the signs that foreshadow catastrophes and the confidence they have succeeded in giving the public in a future which will inevitably be better than the past." [55]

Perhaps even greater was the illusion of those who were conscious of the imminence of a great war but were convinced that it would be the war to end all wars, the last necessary bit of violence that would destroy the relics of the old order and by founding democratic government in every nation, remove the causes of war forever. Renouvier exposed these illusions.[56] He also predicted that the basic situation would reemerge: "It

53. *Esquisse*, II, 348.
54. Méry, *Critique du christianisme*, II, 10.
55. *Personnalisme*, 73.
56. *Histoire*, IV, 703.

is evident that the present unstable equilibrium must give way, broken by war, to a new system of equilibrium analogous to the old. To suppose that this time a general congress of nations would find a firm and durable solution to all the social and political problems of today's world is to expect something of which there is no serious likelihood." [57]

The wars and preparations for war of the nineteenth century patently contradicted the popular conception of progress. "The most visible fact about Europe, contrary to the prophecies of the humanitarian and socialist sects and to the inductions of the philosophers of progress, is the augmentation of the dimensions of war, if I may put it that way, in both breadth and depth, accompanied by an unlimited extension of the military servitude of citizens." [58] This, rather than peace, was the result of democratization: Wars had become wars of peoples, not princes, and their propensity to raise the stakes, to see wars as struggles for survival or agents of progress, had been favored by historicism and evolutionism in philosophy. [59]

Scientific thought, another fetish of the progressives, had been put to the service of destruction. Far from offering hope for the end of war, it could only make war more destructive: "Science furnishes the art of destruction with new instruments of great power and it is not science which will teach men to leave them unused." [60] Renouvier saw no prospect for the end of war.

It was not that he was unsympathetic to peace movements or considered them a waste of time, but such efforts would never be enough to overcome the forces in favor of the settlement of disagreements by force. Thus his sympathy did not prevent Renouvier from explaining why the idea of international courts, promoted by the Hague Conference, would not work (even if some limited utility was to be hoped for from voluntary arbitration agreements). [61] The conditions for a real peace among nations were to be found in the establishment of justice in the minds and conduct

57. *Personnalisme*, 208.
58. *Histoire*, IV, 726.
59. *Ibid.*, 723, 727.
60. *Monadologie*, 422.
61. *Histoire*, IV, 703; *Personnalisme*, 195–97.

of individuals. Thus Renouvier, while not denying utility to collective action or institutional structures, reminded us that they can only palliate the evil in man and will never lead to its radical elimination. The conditions for enduring peace had been laid down in Kant's *Essay on Perpetual Peace,* but in Renouvier's opinion, Kant was much too optimistic about their realization, falling into the error of the optimistic philosophies of history.[62]

Imbued with the history of classical civilization, Renouvier feared a fate for the West analogous to that of the Greek and Roman worlds. What would be the result "if after having lost their religion, domestic customs, and their characteristic ideas with respect to public manners and morals, [the modern Western peoples] should also find themselves unable to realize their ideals of justice or to firmly establish liberty"?[63] More than war, Renouvier feared the loss of private and civic virtue, especially that men would not prove themselves worthy of political freedom and would thus fall under new despotisms.[64]

In the last weeks of his life, Renouvier confided to Louis Prat his fears of a new Dark Ages.

> I hope I'm wrong, but it seems to me that we are watching the beginning of an intellectual and moral decadence which will lead us rapidly to a new night of the mind and the heart. Customs, fashions, more or less forced on men, mechanisms which appear to make life easier and of which men are proud, but no serious philosophic or scientific or even literary culture. Perhaps, here or there, a few little islands—as during the Middle Ages— where very rare minds will have the desire or the will to live a human life. That's all. The men of tomorrow will still know how to amuse and distract themselves but the spirit of free enquiry will have disappeared almost completely in them. They will only

62. *Personnalisme,* 194–95; *Histoire,* IV, 707–10.

63. *Monadologie,* 422. There is an interesting parallel in the analysis of John Lukacs, in *Passing of the Modern Age* (New York, 1970).

64. Méry, *Critique du christianisme,* II, 505, quoting Renouvier's letter to H. Loyson, February 13, 1889.

be able to interest themselves in satisfying their immediate appetites.

One must assume that this night will last a long time. The awakening of mind and heart will nonetheless take place, I want to believe.[65]

Judging from the tenor of today's debates over the state of Western culture (the week of writing this paragraph saw the publication of two widely heralded cries of alarm by Alain Finkielkraut and Bernard-Henri Lévy), the process of decay may have been somewhat slower than Renouvier feared.[66] But the significance of what has been, and is being, lost appears more clearly in our time. Despairing at moments of victory, Renouvier never lost his commitment to the struggle for a human culture and the practice of liberty. As long as today's pessimists are of the same combative temperament, we will not have sunk into that new Alexandrine age Renouvier saw growing in his day.

65. Prat, *Renouvier,* 259–60.
66. Alain Finkielkraut, *Défaite de la pensée* (Paris, 1987), and Bernard-Henri Lévy, *Eloge des intellectuels* (Paris, 1987); also, quite recently, Bruno Lussato and Gérard Messadié, *Bouillon de culture* (Paris, 1986), and Michel Henry, *La Barbarie* (Paris, 1987).

BIBLIOGRAPHY

PRINCIPAL WORKS OF CHARLES RENOUVIER

Les Derniers entretiens, recueillis par Louis Prat. Paris, 1930.

Les Dilemmes de la métaphysique pure. Paris, 1901.

Esquisse d'une classification systématique des doctrines philosophiques. 2 vols. Paris, 1885–86.

Essais de critique générale. Premier esssai. Analyse générale de la connaissance. Bornes de la connaissance. Plus un appendice sur les principes généraux de la logique et des mathématiques. Paris, 1854. A second edition, revised and expanded, was published under the title *Essais de critique générale. Premier essai. Traité de logique générale et de logique formelle.* 3 vols. Paris, 1875.

Essais de critique générale. Deuxième essai. L'homme: la raison, la passion, la liberté, la certitude, la probabilité morale. Paris, 1859. Second edition: *Essais de critique générale. Deuxième essai. Traité de psychologie rationnelle.* 3 vols. Paris, 1875.

Essais de critique générale. Troisième essai. Les principes de la nature. Paris, 1864. Second edition: *Les Principes de la nature.* 2 vols. Paris, 1892.

Essais de critique générale. Quatrième essai. Introduction à la philosophie analytique de l'histoire. Paris, 1864. Second edition: *Introduction à la philosophie analytique de l'histoire, Les idées; les religions; les systèmes.* Paris, 1896.

Histoire et solution des problèmes métaphysiques. Paris, 1901.

Manuel de philosophie ancienne. 2 vols. Paris, 1844.

Manuel de philosophie moderne. Paris, 1842.

Manuel républicain de l'homme et du citoyen. Paris, 1848. Second edition: *Manuel républicain de l'homme et du citoyen, précédé d'une préface en réponse aux critiques et suivi d'une nouvelle déclaration des droits de l'homme et du citoyen.* Paris, 1848. New edition, with introduction by Jules Thomas, Paris, 1904. New edition, with introduction by Maurice Agulhon, Paris, 1981.

Le Personnalisme, suivi d'une étude sur la perception externe et sur la force. Paris, 1903; 2nd ed. Paris, 1926.

Petit traité de morale à l'usage des écoles primaires laïques. Paris, 1879.

Philosophie analytique de l'histoire: les idées; les religions; les systèmes. 4 vols. Paris, 1896–98.

Science de la morale. 2 vols. Paris, 1869.

Uchronie: l'utopie dans l'histoire; esquisse historique du développement de la civilisation européenne tel qu'il n'a pas été, tel qu'il aurait pu être. Paris, 1876.

Victor Hugo le philosophe. Paris, 1900.

Victor Hugo le poète. Paris, 1893.

And Charles Fauvety. *Organisation communale et centrale de la République, projet présenté à la nation pour l'organisation de la commune, de l'enseignement, de la force publique, de la justice, des finances, de l'etat,* par les citoyens H. Bellouard, Benoît (du Rhone), F. Charrassin, A. Chouippe, Erdan, C. Fauvety, Gilardeau, C. Renouvier, J. Serget, etc., etc. Paris, 1851.

And Louis Prat. *La Nouvelle Monadologie.* Paris, 1899.

And William James. "Correspondance de Charles Renouvier et de William James" (edited by Ralph Barton Perry), *Revue de métaphysique et de morale,* XXXVI (1929), 1–35, 193–222.

And Charles Secrétan. *Correspondance de Renouvier et Secrétan.* Paris, 1911.

As editor. *La Critique philosophique.* Paris, 1872–89.
    La Critique religieuse. Paris, 1879–85.

SECONDARY SOURCES

Works Cited

Abbagnano, Nicola. *Storia della filosofia.* Vol. II of 2 vols in 3. Turin, 1950.

Adler, Mortimer J. *The Idea of Freedom: A Dialectical Examination of the Conceptions of Freedom.* 2 vols. Garden City, N.Y., 1958.

Archambault, Paul. *Renouvier.* Paris, 1911.

Arnal, Jean. *L'Hypothèse suprême en théodicéé d'après Charles Renouvier.* Mazamet, France, 1904.

Ascher, Maurice. *Renouvier und der französische Neu-Kriticismus*. Bern, 1900.

Barth, Karl. *Protestant Thought: From Rousseau to Ritschl*. New York, 1959.

Baur, Ludwig. Obituary on Renouvier. *Philosophisches Jahrbuch*, XVIII (1905), 452–53.

Benda, Julien. "Les Idées d'un républicain en 1872." *Nouvelle Revue française*, XXXVII (1931), 23–28, 215–27.

———. *La Trahison des clercs*. Paris, 1927.

Benrubi, Isaac. *Les Sources et les courants de la philosophie contemporaine en France*. 2 vols. Paris, 1933.

———. *Contemporary Thought of France*. Translated by Ernest B. Dicker. New York, 1926.

Bertier de Sauvigny, Guillaume de. *The Bourbon Restoration*. Philadelphia, 1966.

Beurier. "Renouvier et le criticisme français." *Revue philosophique de la France et de l'étranger* (1877), 321–56, 470–96, 576–608.

Blumenthal, Henry. *American and French Culture, 1800–1900: Interchanges in Art, Science, Literature, and Society*. Baton Rouge, 1975.

Boas, George. "The History of Philosophy." In *Philosophic Thought in France and the United States,* edited by Marvin Farber. 2nd ed. Albany, N.Y., 1968.

Borne, Etienne. *Les Nouveaux Inquisiteurs*. Paris, 1983.

Botana, Natalio R. *La Libertad politica y su historia*. Buenos Aires, 1991.

Boutroux, Emile. "La Philosophie d'A. Comte et la métaphysique." *Revue des cours et conférences,* X (1901–1902-I), 796–803; X (1902-II), 206–13, 547–54, 735–41, 741–47; XI (1902–1903-I), 57–64, 145–53.

———. "La Philosophie en France depuis 1867." *Revue de métaphysique et de morale,* XVI (1908), 683–716.

Bouveresse, Jacques. *Le Philosophe chez les autophages*. Paris, 1984.

———. *Rationalité et cynisme*. Paris, 1984.

Brunschwicg, Léon. *Le Progrès de la conscience dans la philosophie occidentale*. 2 vols. Paris, 1927.

Brunschwicg, Léon, and Elie Halévy. "L'Année philosophique en 1893." *Revue de métaphysique et de morale,* II (1894), 473–96, 563–90.

Cassirer, Ernst. "Das Problem des Unendlichen und Renouviers Gesetz der Zahl." In *Philosophisches Abhandlungen, Hermann Cohen zum 70, Geburtstag gewidmet*. Berlin, 1910.

———. Review of Renouvier, *Essais de critique générale. Premier essai. Traité de logique générale et de logique formelle* (2nd ed.). In *Die Geisteswissenschaften,* XXIII (1913), 634–35.

Cavallari, Giovanna. *Charles Renouvier, filosofo della liberal-democrazia*. Naples, 1979.

Collina, Vittore. *Plurale filosofico e radicalismo: saggio sul pensiero politica di Charles Renouvier (1815–1903)*. Bologna, 1980.

Conry, Yvette. *L'Introduction du darwinisme en France au XIXe siècle*. Paris, 1974.

Cornwell, Irène. *Les Principes du droit dans la philosophie de Charles Renouvier: le droit international*. Paris, 1924.

Cournot, A.-A. *Considérations sur la marche des idées et des événements dans les temps modernes*. Paris, 1973. Vol. IV of Cournot, *Oeuvres complètes,* edited by André Robinet. 14 vols.

Dauriac, Lionel. "Les Moments de la philosophie de Charles Renouvier." *Bulletin de la société française de philosophie,* IV (1904), 23–46.

———. "Le Testament philosophique de Renouvier." *Revue philosophique* (1904), 337–58.

———. "Un Episode de l'histoire de la philosophie française vers la fin du XIXe siècle: souvenirs personnels." *Critique philosophique* (1887-II), 272–97.

Delbos, Victor. *La Philosophie française*. Paris, 1919.

———. *La Philosophie pratique de Kant*. Paris, 1904.

Droit, Roger-Pol. "Le Spectre du bouddhisme." *Magazine littéraire,* No. 279 (July–August, 1990), 45–47.

Dumas, Jean-Louis, "Renouvier." In *Dictionnaire des philosophes,* edited by Dénis Huisman. 2 vols. Paris, 1984.

Feigel, Friedrich K. *Charles Renouvier's Philosophie der praktischen Vernunft: kritisch beleuchtet*. Wittenberg, 1908.

Ferrari, Joseph. *Les Philosophes salariés*. 1849; rpr. Paris, 1980.

Ferry, Luc. *Le Système des philosophies de l'histoire*. Paris, 1984. Vol. II of Luc Ferry and Alain Renaut, *Philosophie politique*. 3 vols.

Ferry, Luc, and Alain Renaut. *Des droits de l'homme à l'idée républicaine*. Paris, 1985. Vol. III of Luc Ferry and Alain Renaut, *Philosophie politique*. 3 vols.

———. *La Pensée 68: essai sur l'anti-humanisme contemporaine*. Paris, 1985.

Finkielkraut, Alain. *La Défaite de la pensée*. Paris, 1987.

Foucher, Louis. *La Jeunesse de Renouvier et sa première philosophie, 1815–1854, suivi d'une bibliographie chronologique de Charles Renouvier*. Paris, 1927.

———. "Le Sens de la dernière philosophie de Renouvier." *Revue philosophique,* CXXXIV (1944), 317–28.

Franck, Adolphe. *Moralistes et philosophes*. Paris, 1872.

Galli, Gallo. *Studi storico-critico sulla filosofia di Ch. Renouvier*. Vol. I. Gubbio, 1933. Vol. II. Rome, 1935.

Glaize, Paul. "La Philosophie de M. Renouvier." *Morale indépendante,* September 13, 1869, pp. 49–51.

Halévy, Daniel. "Une lettre de Daniel Halévy." *Nouvelle Revue française,* XXXV (1930), 719–20.

Hamelin, Octave. "La Philosophie analytique de l'histoire de M. Renouvier." *Année philosophique* (1898), 21–48.

———. *Le Système de Renouvier.* Paris, 1927.

Hodgson, Shadworth. "M. Renouvier's Philosophy." *Mind* (1881), 31–61, 173–211.

Höffding, Harald. *Philosophes contemporaines.* Translated by A. Trémesaygues. Paris, 1908.

Hofstadter, Douglas, *Gödel, Escher, Bach: An Eternal Golden Braid.* New York, 1979.

Janet, Paul. "Le Mouvement philosophique." *Temps,* March 8, 1876.

Johnson, Douglas. "Jules Ferry et les protestants." In *Jules Ferry, fondateur de la République,* edited by François Furet. Paris, 1985.

Julliard, Jacques. *La Faute à Rousseau: essai sur les conséquences historiques de l'idée de souveraineté populaire.* Paris, 1985.

Kant, Immanuel. *Groundwork of the Metaphysic of Morals.* Translated by H. J. Paton. 1948; rpr. New York, 1964.

Kaufmann, Walter. *Goethe, Kant, and Hegel.* New York, 1980. Vol. I of Kaufmann, *Discovering the Mind.* 2 vols.

Krieger, Leonard. *The German Idea of Freedom.* Boston, 1957.

Laberthonnière, Father Lucien. *Critique du laïcisme.* Paris, 1948. Vol. VI of Laberthonnière, *Oeuvres.* [8 vols.?]

———. *Esquisse d'une philosophie personnaliste.* Paris, 1942. Vol. VIII of Laberthonnière, *Oeuvres.* [8 vols?]

Lacroix, Jean. *Vocation personnelle et tradition nationale.* Paris, 1942.

Lehman, David. *Signs of the Times: Deconstruction and the Fall of Paul de Man.* New York, 1991.

Le Savoureux, Robert. *L'Entreprise philosophique de Renouvier.* Paris, n.d. [1912?]

Lévy, Bernard-Henri. *Eloge des intellectuels.* Paris, 1987.

Littré, Emile. "Education politique." *Philosophie positive,* XVII (1876), 421–27.

Lukacs, John. *Confessions of an Original Sinner.* New York, 1990.

Mayeur, Jean-Marie. "La Révolution française est un bloc. . . ." *Commentaire,* XII (1989), 145–52.

Méry, Marcel. *La Critique du christianisme chez Renouvier.* 2 vols. Paris, 1952.

Miéville, Henri. *La Philosophie de M. Renouvier et le problème de la connaissance religieuse.* Lausanne, 1902.

Milhaud, Gaston. *La Philosophie de Charles Renouvier.* Paris, 1927.

Mill, John Stuart. *Auguste Comte and Positivism.* London, 1866.

————. *The Later Letters of John Stuart Mill, 1849–1873*. Edited by Francis E. Mineka and Dwight N. Lindley. Vol. IV of 4 vols. Toronto, 1972.

Moisant, Xavier. *Psychologie de l'incroyant*. Paris, 1908.

Mouy, Paul. *L'Idée de progrès dans la philosophie de Renouvier*. Paris, 1927.

Nicolet, Claude. "Jules Ferry et la tradition positiviste." In *Jules Ferry, fondateur de la république*, edited by François Furet. Paris, 1985.

Nisbet, Robert. *History of the Idea of Progress*. New York, 1980.

Ollé-Laprune, Léon. *De la certitude morale*. Paris, 1880.

Parodi, Dominique. *Du positivisme à l'idéalisme: études critiques: philosophies d'hier et d'aujourd'hui*. Paris, 1930.

————. *Du positivisme à l'idéalisme: philosophies d'hier, études critiques*. Paris, 1930. (Despite the confusing titles and same publication date, these are two entirely distinct works.)

Pascal, Blaise. *Les Pensées de Pascal*. Edited by Francis Kaplan. Paris, 1982.

Pasquali, Antonio. *Fundamentos gnoseològicos para una ciencia de la moral: ensayo sobre la formacion de une teoria especial del conocimiento moral en las filosofias de Kant, Lequier, Renouvier y Bergson*. Caracas, 1963.

Picard, Roger. *Les Idées sociales de Renouvier*. Paris, 1908.

Pillon, François. "Un Ouvrage récent sur la philosophie de Charles Renouvier." *Année philosophique* (1905), 95–147.

————. Review of Victor Delbos, *Philosophie pratique de Kant*. In *Année philosophique* (1905), 267–69.

————. Review of William James, *L'Expérience religieuse, essai de psychologie descriptive* (*The Varieties of Religious Experience*). In *Année philosophique* (1905), 214–19.

Popper, Karl. *The High Tide of Prophecy: Hegel, Marx, and the Aftermath*. London, 1945. Vol. II of Popper, *The Open Society and Its Enemies*. 2 vols.

Prat, Louis. *Charles Renouvier, philosophe: sa doctrine, sa vie*. Pamiers, 1937.

Prélot, Marcel. *Histoire des idées politiques*. 8th ed. Paris, n.d.

Proudhon, Pierre-Joseph. *De la justice dans la révolution et dans l'eglise*. Paris, 1932. Vol. VIII of Proudhon, *Oeuvres complètes*, edited by Célestin Bouglé and Henri Moysset. 15 vols.

Ravaisson, Félix. *La Philosophie en France au XIXe siècle*. Paris, 1868; 5th ed. Paris, 1904; rpr. Paris, 1983.

Richard, Gaston. *La Question sociale et le mouvement philosophique au XIXe siècle*. Paris, 1914.

Rorty, Richard. *Contingency, Irony, and Solidarity*. Cambridge, Mass., 1989.

Roure, Lucien. *Doctrines et problèmes*. Paris, 1900.

Schloesing, Armand. "Le Criticisme de M. Renouvier." *Revue chrétienne* (1882), 206–16, 266–78, 377–92.

Scott, John A. *Republican Ideas and the Liberal Tradition in France, 1870–1914.* New York, 1966.

Secrétan, Charles. Review of Renouvier, *Manuel de philosophie moderne.* In *Semeur: journal religieux, politique, philosophique et littéraire,* XI (1842), 362–66, 378–84, 385–91.

Sertillanges, A.-D. *L'Idée de création et ses retentissements en philosophie.* Paris, 1945.

Singer, Barnett. *Modern France: Mind, Politics, Society.* Seattle, 1980.

Spencer, Herbert. "The Man *Versus* the State." In Spencer, *The Man Versus the State,* edited by Donald Macrae. Baltimore, 1969.

Spragens, Thomas A., Jr. *The Irony of Liberal Reason.* Chicago, 1981.

Théveau, Paul, and Pierre Charlot. *D'une république à l'autre: la période réaliste.* Paris, 1981. Vol. XII of Théveau and Charlot, *Histoire de la pensée française.* 12 vols.

Thibaudet, Albert. "Réflexions." *Nouvelle Revue française,* XXXV (1930), 542–54.

Tint, Herbert. "The Search for a Laic Morality under the French Third Republic: Renouvier and the 'Critique philosophique.'" *Sociological Review,* V (1957), 5–26.

Vallois, Maximilien. *La Formation de l'influence kantienne en France.* Paris, 1924.

Verneaux, Roger. "Le Criticisme de Dauriac." *Revue philosophique de la France et de l'étranger,* CXXXIII (1942–43), 97–108.

———. *L'Idéalisme de Renouvier.* Paris, 1943.

———. *Renouvier, disciple et critique de Kant.* Paris, 1945.

Waelti, Elisabeth. *La Morale kantienne de Charles Renouvier et son influence sur la constitution de la morale laïque dans la deuxième moitié du XIXe siècle en France.* Geneva, 1947.

Weill, Georges. *Histoire de l'idée laïque en France au XIXe siècle.* 2nd ed. Paris, 1929.

Works Consulted or Mentioned

Azouvi, François, and Dominque Bourel. *De Königsberg à Paris: la réception de Kant en France (1788–1804).* Paris, 1991.

Besançon, Alain. *Les Origines intellectuelles du léninisme.* Paris, 1977.

Bloch, Olivier-René. "Marx, Renouvier et l'histoire du matérialisme." *Pensée,* No. 191 (1977), 3–42.

Bois, H. "L'Influence de Lequier sur Renouvier." In *Recueil de l'académie des sciences, belles-lettres et arts de Tarn-et-Garonne (1910).* Montauban, 1911.

Bouglé, Célestin. "Une Visite à Renouvier." In literary supplement to *Figaro*, June 3, 1911.

Broch, Hermann. *Huguenau oder die Sachlichkeit.* Frankfurt am Main, 1931. Vol. III of Broch, *Die Schlafwandler.* French edition: *Les Somnambules.* Paris, 1957.

Bruckner, Pascal. *Le Sanglot de l'homme blanc: tiers-monde, culpabilité, haine de soi.* Paris, 1983.

Buquet, Paul. "Charles Renouvier." *Revue socialiste,* II (1903), 385–94.

Canivez, André. *Jules Lagneau, professeur de philosophie: essai sur la condition du professeur de philosophie jusqu'à la fin du XIXe siècle.* 2 vols. Paris, 1965.

Charléty, Sebastien. *Histoire du Saint-Simonisme.* Paris, 1896.

Clark, Linda L. *Social Darwinism in France.* University, Ala., 1984.

Clive, John. *Not by Fact Alone: Essays on the Writing and Reading of History.* New York, 1989.

Coignet, C. "Science de la morale, par Ch. Renouvier." *Morale indépendante,* May 30, 1869, pp. 345–47; June 6, 1869, pp. 353–55; June 27, 1869, pp. 378–79; July 4, 1869, pp. 385–87; July 11, 1869, pp. 393–95.

Compayré, G. "Uchronie, par Renouvier." *Revue philosophique,* II (1876), 294–303.

Darlu, A. "La Morale de Renouvier." *Revue de métaphysique et de morale,* XII (1904), 1–18.

Dauriac, Lionel. "Le Philosophe Charles Renouvier." *Revue latine,* III (1904), 370–81.

Delbez, Louis, *Les Grands courants de la pensée politique française depuis le XIXe siècle.* Paris, 1970.

Dumas, Jean-Louis. "Renouvier critique de Hegel." *Revue de métaphysique et de morale,* LXXVI (1971), 32–52.

Duperrut, Frank. "Charles Renouvier." *Revue de théologie et de philosophie,* XXXVII (1904), 31–41.

Foucher, Louis. "La Notion de l'immortalité de l'âme dans la philosophie française du XIXe siècle." *Revue des sciences philosophiques et théologiques* (1932), 25–53, 186–218, 562–87.

Fouillée, Alfred. *Critique des systèmes de morale contemporains.* Paris, 1883.

Franchi, Ausonio. "Théorie de la connaissance par Charles Renouvier." *La Revue* (June, 1855), 260–69.

Franck, Adolphe. *Moralistes et philosophes.* Paris, 1872.

Furet, François. *Penser la révolution française.* Paris, 1978.

Girard, Louis. *Les Libéraux français, 1814–1875.* Paris, 1985.

Goulemot, Jean Marie. "Candide militant: La littérature française et la philosophie des lumières dans quelques revues communistes de 1944 à la mort de Joseph Staline." *Libre*, VII (1980), 199–245.

Grin, Edmond. "Charles Renouvier, homme de la continuité bien que philosophe du discontinu." *Etudes théologiques et religieuses* (1957), 137–60.

Guiral, Pierre. *Adolphe Thiers: ou la nécessité en politique*. Paris, 1986.

Henry, Michel. *La Barbarie*. Paris, 1987.

Hoffman, Robert. L. *Revolutionary Justice: The Social and Political Theory of P. J. Proudhon*. Carbondale, Ill., 1972.

Janssens, Edgar. "Charles Renouvier." *Revue néo-scolastique*, X (1903), 390–93.

Jardin, André. *Alexis de Tocqueville, 1805–1859*. Paris, 1984.

———. *Histoire du libéralisme politique, de la crise de l'absolutisme à la constitution de 1875*. Paris, 1985.

Kauffman, Walter. *Without Guilt or Justice: From Decidophobia to Autonomy*. New York, 1973.

Lamberti, Jean-Claude. *Tocqueville et les deux démocraties*. Paris, 1983.

Lechalas, G. "*Les principes de la nature* (2e ed.), par Ch. Renouvier." *Revue philosophique*, XXXIV (1892), 628–46.

Lefort, Claude. *Essais sur le politique (XIXe-XXe siècles)*. Paris, 1986.

Leroux, Emmanuel. "La Philosophie morale en France depuis la guerre." *Revue philosophique*, CIX (1930), 43–78.

Leroy, Maxime. *La Vie véritable de comte Henri de Saint-Simon*. Paris, 1925.

Logue, William. "French Political Thought in the 1980s: Return to the Rights of Man?" *Proceedings of the Annual Meeting of the Western Society for French History*, XVI (1989), 283–90.

———. *From Philosophy to Sociology: The Evolution of French Liberalism, 1870–1914*. DeKalb, Ill., 1983.

Lotze, Hermann. "L'Infini actuel est-il contradictoire? Réponse de M. Lotze à M. Renouvier." *Revue philosophique*, IX (1880), 481–92.

Loubère, Leo. *Louis Blanc: His Life and His Contribution to the Rise of French Jacobin-Socialism*. Evanston, 1961.

Lukacs, John. *Passing of the Modern Age*. New York, 1970.

Lussato, Bruno, and Gérard Messadié. *Bouillon de culture*. Paris, 1986.

Manent, Pierre. *Histoire intellectuelle du libéralisme: dix leçons*. Paris, 1987.

———. *Les Libéraux*. Paris, 1986.

———. *Tocqueville et la nature de la démocratie*. Paris, 1982.

Manuel, Frank E. *The New World of Henri Saint-Simon*. Cambridge, Mass., 1956.

————. *The Prophets of Paris.* Cambridge, Mass., 1962.

Michel, Henry. "Charles Renouvier." *Temps,* September 4, 1903.

————. *L'Idée de l'etat: essai critique sur l'histoire des théories sociales et politiques en France depuis la révolution.* Paris, 1896.

Molnar, Thomas. *The Counter-Revolution.* New York, 1969.

————. *The Decline of the Intellectual.* New Rochelle, N.Y., 1961.

Moses, Claire Goldberg. *French Feminism in the Nineteenth Century.* Albany, N.Y., 1984.

Parodi, Dominique. *Le Problème moral et la pensée contemporaine.* Paris, 1909.

Philonenko, Alexis. *La Liberté humaine dans la philosophie de Fichte.* Paris, 1966.

Pisier-Kouchner, Evelyne. "L'Obéissance et la loi: le droit." In *Histoire des idéologies,* edited by François Châtelet. Vol. III. Paris, 1978.

Platz, Wilhelm. *Charles Renouvier als Kritiker der französischen Kultur.* Bonn, 1934.

Pyguillem, Gérard. *Charles Renouvier: conférence donnée au lycée de Prades, le 9 mai 1970.* Prades, France, 1971.

Quine, W. V. "Has Philosophy Lost Contact With People?" In Quine, *Theories and Things.* Cambridge, Mass., 1981.

Ravisson, Félix. *De l'habitude.* Paris, 1838.

Renaut, Alain. *Le Système du droit: philosophie et droit dans la pensée de Fichte.* Paris, 1986.

Revel, Jean-François. *La Tentation totalitaire.* Paris, 1976.

Reymond, A. Review of *La Philosophie de M. Renouvier et le problème de la connaissance religieuse,* by Henri Miéville. In *Revue de théologie et de philosophie,* XXXVII (1904), 196–204.

Rorty, Richard. *Philosophy and the Mirror of Nature.* Princeton, N.J., 1979.

Séailles, Gabriel. *La Philosophie de Charles Renouvier: introduction à l'étude du néo-criticisme.* Paris, 1905.

Shklar, Judith N. *Ordinary Vices.* Cambridge, Mass., 1984.

Spitzer, Alan B. *The Revolutionary Theories of Louis Auguste Blanqui.* New York, 1957.

Stock-Morton, Phyllis. *Moral Education for a Secular Society: The Development of Morale Laique in Nineteenth Century France.* Albany, N.Y., 1988.

Taine, Hippolyte. "Quelques ouvrages philosophiques récents." *Journal des débats,* June 27, 1867.

Talmon, Jacob L. *Political Messianism: The Romantic Phase.* New York, 1960.

Vyverberg, Henry. *Historical Pessimism in the French Enlightenment.* Cambridge, Mass., 1958.

Waline, Marcel. *L'Individualisme et le droit.* 2nd ed. Paris, 1949.

Weil, Eric. *Philosophie politique.* Paris, 1956.

Welch, Cheryl B. *Liberty and Utility: The French Idéologues and the Transformation of Liberalism.* New York, 1984.

Wyrouboff, Georges. Review of 2nd ed. of first and second *Essais de critique générale.* In *Revue de la philosophie positive,* XVII (1876), 155–57.

Yang, Pao-San. *La Psychologie de l'intelligence chez Renouvier: etude spéciale de la théorie du vertige mental.* Paris, 1930.

INDEX